Politics
A New Approach

David Roberts

Causeway Books

Causeway Press Ltd
PO Box 13, Ormskirk, Lancashire L39 5HP

British Library Cataloguing in Publication Data
Roberts, David, 1948 April 15-
    Politics: a new approach.
    1. Great Britain—Politics and government
    —18th century   2. Great Britain—
    Politics and government—19th century
    3. Great Britain—Politics and government
    —20th century
    I. Title
    320.941   JN210

ISBN 0 946183 25 2

Published 1986

Phototypesetting by Bookform, Formby, Merseyside
Printed and bound by Robert Hartnoll (1985) Ltd, Bodmin, Cornwall

Preface

Politics: A New Approach provides a comprehensive introduction to the study of British politics and government for GCSE. Its format and content have been designed to meet the requirements of the new examinations in this subject. Extensive use is made of data response exercises which contain questions of varying degrees of difficulty. These encourage students to be active learners, whether as members of a class or in pursuing their own course of study. Source material, appropriately abridged or adapted, has been selected for its relevance and interest. No prior knowledge of the subject is assumed as concepts and terms are explained as they are introduced.

The book should also prove useful for students new to the subject at 'A' Level, at BTEC National level (Public Administration) and for those taking pre-vocational courses with a politics component. It aims to integrate a conceptual approach within a framework that introduces the student to the main political institutions and processes. Political issues, events and argument are used to illustrate and give meaning to the workings of the political system. Although comparisons are drawn with other societies, the book is concerned mainly with the government and politics of Britain.

Many students display a healthy scepticism towards politics and government and can be deterred by the sometimes reverential tones of the traditional textbook. **Politics: A New Approach** acknowledges the often understandable doubts and suspicions believing that they can be used to facilitate, rather than discourage, a serious study of the political process.

In writing the book I have received assistance, advice and encouragement from a number of people. In particular, thanks are due to Jim Capie, Barbara Francis and Richard Smith all of whom helped in different ways. I am especially grateful to Mike Haralambos for his invaluable advice and enthusiastic support throughout the project. Finally, I should like to thank Anne for practical help and support and for cheerfully tolerating the distractions of the past twelve months.

David Roberts
January 1986

Contents

Acknowledgements

We are grateful to the following for permission to reproduce photographs and artwork.

Animal Protection Alliance, p. 114
BBC Hulton Picture Library, p. 328
Campaign for Nuclear Disarmament, p. 126
Channel 4, p. 64
Department of the Environment, cover and p. 222
Format Photographers and Jenny Matthews, p. 41; and Sheila Gray, pp. 94, 123; and Brenda Prince, p. 268
Free Association Books, p. 246 (from **Is Anybody Out There?** by J.F. Batellier, London, 1984)
Greater London Council, pp. 286, 287
Lancashire Library, Preston District, pp. 9, 10 (from **The Political Alphabet** by George Cruikshank)
National Museum of Labour History, p. 101
Network Photographers, pp. 5, 67, 196, 238, 318
New Statesman, p. 46
The Photo Source, pp. 85, 159, 214, 270
Public Information Office, House of Commons Library, p. 147
Punch, pp. 16, 313
Rex Features, pp. 20, 117
Serjeant at Arms, House of Commons, p. 146
Antony Winterbottom – Spiral Studio Graphics, pp. 14, 23, 36, 50, 69, 75, 90, 136, 139, 151, 173, 199, 208, 216, 233, 241, 295, 267, 280, 293, 308, 316

Extracts reproduced from YES MINISTER VOLUME 3 by Jonathan Lynn and Antony Jay, NO MINISTER by Hugo Young and Anne Sloman and POLITICS AND YOU with the permission of the British Broadcasting Corporation.

Every effort has been made to locate the copyright owners of material quoted in the text. Any omissions brought to our attention are regretted and will be credited in subsequent printings.

To
Anne, Sally and Ben

Section 1 Power, People and Politics

In this section some of the central terms and ideas in the study of government and politics are introduced. Questions about how **decisions** are made, and who makes them, and where **power** lies are the main concerns of any examination of political affairs. They also open up issues about **democracy**, and help in assessing the extent to which the political system in Britain is democratic. The questions of power and democracy are returned to specifically at the end of the book. But they are considered throughout. So, too, are the roles of individuals in the political system. The idea or concept of **political socialization** – the process by which people come to learn and to form their political attitudes and beliefs – is therefore examined in this first section.

1 Decision-making and power

Politics is about decision-making and power. It is concerned with how people in groups reach decisions and implement them (put them into effect). Political power is involved in both of these: the power that some people have over others in seeing that their decisions are (a) accepted, and (b) carried out. The following passage examines this process.

Because there are so many groups in society, each wanting different things, government is a difficult business – both at national and local level.

Groups and individuals who disagree must find ways of living and working together if society is not to break down. This is a basic problem of politics; and, to put it very simply, there are two sorts of solutions. One way of dealing with people who disagree with us is to shoot them, hit them over the head or lock them up. This approach can be used by conflicting groups within a society, or by a government which gives out orders and uses force to eliminate opposition.

The other kind of solution to the problem of conflict is the one generally favoured in most societies. It is to work out methods of decision-making which all groups can accept as fair – even when they do not get their own way. At government level, this is only likely to work if the groups directly concerned in particular decisions are consulted. Without proper consultation there is always a danger that decisions will not be accepted.

Political activity is of course not just concerned with making decisions but also with carrying them out. Those who are responsible for managing the affairs of a society require some sort of **power** in order to make their decisions effective. Consequently the study of politics is to a large extent a study of the power that some have over others – the form it takes, the groups or individuals who possess it, and the uses to which it is put.

Those who seek political power are often talked of in uncomplimentary ways. Politicians are accused of being 'power mad', and we are told that power corrupts people, making them dishonest and self-seeking. It is always easy to claim that politicians want power in order to 'feather their own nests' or simply to feel important. But we cannot get away from the fact that in a modern state **some people** have to take essential decisions; and they have to be given power to carry them out.

Everyone has views about what is good or bad in society, and about the sorts of changes that need to be made. Political power is essential if any such changes are to be brought about. The really important question is not whether some should have power over others, but whether power is put to good use. Are political leaders taking account of the wishes of the people? And if they are not is it possible to replace them?

Political power is not always to be found in the most obvious places. In Britain for example it might seem that political power is largely concentrated in the hands of MPs at Westminster. But in fact many groups and individuals outside Parliament have power to influence political decisions, including leaders of big business, the trade unions and the civil service. So when we look at the British political system we should keep firmly in mind the question 'Where does power lie?'

(from **British Government** by Philip Gabriel, Longman, London, 1981, pp. 3-4, 8)

1. From your knowledge of current affairs, provide one example of a disagreement between two or more groups. Clearly state
   a what the disagreement is about   (2)
   b the groups involved   (2)
2. Explain the two types of solutions to political conflict.   (4)
3. What is political power?   (4)
4. Give **two** reasons why people may seek political power.   (4)
5. Which groups do you think are the most powerful in British society? Give reasons for your answer.   (4)

2 Political socialization

Sociologists use the term **socialization** to refer to the process whereby individuals learn the beliefs, attitudes, values (aims that are regarded as worthwhile) and behaviour that are expected or customary in their society.

Political socialization, therefore, is the process by which people acquire certain **political** attitudes, beliefs and ways of behaving. These may involve attitudes to political parties, opinions on particular issues, and ideas and beliefs about the system of government in general.

It should not be thought, however, that people passively accept or adopt all the political attitudes and beliefs that confront them. Socialization is a process which involves **interacting** with others, and individuals develop the ability to think about and reflect upon ideas. Because of this it is not possible to predict exactly how a particular individual will, for example, cast his vote at an election. Generalizations about the outcomes of political socialization are made in terms of trends or tendencies about large groups. For instance, it has been observed that as a result of political socialization, a high proportion of people whose parents regularly voted for the Conservative Party will themselves vote for that party. But not everybody who falls into this category will vote Conservative.

The following passage looks at some examples of the major sources of influence on people's political socialization. These sources of influence are sometimes called the **agencies** of socialization.

> Through the process of socialization, people come to form a view of society and of how they themselves fit into it. They develop certain beliefs, values and ways of seeing things, and hold certain ideas about their own roles and the roles of other people. It is usually thought that the family is the most important agency of socialization, but there are other influences, too, such as education, the workplace, friends and the neighbourhood. **Political** socialization is part of this wider socialization process. The sorts of attitudes that people have to the political system, and the roles they see themselves playing within it, will vary according to their political socialization.
>
> The socialization of most people does not lead them into an active political role. When government decisions and actions affect their own lives, they may well talk about politics. The majority of people turn out to vote at elections. But relatively few people extend their political activities much further. In some cases, though, it is easy to see how an active interest in politics runs in families. In the Conservative Party, for example, the Churchills and the MacMillans are both well-known 'political' families. Michael Foot and Tony Benn of the Labour Party both had fathers who had been MPs, as did Roy Jenkins of the Social Democratic Party.
>
> It is not necessary to think only of Parliament, however, to recognize the influence of the family. Children soon become aware of differences in the ways boys and girls are often expected to behave. These differences may follow from the different roles they see their parents playing at home. In many families, active participation in politics may still be thought of as more appropriate to men rather than women. There are very few women MPs, and sex differences in political socialization could be a major reason for this.
>
> Some of the political socialization that takes place within the family may be intentional. But perhaps of greater importance is the unintentional exposure of a child to political

Debate at Oxford University Union, 1984. For these students a political career is seen as a fairly 'normal' option.

views and attitudes. He or she may hear views expressed about political leaders or events and, over a period of time, begin to adopt them. More general attitudes – such as respect, or the lack of it, for governments or positions of authority – might be formed in a similar way.

Many prominent politicians were educated at major public schools and the older universities (particularly Oxford and Cambridge). These educational institutions encourage the development of certain attitudes and expectations about leadership and power. For many of their students, a political career is not seen as unusual but as a fairly 'normal' option at some stage in their lives. Within the state education system political education is now accepted in some schools. But most adults today, and those of previous generations, were not encouraged or prepared at school to expect to take an active role in politics.

(adapted from **Politics and Government** by Tom Brennan, Cambridge University Press, Cambridge, 1982, pp. 112–4 and **The Civic Culture** by G. A. Almond and S. Verba, Princeton University Press, Princeton, 1963, p. 269)

1. Why is the family thought to be the most important socializing agency? (2)
2. Give one example of intentional and one example of unintentional political socialization that can occur in the family. (2)
3. a What factors referred to in the passage might explain why so few people are active in politics? (3)
   b What additional reasons can you suggest? (2)
4. a In what ways is the political socialization of those who attend public schools likely to differ from those attending state schools? (2)
   b From your own experience, consider ways in which schools may contribute unintentionally or indirectly to political socialization. (2)
5. a Besides the family and education, what other agencies of socialization are referred to in the passage? (2)
   b In what ways might each of these other factors contribute to an individual's political socialization? (3)
   c Name any other possible influences in society – not included in the passage – which might be imporant in political socialization. (2)

3 Democracy (1)

Relatively few people are active in politics. But a requirement of democracy is that people should be able to have a say about matters which affect their lives. There are different views about how this should operate and how far it should go. The following passage examines the development of ideas about democracy and how the term has been interpreted at different times and in different places.

The word democracy comes from two Greek words meaning 'people power'. In ancient Greece democracy was the form of government in which all qualified citizens were allowed to **participate** in the government of their cities. The citizen was expected to play a positive role in government rather than giving the task of ruling to others. This **direct** form of democracy has been seen as the purest form of democracy. However, even in Greece, large sections of the population – notably slaves, women and children – were not regarded as 'qualified citizens' and therefore were denied participation.

Two distinct views of democracy developed in nineteenth century Britain. With the first view, democracy meant people being involved in decision-making and in being able to control their working lives as well as influencing political events. The second view expressed a less direct form of democracy. It was limited to the idea that people should have some say in selecting a government. If **direct** democracy was impossible in a large industrial society then a **representative** democracy (in which the people elect representatives to assist in government) was seen as the practical alternative. This second type would mean that most people should be entitled to vote rather than, as with the first view, enabling them to actively participate in government. It is the second view – representative democracy – that has formed the main approach to political thinking in Britain.

However, some feel that with this arrangement the people are relegated to mere votecasters. They say that voting should be only one aspect of democracy and that people should be able to involve themselves more actively in political affairs.

Decision-making in societies referred to as 'socialist', such as the USSR, is also claimed to be democratic. The idea is that decisions made by political leaders are based on information and opinion flowing upwards from local, or 'grass-roots', level. The people have the right to express their views on these decisions which may then be altered by the leaders after taking account of the people's views. A final policy is then formed which all the people are expected to abide by. Some critics of this type of democracy say that, in practice, it can run into problems. Some decisions may need to be made quickly, with little time for drawn-out procedures of consultation and discussion at grass-roots level. Political leaders may also try to prevent or discourage too much questioning or criticism of their decisions.

(adapted from **Basic Political Concepts** by Alan Renwick and Ian Swinburn, Hutchinson, London, 1980, pp. 124–36)

1. a Why are the cities of ancient Greece referred to as **direct** democracies? (2)

  b In what ways might they be regarded as undemocratic today?
  (2)
2. a Why might a direct democracy be impossible in a large
     industrial society? (2)
  b How does a representative democracy differ from a direct
     democracy? (3)
  c Why do some people think that the British form of represent-
     ative democracy is too limited? (2)
3. a In what sense might the political systems of socialist societies
     be called democratic? (3)
  b How have they been criticized? (2)
4. Suggest ways in which people could actively participate in
   political affairs in addition to voting at elections. (4)

4 Democracy (2)

Nearly all governments around the world would claim that their
political systems are democratic. But democracy is not a precise
word. It means different things to different people. How
democracy is viewed may depend very much on the society in
which the individual is brought up and on his or her political
socialization. The following passage emphasizes this point and
then examines some of the characteristics that might be found in a
representative democracy.

  'Democracy may exist in more than one form and all societies,
  including Britain, have some flaws in their claims to being
  democratic.' Many people who live in the 'liberal democracies'
  of the Western world (such as those in North America and
  Western Europe) say that other societies are undemocratic
  because their political systems seem so unlike those of the
  West. Yet many societies have characteristics of democracy
  which people in this country may be unwilling to see. At the
  same time, it is possible to recognize undemocratic aspects in
  the British system.
    What are the main ideas associated with representative
  democracies? A government must arise out of public opinion
  and be answerable to the public. This means a government
  taking account of the wishes of the people and publicly

D is a DESPOT, in whom ye may see
A symbol of all who hate the word–FREE

(from **Political Alphabet** by George Cruikshank)

explaining and justifying its actions. It also means that the people have opportunities to change the government by choosing an alternative. This would require regular elections and a system of checks to prevent one group of people from having too much power. Power concentrated in the hands of one group or a single person can lead to a denial of other features expected in a democracy. For example, it is often thought that governments should act for the benefit of the nation as a whole and not in the interests of a particular group or class. There should be tolerance towards minority groups. Free speech and a free press should exist. People should have the freedom to meet together when and with whom they wish.

To guarantee these freedoms it is necessary to have an

Q stands for QUESTION–How long shall this be
A portrait of MAN–destin'd to be free?

(from **Political Alphabet** by George Cruikshank)

independent system of law courts free from government interference. To prevent the concentration of power, the main functions of government should be divided and each function should be controlled by different groups of people. This would mean that the functions of making laws, carrying out the law and deciding if and when the law has been broken, should not all be the responsibility of the same people.

(adapted from **Basic Political Concepts** by Alan Renwick and Ian Swinburn, Hutchinson, London, 1980, pp. 124, 142–8)

1. List five characteristics of a representative democracy.   (5)
2. What do you think is meant by the term 'a free press'?   (2)
3. a Which of the features mentioned in the passage could be described as 'freedom of assembly'?   (2)
   b Why is this important for democracy?   (2)

4. a What are the main functions of government referred to in the
      passage?   (3)
   b Why is it thought necessary that each function should be
      carried out by different groups of people?   (2)
5. Suggest other features that might be considered desirable in a
   democracy.   (4)

Section 2 Elections

The extent to which the democratic features outlined in the previous section can be found in Britain will be examined at various stages of the book. Britain is often described as a representative democracy because elections take place. Every so often individuals are put forward to stand as candidates at elections in the hope of being selected to represent the people.

There are three main types of elections that take place throughout the United Kingdom as a whole and at which the vast majority of the adult population is entitled to vote:

1. **General elections** – to elect 650 Members of Parliament (MPs) to the House of Commons. These are the 'parliamentary elections'.

2. **Local elections** – to elect local councils of various types which take on responsibilities for running certain local services such as education and housing.

3. **European elections** – to elect the UK Members of the European Parliament.

This section is concerned with the first of these: the general, or parliamentary election. The arrangements and procedures which make up the British system of elections are presented and the debates over whether the system should be changed and, if so, how, are then examined.

1 Constituencies and candidates

For election purposes the United Kingdom is now divided into 650 geographical areas or parliamentary constituencies. England has 523 constituencies, Scotland 72, Wales 38, and Northern Ireland 17. Each constituency 'returns' one MP to Parliament: this is the candidate who receives the largest number of votes in that constituency at an election. Candidates do not have to belong to a political party in order to stand for election, although independent candidates are rarely successful. The Conservative and Labour parties usually put forward candidates in the vast majority of constituencies. For the 1983 general election the Liberal Party and the Social Democratic Party formed an electoral alliance and between them fielded candidates in almost all the constituencies in Britain. Other parties which put up candidates in particular regions of the United Kingdom included the Scottish National Party, Plaid Cymru (Wales), and, in Northern Ireland, Ulster Unionists, Ulster Democratic Unionists, Ulster Popular Unionists, Provisional Sinn Fein, and the Social and Democratic Labour Party.

The following extract looks at the size of constituencies in terms of geographical area and electorate (the number of people entitled to vote). The legal requirements concerning candidates for election are also described.

At the 1983 General Election 2,579 candidates stood for election to Parliament. The 650 constituencies varied considerably in population and geographical area, but the average electorate in each constituency was about 67,000. The Western Isles with the smallest electorate of only about 23,000 was one of the largest in geographical area. The Isle of Wight with the largest electorate of about 94,000 was geographically confined to quite a small area. Discrepancies of population and geographical area derive mainly from the fact that the population has expanded in some parts of the country – for example, East Anglia and the South-West of England – and contracted in other parts – for example, the inner-city areas of London, Birmingham and Glasgow. The independent Boundary Commissions attempt every ten to fifteen years to take account of the movements in population by re-drawing the boundaries of constituencies where necessary.

Any British citizen who is resident in this country and who will be at least 21 years old when the new Parliament meets, is legally entitled to stand for election to the House of Commons. The only provisos are that he must get ten qualified voters in the constituency to sign his nomination papers and he must deposit a sum of £500 which is refunded to him after the election if he gets more than 5 per cent of the votes cast. There is no requirement that candidates should reside in the constituency for which they seek election and

'Only problem now is which party do I stand for?'

only a few categories of people are automatically disqualified from standing for Parliament. (These include 'certified lunatics', convicted prisoners serving sentences of more than one year, members of the House of Lords, people serving in the civil service, the armed services and the police, and clergymen of certain churches.)

Each candidate is restricted by law to a maximum expenditure during the election campaign. Each candidate has to have an Agent who is legally responsible for seeing that all aspects of election law are observed. The Agent also serves in most cases as the local campaign manager for his candidate, although this is not part of his legal duties.

(from **Mastering British Politics** by F. N. Forman, Macmillan, Basingstoke and London, 1985, pp. 22–4, with minor additions)

1. Referring to the constituencies of the Western Isles and the Isle of Wight, explain why constituencies cannot all contain roughly equal numbers of voters. (4)
2. a What function is performed by the Boundary Commissions? (2)
   b Why are the Boundary Commissions expected to act independently of the interests of political parties? (2)
3. Why do you think that candidates are required
   a to pay a deposit, refundable on obtaining a certain proportion of the votes? (2)
   b to be nominated by ten electors of the constituency? (2)
4. Briefly describe the functions of an election agent. (2)
5. Why are candidates limited in the amount of money they can spend on their election campaigns? (2)
6. Select **one** of the categories of people not permitted to stand for election to the House of Commons, and
   a suggest why they are excluded (2)
   b outline a case for their being allowed to become candidates. (2)

2 The vote

All people aged 18 or over who have British nationality (plus citizens of the Republic of Ireland resident in Britain) are qualified to vote at a general election, with the following exceptions:

- members of the House of Lords
- people serving prison sentences of more than twelve months
- individuals certified as 'insane'
- any person convicted of corrupt practices at elections during the previous five years.

To be eligible to cast a vote a person must be included on the register of electors for his area. Each household is obliged to complete a form each year giving the names of each person old enough to vote.

Although he or she does not have to use it, each elector has one vote. This has not always been the case. Similarly, it is not all that long ago when only a small proportion of the population was entitled to vote, as the following extract shows.

PUNCH, OR THE LONDON CHARIVARI.—May 10, 1905.

THE DIGNITY OF THE FRANCHISE.

QUALIFIED VOTER. "AH, YOU MAY PAY RATES AN' TAXES, AN' YOU MAY 'AVE RESPONSERBILITIES AN' ALL; BUT WHEN IT COMES TO *VOTIN'*, YOU MUST LEAVE IT TO *US MEN!*"

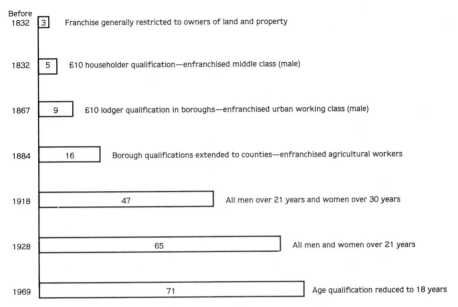

Growth of the electorate: effect of Reform Acts 1832–1969

Before 1832 — **3** — Franchise generally restricted to owners of land and property

1832 — **5** — £10 householder qualification—enfranchised middle class (male)

1867 — **9** — £10 lodger qualification in boroughs—enfranchised urban working class (male)

1884 — **16** — Borough qualifications extended to counties—enfranchised agricultural workers

1918 — **47** — All men over 21 years and women over 30 years

1928 — **65** — All men and women over 21 years

1969 — **71** — Age qualification reduced to 18 years

Electorate as percentage of total population

For centuries, the House of Commons was elected by a small minority of the population, mostly freehold owners of land. The franchise or right to vote was gradually extended to all adult citizens by a series of Acts of Parliament starting with the Great Reform Act 1832 (see diagram above). Most men were enfranchised by the end of the nineteenth century, but the democratic goal of universal suffrage – votes for all adult men and women – was not attained until 1928. Even then, the franchise fell short of full equality because a limited number of people, comprising university graduates and owners of businesses, were entitled to more than one vote. The abolition of plural voting, in 1948, established the democratic principle of 'one person, one vote'. The most recent and perhaps final step in the development of the franchise was the reduction of the voting age to eighteen by the Representation of the People Act 1969.

Political rights have not been achieved by the mass of the

people without a hard struggle. The voting demands of working men were first forcibly expressed in the massive meetings and demonstrations organized in support of the 'People's Charter' during the years following the 1832 Reform Act. The struggle for votes for women was even more bitterly fought, in the early part of this century, with militant suffragettes attacking property and suffering imprisonment, hunger strikes, and forced feeding. Neither the chartists nor the suffragettes were immediately successful, but both movements established claims that could not be denied in the end.

(from **Parliament and Its Work** by Keith Marder, Wheaton, Exeter, 1979, p. 4)

1. Explain the meaning of the following terms: **electorate, franchise, universal suffrage, plural voting.** (4)
2. a In what year did men and women first become entitled to vote on an equal basis? (2)
   b When did working class men in the towns first gain the vote? (2)
3. From the information in the extract, identify the **demands** and the **methods used** by
   a the chartists (2)
   b the suffragettes (2)
4. a Why do you think the voting age was reduced to 18 in 1969? (2)
   b Suggest arguments for and against a further reduction to 16 years. (4)
5. Suggest reasons why it has often required a 'hard struggle' to achieve extensions to the franchise. (2)

3 The general election

The people chased the Conservative candidate half a mile and threw him into a pond full of duckweed. People took politics seriously in those days. They used to begin storing up rotten eggs weeks before an election.

(from **Coming up for Air** by George Orwell, referring to an election in the early years of this century)

For many people, a general election is one of the few times they will take part directly in a political act of national significance. Usually over 70% of the electorate turns out to vote, and the election results, as well as the weeks of campaigning beforehand, will be extensively covered by television, radio and the newspapers.

At a general election people have the opportunity to vote for a candidate representing a party which hopes to be able to form the next government. Although, by law, elections must be held at least once every five years, they often take place more frequently. This could happen if a government is defeated on a vote of 'no confidence' in the House of Commons. It would show that the government could no longer maintain the support of a majority of MPs and it would then be expected to resign. Although this is not a regular occurrence, it did happen to the Labour Government in 1979. The Prime Minister, Jim Callaghan, asked the Queen to 'dissolve' Parliament and a general election was held a few weeks later. A more likely reason for an early general election is that the Prime Minister, who decides the date when the election shall be held, will try to select a time when support for his or her party among the electorate appears to be strongest.

The following passage indicates the procedures of election day and, using the 1983 general election as an illustration, looks at what happens during the campaign leading up to it.

In the second week of May, 1983, Margaret Thatcher announced that there would be a general election on 9 June. Usually, by the time an election is called, the different parties in each constituency will have already chosen their candidates, and the national and local party organizations will be ready for the election campaign. However, in May 1983, although the Conservatives were well organized, neither the Alliance nor Labour were properly prepared for fighting an election. Margaret Thatcher would have liked to complete her full five-year term (ending in 1984). But a number of factors – predictions about the state of the economy, results of opinion polls, disputes within the Labour Party, etc. – led to calls for an early election.

For the election campaign, each of the parties prepare long manifestos. These manifestos inform the electorate of what the parties intend to do if they win the election and form the

Margaret Thatcher after winning the 1983 general election.

new government. They are given extensive coverage in the media. The party leaders go around the country making speeches and they also appear in party political broadcasts on television. In fact television is probably their most important link with the public, although it can be overdone. One survey indicated that over 50% of those asked thought there was too much television coverage of the 1983 election. The performance of party leaders in handling the tough questioning of the television interviewers, such as Brian Walden and Robin Day, may well have had some effect on the election result. Michael Foot 'was generally thought to be worst – vague, rambling and verbose'. Survey results indicated that the Labour Party might have been far more popular with a different leader. Roy Jenkins (SDP leader) was said to be 'ineffective' and 'pompous'. Margaret Thatcher was 'generally impressive', but David Steel 'was the only leader to emerge with full marks: a poor platform speaker, he proved brilliant on the more intimate stage of television'.

As part of the parties' campaign at local level, printed personal statements by the candidates are delivered to each household. They will usually mention some points from the national party manifestos, but will also contain some local details. A photograph and some information about the candidate will probably be included. Active party members will be busy canvassing – knocking on doors to discover who is likely to vote for their own particular candidate. On voting day, these electors can be reminded to go and cast their vote. In addition to canvassing there will be local meetings, and posters will be put up in the streets and in people's windows.

A ballot paper

BROWN **Independent**	
CLARKE **Labour**	
JONES **Liberal**	
REYNOLDS **Conservative**	

On the day of the election, polling stations – usually local schools, libraries and village halls – are open from early morning to late evening. All people on the electoral register should have received a card telling them where they can vote. At the polling station they will be given a ballot paper which gives the candidates' names and parties (see previous page). The voter puts a cross by the candidate of her choice, and voting is done in secret.

Votes will be counted, usually the same night, at a central location in the constituency such as the Town Hall. Television and radio broadcast the results from around the country, as they are announced, until the early hours of the following morning. By this time, the overall outcome of the general election – in terms of which party is likely to form the next government – is usually known.

(adapted from **The General Election** produced by the British Youth Council [Political Education Series] and **British Politics Today** by Bill Jones and Dennis Kavanagh, Manchester University Press, Manchester, 1983, pp. 179–83)

1. Identify the leaders of the following parties at the time of the 1983 general election
   a Conservative Party   (1)
   b Labour Party   (1)
   c Social Democratic Party   (1)
2. a Give two reasons why a general election may take place before a government has completed its full term.   (2)
   b Which of these applied in 1983?   (1)
3. a What role does television play during the period of an election?   (3)
   b In what ways might it affect the outcome of an election?   (2)
4. a How can a local party member help during an election campaign?   (3)
   b Why is the election campaign at national level probably more influential than the local campaign?   (3)
5. a Why is voting carried out by secret ballot?   (1)
   b In some countries, such as Australia, all electors are legally required to vote. Should voting be compulsory in Britain? Give reasons.   (2)

4 The British electoral system

The British system of elections is known as the 'first past the post' system. In each constituency the candidate receiving the highest number of votes wins a seat in the House of Commons, becoming the Member of Parliament for that constituency. The difference between the number of votes cast for the winning candidate and those received by his/her closest rival is called the **majority**. In some constituencies the majorities may be very large, running into many thousands of votes. These are known as **safe seats**, especially if a large majority is obtained by the same political party in successive elections. In other constituencies the results can be very close, with the successful candidate winning by only a narrow margin of votes: hence the term **marginal seats** or **marginals**. In the 1983 general election, for example, there were 19 seats with majorities of fewer than 500 votes.

If one political party wins more constituencies than all the other parties put together, it will have an **overall majority** of seats in the

House of Commons. The Queen will invite the party leader to become the Prime Minister and to form the new government. If no party has an overall majority, agreements may have to be made between two or more parties on how a government should be formed. They could arrange a **coalition** by forming a government composed of members from each of the parties involved in the agreement.

Some of the terms introduced above and some of the effects of the British electoral system are illustrated in the following tables.

Results from two constituencies at the 1983 general election

Blaenau Gwent

Candidate	Party	Votes
G. Atkinson	Liberal/Alliance	6,408
M. Foot	Labour	30,113
S. Morgan	Plaid Cymru	1,624
T. Morgan	Conservative	4,816

Leicester, South

Candidate	Party	Votes
C. Davis	Ecology	495
J. Marshall	Labour	21,417
C. Pickard	British National Party	280
R. Renold	Liberal/Alliance	9,410
D. Roberts	Workers Party for a Workers State	161
D. Spencer	Conservative	21,424

1. a Name the winning candidate and party in each of the constituencies shown above. (2)
   b Which of these constituencies is the 'marginal'? (1)
   c Why might votes cast in safe-seats sometimes be referred to as 'wasted' votes? (3)

UK General Election Results, 9 June, 1983

Party	Total Votes	% Share of Total	Number of Seats (MPs)
Conservative	13,012,602	42.4	397
Labour	8,457,124	27.6	209
Liberal/SDP Alliance	7,780,587	25.4	23
Scottish Nationalist	331,975	1.1	2
Plaid Cymru	125,309	0.4	2
Others	963,308	3.1	17
Totals	30,670,905	100.0	650

2. a From which party was the new government formed? (1)
   b Calculate the winning party's overall majority. (2)
   c Using the information in the table, explain why the Labour Party won far more seats than the Liberal/SDP Alliance despite their shares of the total votes being fairly close. (3)
3. In 1951 the Labour Party obtained the highest number of votes cast in the country but the Conservative Party won the election. In the general election of February, 1974, the reverse occurred. How can such situations arise? (3)
4. In what ways might the 'first past the post' electoral system be considered 'unfair'? (5)

5 Should the electoral system be changed?

Defenders of the present electoral system claim that it produces strong and effective government, based largely on a two-party system in Parliament. A common outcome of general elections has been that one party has an overall majority of seats in the house of Commons. This means that the government can usually rely on the voting support of MPs in its own party to agree to its policies. In this way it can make laws and carry out the promises it made to the electorate during the election campaign. The British electoral system is also simple. It is easy for the voters to understand and the election result is quickly known.

However, some people believe that the 'first past the post' system is unsatisfactory and should be changed. The following extract, from a report by the Liberal/SDP Alliance, details a number of criticisms of the present system.

The 'first past the post' system of election may be seen by many in the Labour and Conservative parties as part of the natural order of things. Yet today Britain is the only democracy in Europe to employ the system.

It is commonly defended on the ground that it makes for effective and stable government, and that this is more important than the election of representatives who in total reflect as nearly as possible the opinions and wishes of all the voters. In a multi-party situation the first past the post system is in fact less likely to deliver 'strong government', but even if it did would this be a good thing? Under our system any government which has an absolute [overall] majority in the House of Commons (however small) is a 'strong government'. This means that over the period between general elections it can force through legislation, however partisan, and recent history has shown that governments do not hesitate to do so. This is the condition which Lord Hailsham has described as 'elective dictatorship'.

Yet since the war, no party and hence no government has achieved 50% of the vote.

This is particularly dangerous at a time when both the Conservative and Labour parties (partly as a consequence of the electoral system) have become more extreme. An alternation of 'strong governments' put into power by a minority of voters may now lead to each government putting through extremist measures which are desired by only a minority of the voters, and which the next government will then try to reverse whilst at the same time putting through extremist measures of its own. This scenario repeated at intervals of five years or less is hardly likely to enable the country to succeed economically or in any other way.

Thus in recent years the first past the post system has not given Britain stable government. Indeed, the consequence of continual lurches in policy has been instability of a most damaging kind. This can be seen clearly in the field of economic and industrial policy. The steel industry, in the words of Lord Caldecote, 'has been a political shuttlecock for a quarter of a century. Threatened with nationalization, nationalized, denationalized, renationalized, now reduced … to a shambles. In no other country has so much waste and human misery been caused by fundamental changes of government policy resulting from our two-party adversary electoral system.'

Single-party majority governments, therefore, are unlikely to provide strong and effective government. Indeed recent changes in the working of the electoral system have made the first past the post system even less defensible. Less of the electorate have been willing to vote for the Conservative and Labour parties, and many have preferred to vote for Liberal or Nationalist candidates. The consequence is that governments have been gaining absolute parliamentary majorities on much smaller percentages of the popular vote. In October, 1974, the Labour government secured the support of only 39.2% of those who voted, and just over one-quarter of the electorate. In 1979, the Conservatives gained 43.9% of the vote, enjoying the support of around one-third of the electorate.

(from **Electoral Reform: First Report of the Joint Liberal/SDP Alliance Commission on Constitutional Reform**, Poland Street Publications, London, 1982, pp. 3–4)

The Alliance report goes on to say that the first past the post system exaggerates regional differences in party support. Labour is under-represented in the South and rural areas, the Conservatives in the North and some urban areas. It claims that these political parties may therefore be unduly influenced by the interests of particular regions and classes and insensitive to the needs of others. The report states that, in the past, the present system has discriminated against the Liberal Party because support for the Liberals was evenly spread geographically. Furthermore, the Liberals have been even more under-represented than those smaller parties which are connected with only one part of the United Kingdom. For example: 'In October 1974, the Liberals with 18.3% of the vote won 13 seats, while the SNP Scottish National Party with only 2.9% of the total UK vote secured 11 seats.' (p. 6)

A different electoral system – with parties being represented in Parliament in proportion to their support among the electorate as a whole – would be more likely to result in coalition governments. But the Alliance report does not see this as a bad thing. It argues that coalitions force the parties to negotiate and strive for agreement, and this is seen as preferable to the present 'confrontational approach' of British politics. It also points out that coalition governments seem to have been successful in Scandinavian countries and in West Germany.

1. Why are the Alliance parties the strongest critics of the present electoral system? (2)
2. Explain Lord Hailsham's phrase 'elective dictatorship.' (2)
3. In what sense have all governments since 1945 been 'minority governments'? (1)

4. What evidence is provided for the claim that the electoral system has produced unstable government? (3)
5. a Using information from the above passage and from the 1983 general election results (given in Section 2.4), show how the Liberal Party and the Liberal/SDP Alliance have failed to win seats in proportion to their support amongst the voters as a whole. (5)
   b Why does this situation occur? (3)
6. a What is the advantage claimed for coalition governments? (2)
   b What disadvantages could there be? (2)

6 Electoral reform

Because of the sorts of criticisms referred to in the previous extract (2.5), various suggestions have been made about how to reform the present electoral system. Some of these suggestions aim to remove the possibility whereby, under the first past the post system, a candidate can win a seat and yet receive fewer than half the votes cast in his or her constituency. Other proposals go further by also encouraging a more **proportional representation** at national level. The aim is to ensure that the different parties obtain seats in the House of Commons more in line with their levels of support amongst the electorate as a whole. The following passage explains two of the more commonly recommended ideas for electoral reform and presents some of their advantages and problems.

The voter is given very little choice under the present electoral system. All he can do is mark a cross by the name of the candidate standing for his preferred party. With a system that allows **preferential** voting, however, the voter can rank candidates in order of preference. Such a reform to the electoral system would be easy to arrange as the present single-member constituencies (one MP for each of the 650 constituencies) could be retained. In this case, the new system is referred to as the **Alternative Vote**. Instead of a single mark for one candidate, the voter can indicate his preferences among the different candidates: 1,2,3, and so on. If one candidate gets over half the total first-preference votes cast he becomes the MP for that constituency. If no candidate receives over half the total, then the one with the least number of votes is eliminated from the count. His ballot papers are then examined and added to the votes of the remaining candidates according to the second preferences shown on them. This procedure continues until one candidate has over 50% of the total votes and emerges as the winner. The successful candidate in every constituency can therefore claim to have at least some supprt from a majority of the voters.

The Alternative Vote system, however, would not necessarily improve the under-representation of some parties that occurs with the present system. To have preferential voting **and** a system of proportional representation (PR), the **Single Transferable Vote** has been recommended by some people (including members of the SDP and Liberal Party). As with the Alternative Vote, the voter places the candidates in order of preference. Each party could put forward a number of candidates. Electors loyal to one party could choose to rank only their party's candidates. But voters could decide to list candidates from more than one party. They might wish to base their choices on reasons other than party identification.

With STV, the method of counting the votes and calculating which of the candidates are to be elected is relatively complicated. To secure election, candidates have to reach a certain quota of votes, worked out according to a precise formula. Once a candidate has reached the quota, any of his surplus votes are distributed among the other candidates according to the second preferences on the ballot papers. The advantage claimed for this is that it avoids the 'wasted votes' of the present system. Introducing STV, however, would involve a big change to the present constituency system. Boundaries would have to be completely redrawn and there would be fewer, and larger, constituencies. For example, a large city under the present system may have, say, seven constituencies each returning one MP to Parliament. With STV it could be changed into one large constituency electing seven MPs. Each of the major parties would put up several candidates, and there would also be candidates from the smaller parties. Voters might therefore be faced with a ballot paper containing over 30 names from which to organize their preferences.

The STV method of proportional representation is used in some countries, such as the Republic of Ireland and Australia. Some trade unions in this country have also adopted it. Multi-member constituencies would give people a choice of Parliamentary representatives should they wish an MP to take up a problem on their behalf. But because the constituencies would be larger, the present advantage of having a **local** MP could be lost. STV would produce a more **representative** House of Commons, but it would probably result in coalition governments. Coalitions can lead to fudged decisions, with parties not being able to carry out their manifesto promises because of the compromises they would be forced to make.

(adapted from **Westminster Workshop** by R. K. Mosley, Pergamon Press, Oxford, 1979, pp. 21–8 and **Electoral Reform**: First Report of the Joint Liberal/SDP Alliance Commission on Constitutional Reform, Poland Street Publications, London, 1982, pp. 10–23)

1. Sir Winston Churchill claimed that the Alternative Vote system is 'the worst of all possible plans in which the decision is to be determined by the most worthless votes given to the most worthless candidates'.
   a Explain what is meant by this criticism.   (2)
   b According to the passage, what advantage does the Alternative Vote have over the present system of election? (1)
2. a What problems would a multi-member constituency pose for an MP and for his constituents (people living in his constituency)?   (3)
   b What benefits for constituents might result from a multi-member constituency?   (2)
3. a Prepare the outline of a speech to be given by a Liberal Party member calling for the introduction of a system of proportional representation.   (6)
   b Prepare the outline of a reply, indicating the disadvantages of PR and defending the present electoral system.   (6)

7 By-elections

The form of proportional representation discussed in the previous passage (2.6) could be introduced for general elections. But some other system would be required for those occasions when it is necessary to hold an election to find a replacement for an MP for a particular constituency. These take place between general elections and are called by-elections. The following extract explains why they are held and shows how the outcome of a by-election can be very different from that of a general election.

By-elections are most commonly held when MPs die in office or resign. The biggest difference between by-elections and general elections is that the former do not directly decide which party will form the government. (The Labour Government, elected in October 1974, eventually saw its majority disappear after losing a series of by-elections. But it did manage to remain in power until 1979 through pacts and agreements with other parties.)

Voters do not treat by-elections in the same way as general elections. Usually, though not always, the turnout at by-elections is lower than at general elections in the same constituency. The major parties, especially the party in power, often do badly because their supporters stay at home. But by-elections are often excellent for parties such as the Liberals and Nationalists. The most spectacular by-elections in the 1960s and 1970s were those in which Liberals and Nationalists captured formerly safe seats from the major parties. For example, Gwynfor Evans won Camarthen for Plaid Cymru in 1966; Winifred Ewing won Hamilton as a Scottish Nationalist in 1967; and the Liberals triumphed in a number of by-elections such as Isle of Ely and Berwick on Tweed in 1973 and Liverpool Edge Hill in 1979.

Often, indeed, minor parties do better at by-elections than at the following general election, and their best results frequently occur in what were previously safe seats. For an example of how the safeness of the seat affected voters' calculations, we may look at Berwick on Tweed, a safe Conservative seat where a by-election took place in 1973 because of the resignation of Mr. Anthony Lambton after he admitted to accusations of associating with prostitutes and possessing cannabis. (It is not, of course, a legal offence for a MP to have intercourse with a prostitute. But, since he was a junior defence minister, Lambton risked being blackmailed or having defence secrets passed on to hostile powers.) At the by-election, it is plain that a large number of Conservative voters supported the Liberal. Many of them no doubt felt that as it was a safe seat it could do the party no harm for them to register their protest in this way. But at the same time Labour voters could see that their party had no chance of winning and that it was in their best interests to vote Liberal 'to keep the Tories out'. With both these processes working it was probably easier for the Liberal to win the seat than if it had been marginal as between Conservative and Labour.

(from **Elections** by Iain McLean, Longman, London, 1983, pp. 69–71, with minor additions)

1. a How does a by-election differ from a general election?   (2)
   b Why are by-elections held?   (2)
2. Explain why each of the following might occur at a by-election when compared with a general election:
   a lower turnout   (2)
   b greater support for a smaller party   (2)
   c the loss of a safe seat   (2)
3. The following election results all refer to the **Crosby** constituency.

1979 General Election

(Electorate: 81,208)

R. Page (Conservative)	34,768
A. Mulhearn (Labour)	15,496
A. Hill (Liberal)	9,302
P. Hussey (Ecology)	1,489

Conservative majority: 19,272
Turnout: 75%

By-election, 26 November, 1981

S. Williams (SDP/Liberal Alliance)	28,118
J. Butcher (Conservative)	22,829
J. Backhouse (Labour)	5,450
R. Small (Ecology)	480
T. Biscuit-Barrel (Looney Society)	223
T. Keen (C-L Alliance)	99
W. Boakes (Public Safety)	36
J. Kennedy (Suspended Students)	31
D. Potter (Humanitarian)	31

SDP/Liberal Alliance majority: 5,289
Turnout: 70%

1983 General Election

(Electorate: 83,274)

G. Thornton (Conservative)	30,604
S. Williams (SDP/Alliance)	27,203
R. Waring (Labour)	6,611
P. Hussey (Ecology)	415

Conservative majority: 3,401
Turnout: 78%

a Identify **four** points about by-elections made in the extract which could be supported by evidence from the above results. Clearly indicate the evidence for each point.   (8)

b A by-election often attracts a greater number of candidates than at a general election in the same constituency. Why do you think this is?   (2)

Section 3 Voting Behaviour

How do electors decide who to vote for at election times? Why do some people vote for the Conservative party, others for Labour and yet others for one of the Alliance parties? Why do some voters support one of the smaller parties whilst a significant number of electors do not use their vote at all?

When deciding how (or whether) to cast their vote, do most people study the manifestos put out by each of the parties and vote for the party offering what seems to them to be the best policies? Or do they vote according to what they know about the candidates standing in their constituencies? Or do voters tend to form a general image of the parties and vote accordingly? Section 1.2 examined the various agencies of political socialization – the family, education, and so on – and the role they play in helping to form an individual's political attitudes and beliefs. It might be expected that people with similar socialization experiences come to form similar images of, and general attitudes to, political parties. Political scientists studying voting behaviour have found that there are often **some** connections between the way people vote and, for example, their class, sex, age, and the region of the country in which they live.

This section examines some of these questions and connections.

1 Voting and class (1)

The connection with voting behaviour that has been studied more than any other is class. Social class can be defined in a number of different ways but a major distinction is often made, on the basis of occupation, between the middle class and the working class. According to this division the middle class consists of those in professional, business and other non-manual jobs, and the working class those in manual occupations. This type of classification is in many ways unsatisfactory. Married women, for instance, are generally classified according to their husband's occupation without taking account of any paid work they themselves carry out. It can also be argued that social class involves more than merely the job a person happens to be doing at a particular time. Nevertheless, occupational categories do provide a straightforward, if rather rough-and-ready, guide for the purpose of studying class differences in voting behaviour amongst the electorate as a whole.

The British Labour Party has traditionally been associated with the interests of the working class while the Conservative Party has been seen as defending those of the more wealthy and privileged in society (the upper and middle classes). If people always voted according to their class interests the Labour Party would be continuously in power (as the working class makes up a greater proportion of the electorate than the other classes). But this has not been the case. In half of the general elections since 1945 the Conservative Party has received more votes than the Labour Party. This suggests that a significant proportion of the working class votes for parties other than Labour. Up to the mid-1970s about one-third of the working class vote went to the Conservative Party at each election. This amounted to about half of the Conservatives' total vote. In 1959, the Labour Party lost its third election in succession. Consequently, these working class Conservative voters became the subject of attention. The following passage presents a number of arguments that were put forward about 'cross-class' voting (why some electors were apparently voting against their class interests).

> 'It's a large, late Victorian terraced house in a fashionable part of town. In the dingy two-room basement lives a retired hospital porter, his wife and their grown-up son. They read the **Daily Express** and vote Conservative. Above them, their landlords, a university lecturer and his wife, a school-teacher, occupy the other three floors.' Their joint income is well over double the average income of a married couple and they 'part-own a cottage in the Dordogne. They read the **Morning Star** and **Socialist Worker** and vote Labour'.
>
> This sort of situation is not all that unusual. Although the exact proportions vary from one election to another, about one-sixth of middle class voters have regularly supported the

Labour Party. It has been observed that these 'middle class radicals' were often in occupations concerned with service to the community and social welfare or which emphasized self-expression and creativity. Social work and teaching are two examples. In general, neither of these two jobs are provided by private industry with which the Conservative Party is more closely identified.

However, more significant, in terms of numbers and the outcomes of elections, are the working class voters who vote Conservative. Various explanations have been offered for working class Conservative voting. W. G. Runciman claimed it was to do with how working class electors viewed their own class position. If they saw themselves as 'middle class' they were more likely to vote Conservative than if they regarded themselves as 'working class'. John Goldthorpe found that working class Conservative voters often had friends or family members who were non-manual employees and who voted Tory. Manual workers who lived in working class communities and who did not often mix with other classes were more likely to vote Labour. Others have argued that this is especially noticeable in those working class communities which grew up around single industries such as mining, shipbuilding and dock work. These communities tend to be insulated from middle class values and ideas. They developed their own life-styles, attitudes and beliefs which include strong Labour Party loyalties. Elsewhere, members of the working class may be more exposed to what Frank Parkin has called the 'dominant value system' which is more closely represented by the Conservative Party.

McKenzie and Silver detected two different attitudes among working class Conservatives. There were some who voted Tory because they believed that Conservative politicians were the 'natural rulers of Britain... uniquely qualified to govern by birth, experience and outlook'. McKenzie and Silver labelled these electors **deferential** voters. They 'deferred' to traditional authority, believing that Conservative leaders had superior qualities to those of their own class. The other group of working class Tories were called the **secular** voters. They voted Conservative because they judged this party to be more successful in bringing about benefits such as higher living standards. They believed they would be 'better off' with the Conservative Party in power.

(adapted from 'The tale of the working class Tory' by Tom Forester, **New Society**, 15 October 1981, pp. 97–9 and **Sociology: Themes and Perspectives** by Michael Haralambos with Robin Heald, University Tutorial Press, Slough, 1980, pp. 130–33)

1. a Which is the working class family and which the middle class family in the example at the beginning of the passage?   (2)
   b On what basis have you made the distinction?   (2)
2. a What explanation is offered for middle class Labour voting?   (2)
   b Suggest other reasons.   (2)
3. How does Goldthorpe's explanation of working class Conservative voting differ from that suggested by Runciman?   (4)
4. Distinguish between the 'deferential' and the 'secular' working class Tory voters.   (4)
5. How might explanations of cross-class voting be of interest to politicians?   (4)

2 Voting and class (2)

The debate about working class Tory voting faded as Labour won four of the five general elections from 1964 to October, 1974. Interest was rekindled, however, after its defeat in 1983. It was not only that the Conservatives had won their second election in succession but also that the Labour vote had dropped to such a low level. Some of the arguments of the 1960s re-emerged, although the evidence of the 1979 and 1983 general elections might suggest that class differences in the way people vote are becoming less important. Nevertheless, middle class voters are still more likely to vote for the Conservative Party than for other parties and the Labour Party still relies for the vast majority of its support on the working class.

The 1983 general election was the first to be contested by the Social Democratic Party. The Alliance it formed with the Liberals attracted votes in fairly even proportions from all social classes. This new development in electoral politics has made the analysis of voting behaviour more complicated, as the following extract shows.

In the 1983 general election 'the electorate did not embrace the Conservatives; it rebuffed Labour and flirted with the Alliance. The Labour vote was down to 27.6%, its lowest share since 1918. What needs to be explained about the 1983 election is not why the Conservatives did so well, but why Labour did so badly and the Alliance not quite well enough. The Conservatives owe their triumph, Labour its humiliation, to a direct switch of votes from Labour to the Alliance' (although for every three electors moving from Labour to the Alliance, one switched to the Conservatives and one did not vote at all).

Although social class continues to be a major factor in party choice it has been weakening since the 1950s. There used to be a considerable gap between the proportion of manual workers voting for the Labour Party and the proportion of non-manual employees voting the same way. In the 1959 election this difference stood at 40%. In 1983 it was down to 21%. In the middle classes, particularly among office workers, the relatively small Labour vote has not changed much. And, compared with 1979, the working class

Conservative vote did not rise much. It was more a case of a continuing decline in the number of working class Labour voters, with many moving to the Alliance. In fact the Alliance vote was spread very evenly over all classes.

Can the Labour Party still claim to be the party of the working class? Ivor Crewe's answer is: 'The Labour vote remains largely working class; but the working class has ceased to be largely Labour.' In 1983 only 38% of manual workers voted Labour. It remains the party of the **traditional working class** – those living in council houses, those in Scotland and the North of England, and those working in the public sector (employed by the government, local councils and in the nationalized industries). However, the Labour Party appears to have lost the support of the **new working class**. Among those workers employed by private firms and companies, voting support for Labour and for the Conservatives was more or less equal. Furthermore, the 1983 voting patterns of manual workers who are home-owners, or who live in the South, show that for this group Labour fell into **third** place.

Ivor Crewe concludes his analysis of working class voting behaviour by arguing: 'The old working class is now too small to give Labour electoral victory; the new working class too big to be ignored. By 1983 twice as many manual workers were employed in the private than public sector. Almost as many were home-owners as council tenants. The division of Britain is no longer **between** the classes but **within** the working class.' And he adds that the more secure and better-off sections within this class are growing. Crewe suggests that unless the Labour Party can attract both the 'old' and the 'new' working class, it will be unable to recapture the level of voting support it once had.

(adapted from 'The disturbing truth behind Labour's rout' by Ivor Crewe, **The Guardian** June 13, 1983)

1. What evidence is provided to support the claims that
   a class has become less important in party choice?   (3)
   b the Alliance parties are not class based?   (2)
2. With the help of comments from elsewhere in the passage, explain the first sentence of the extract.   (5)

3. Explain the comment that '...the Labour vote remains largely
working class; but the working class has ceased to be largely
Labour'.   (2)
4. a What is the difference between the 'public' and the 'private'
sector?   (2)
  b How does Ivor Crewe distinguish between the 'traditional' (or
'old') working class and the 'new' working class?   (2)
  c How does he make use of this distinction in reaching his conclusion about what the Labour Party must do to regain its
electoral support?   (4)

3 Sex, age and region

Not all political scientists agree that the link between class and
voting behaviour has significantly declined. Different ways of cate-
gorizing the electorate into particular class groups produce
different sets of figures. But class is not the only factor that has
interested those who study voting patterns. For example, over
many elections surveys consistently indicated that more women
than men voted Conservative. There was a tendency for older
people to vote Conservative and younger voters to support Labour.
Labour received a much higher proportion of the votes from some
ethnic minorities and among trade unionists than did the
Conservatives. In regional terms Labour have traditionally done
better in Scotland, Wales and the north of England, whereas
Conservative support was higher in the south and in the more rural
and suburban parts of England. The following extracts provide
evidence on three of these factors – sex, age and region – to see if
the differences have been maintained in recent general elections.

A permanent feature of all elections until recently was the
higher Conservative vote among women than men. The gap
disappeared in 1979 and has now gone into reverse. For the
first time, and under Britain's first woman Prime Minister,
the Conservatives drew less support from women than men
(although this is disputed by the results of another survey).
The Alliance, not Labour, benefited, taking 4% more votes
among women (28%) than men (24%).
Until 1979 surveys showed that, compared with the old,

An alternative to voting? The People's March for Jobs arriving in central London, 1983.

the young voted Labour in higher proportions. In 1979, for the first time, new voters divided equally between Labour and the Conservatives. This time (1983) Labour came third among new voters taking a mere 17% of their vote, 3% behind the Alliance and 11% behind the Conservatives. That Labour should fail so dismally among the young at a time of severe youth unemployment must seem a mystery. Ironically, unemployment was part of the reason. Among unemployed 18–22 year olds, almost half (47%) did not vote at all.

Conservative support steadily increased from the young to the old, but along a gentler gradient than in the past. The odd group out was the old. Among the over 65s, the Conservative vote dropped by more than the national average, the Labour vote by less. Labour policy on pensions, and the Government's record, could be an explanation, although only a fifth of the over 65s in the survey cited pensions as an important issue. An alternative explanation is that the over 65s are the generation of the 1930s and the Second World War. The majority will have first voted in, and contributed to, the Labour landslide of 1945. Some of the Labour loyalty induced in their formative years will have lasted until today. The Alliance did best among new voters, worst among the over 65s, probably because party loyalties are least fixed in the young and most ingrained in the old.

(from 'The disturbing truth behind Labour's rout' by Ivor Crewe, **The Guardian** June 13, 1983, with minor additions)

Labour (following the 1983 election) now has no seats south of a line from London to Bristol. The party has only 30 out of 260 seats south of a line from the Severn to the Wash (excluding London, just three seats out of 176). In 1945 more than one-third of Labour's wins were in southern England; as recently as October 1974 more than a quarter. The share is now one in seven. Labour has lost 62% of its seats in southern England in nine years. On the other hand, the Conservatives now have no MPs in Glasgow or Liverpool and just one in Manchester. As the table shows, it is not simply a matter of the north-south divide growing deeper. Labour's share of the vote fell by more than the national average in Leeds and Sheffield; but less than the Conservatives' further south of Birmingham.

How The Big Cities Voted

	CON		LAB		LIB/SDP	
	%	Change since '79	%	Change since '79	%	Change since '79
Liverpool	29.3	−6.6	47.2	− 1.8	22.8	+ 8.5
Glasgow	18.8	−7.3	52.0	− 5.0	21.2	+ 15.9
Birmingham	39.0	−5.3	42.3	− 4.1	18.0	+ 10.4
Manchester	30.4	−4.5	50.3	− 4.2	18.0	+ 8.8
Edinburgh	34.9	−4.3	30.7	− 7.0	28.5	+ 16.0
Sheffield	29.4	−2.4	44.2	− 10.0	26.0	+ 12.9
London	43.9	−2.1	29.7	− 9.9	24.9	+ 13.0
Bristol	42.3	−0.8	33.1	− 9.3	23.5	+ 10.6
Leeds	34.8	−1.2	35.5	− 10.8	28.6	+ 12.5
Cardiff	40.6	−0.6	29.9	− 12.4	27.2	+ 14.0

(SDP was not in existence in 1979. 'Lib/SDP change' column is therefore based on a comparison with the 1979 votes for the Liberal Party only.)

(from 'Anatomy of a landslide' by Peter Kellner, **New Statesman**, 17 June, 1983, pp. 7-8, with minor additions)

1. a According to the evidence in the extracts about the 1983

election, are voting patterns becoming more predictable or
less predictable?   (1)
  b Why might it be dangerous to draw definite conclusions from
     the study of one election only?   (2)
2. Suggest reasons why
  a more women than men voted Conservative up to the
     mid-1970s   (2)
  b this may no longer be the case   (2)
3. How can the concept of political socialization help in describing
   one of the suggested reasons for the Labour vote in the over-65
   age group?   (3)
4. Suggest why so many of the young unemployed did not use
  ⟩ their vote in the 1983 election.   (2)
5. From the table, identify the city which provided the highest
   proportion of the votes for
  a the Conservative Party   (1)
  b the Labour Party   (1)
  c the Alliance   (1)
6. Suggest reasons why the Conservatives appear to do less well in
   the large cities.   (3)
7. Because voting is carried out in secret, a lot of the information
   about voting behaviour is obtained from surveys. Why might
   survey data not always be totally accurate?   (2)

4 Policies, issues and images

If some of the traditional indicators of voting behaviour – class,
sex, age – are becoming less predictable, it is perhaps useful to look
at the question from another angle. Are people increasingly voting
according to specific policies, whichever party is putting them
forward, or do general images of political parties play a role? At
each election there are usually one or two issues which become
central to the campaign but which may be absent at the following
election. Particular events, too, can have their effect. The
heightened popularity of the Government – and especially the
Prime Minister – after the Falklands War was still benefiting the
Conservative Party at the 1983 election. On the other hand, the
general images which people form of political parties tend to last a
long time. The first of the following two extracts argues that

images are more important than issues in explaining party choice at elections. The second emphasizes the policies of the parties.

Even though the party system **enables** electors to choose between sets of programmes, it is not true that electors choose between programmes. It is not even true that electors, having only one vote, establish an order of priority and select one 'most important issue' on the basis of which they cast their vote. Studies have shown that the support which electors give to a party is linked, not with 'issues', but with much broader and vaguer general 'images' with which the party is associated. These images often coincide with a certain view of the class system in the country, particularly among Labour electors, a large majority of whom claim that their party is 'for the working class' and that the Conservative party is 'for the rich or big business'. Images are also associated with some general economic social notions, such as the 'Welfare State', 'employment', 'free enterprise' and 'nationalization'.

Images differ from issues, but they are connected to them. Images are influenced by issues in a general fashion: they are influenced by what is going on. They are also influenced by leadership. But they are more persistent than issues, although they are much vaguer. They indicate that the electors have a general view of society and of the way in which the parties fit in the framework of society.

Voting is clearly partly an emotional affair. It is based on prejudices as well as on a rational assessment of society in general. It is based on the view which the electors have of the future society which the parties are trying to build. Party images are the channel through which the party conflict is resolved, every four or five years, at a general election. General elections involve the whole life of the nation. It is natural that they should be decided, not only by views on one or a few fairly specialized questions, but on the whole of the impressions which, rightly or wrongly, electors have of society and of its political forces.

(from **Voters, Parties and Leaders** by J. Blondel, Penguin, Harmondsworth, 1969, pp. 81–4)

Which of the many influences on the vote – leaders, party

policy, self-interest, sheer party loyalty – has the most impact? All have some influence, and disentangling precisely their separate effect is impossible. Yet the evidence (from the survey undertaken by Gallup, for the BBC, involving over 4,000 interviews at the time of the 1983 general election) strongly suggests that, as in previous elections, policies counted for much more than personalities; perceptions of the country's interest more than self-interest.

The decisive dominance of national policy considerations is revealed when the vote in the election is compared with people's choice of parties on different criteria (see the table below).

Party preferences on various questions

	Vote Great Britain 1983 %	Which party has the best policies?	Which party is best for people like you?	Which party has the best team of leaders?	Which party do you generally identify with?	Who would make the best PM?	
Cons.	43	50	43	58	44	Thatcher	46
Lab.	28	25	33	17	38	Foot	13
Lib/SDP	26	24	22	24	16	Steel	35
Others	3	1	2	1	2	Jenkins	6

More people chose the Conservative Party on each of the questions in the table than actually voted for it. This indicates the power of deep-seated Labour loyalties to induce a vote of the heart rather than the mind.

But if policies count, which ones in particular? The most important issue for voters was unemployment (72%), followed way behind by defence (38%), prices (20%) and health (11%). References to strikes fell from 20% in 1979 to 3% in 1983 and mention of taxes from 21% to 4%. Immigration, the hidden mover of votes in the 1960s and 1970s, dropped off the bottom of the political agenda (1%). Unemployment was the dominant issue in voters' minds. Why, then, did Labour do so badly? The answer is that fewer people were convinced that Labour could shorten the dole queues. As a result, unemployment damaged the Conservative vote without repairing Labour's.

The effect of the party leaders cannot be ignored. Not since

Twinkle twinkle, Stainless Steel,
How we love your sex-appeal!
Up above the sordid scrimmage,
Polishing your TV image —
Twinkle twinkle, Stainless Steel,
How much **rust** do you conceal?

John Minnion

the Second World War (probably much earlier) has a major party leader been regarded as so implausible a Prime Minister as Michael Foot. Only 13% picked him as the best potential Prime Minister; and fully 63% picked him as the worst. Foot was more of a liability to his party than Margaret Thatcher was an asset to hers. She was first choice as Prime Minister, but in the eyes of only slightly more people than actually voted Conservative. David Steel had numerous admirers and virtually no detractors. Sifting through the mounds of data produced by the survey, however, one is struck by the way leaders mattered less than policy.

The Alliance failed to poll its potential support for the usual reason – the squeeze on third parties. 59% of potential Alliance supporters explained their decision to vote differently by saying that the Alliance could not win, and a vote for it would only let the Conservatives or Labour in.

(from 'How Labour was trounced all round' by Ivor Crewe in **The Guardian** June 14, 1983, with minor additions)

1. a Give **one** example from the first passage of a party image.   (2)
   b State **two** ways in which images differ from issues.   (2)

2. According to the table in the second extract which question produced the highest response for
   a the Conservative Party? (1)
   b the Labour Party? (1)
3. a What does Blondel (first extract) mean by voting being 'partly an emotional affair'? (2)
   b Which of the comments by Crewe (second extract) seems to lend some support for this view? (2)
   c From what evidence does Crewe make this comment? (2)
4. What evidence is there in the second passage to indicate that issues tend to have a shorter life than images? (2)
5. Blondel states that a party's image can be influenced by leadership. Using information from the second extract, say which party you think would have been most affected by this factor in the 1983 election. (3)
6. What evidence is there to suggest that the Alliance had more support among the electorate than its 1983 share of the vote indicates? (3)

5 Image-making

It might seem from the previous passages in this section that party loyalty has been declining and that policies are playing a greater role in determining how people vote. Nevertheless, the parties themselves are anxious to create, maintain or change their own images which they want to present to the electorate, as the following extract shows.

> Myth matters more than reality in electoral politics. That is why all three major groups use professional advertising agencies: the Conservatives since the mid-1950s, Labour (for the first time) and the Alliance in the election of 1983.
>
> The image-makers have to start with reality. The most important (though not all-important) image is that of the party leader. In 1983, voters put Mrs. Thatcher head and shoulders above Labour's then leader, Mr. Foot, as a potential Prime Minister. The quality most widely recognized – 'good in a crisis', accepted by 60% of the voters – was one she had proved; Mr. Foot scored just 9%.

But reality is also bendable. In 1983, indeed for two years earlier, as inflation fell and unemployment rose, Mrs. Thatcher was presented as (1) determinedly sticking to her policies in order (2) to fulfil her main campaign pledge of 1979, control of inflation.

This was hokum. The main theme of the Conservatives' campaign in 1979 had in fact been tax-cutting and incentives, to get the economy moving. Prices (connected with inflation) played curiously little part. Once elected, the Conservatives instantly redeemed their pledge on incentives, cutting income tax. The economy indeed moved – downwards. But that was the last heard of tax-cutting – its effect was to add four points to an inflation rate already rising fast, the largest at-a-stroke price rise ever engineered by any peacetime government. The election-winning image of 1983 was false.

Could Labour have upset it? Wisely, they did not try. Whatever may have happened earlier, in the end the inflation battle, like the Falklands War, was indeed won. Election experience (and the fate of some Labour attempts to make capital out of the Falklands) shows that (1) trying to dent the other side's image at its strongest point is counter-productive, and (2) voters judge results, not what led up to them.

(from 'The old order changeth' in **The Economist** 15 October, 1983, pp. 21–3)

1. Which of the main parties was the first to use a professional advertising agency? (1)
2. In your own words, explain how the Conservatives' 'election-winning image of 1983 was false'. (3)
3. In your own words, give **two** reasons why Labour did not try to upset the Conservative Party image. (4)
4. To which sections of the electorate (according to class, age, region, etc.) would you target your advertising campaign if you were acting at the next election for
   a the Conservative Party (4)
   b the Labour Party (4)
5. Briefly discuss the view that political parties should not be 'sold' in the same way as breakfast cereals or soap powders. (4)

6 Non-voters and floaters

This section has so far dealt with the way people use their votes. But what of those who do not or cannot use them – the non-voters? Since the Second World War, the non-voting (or abstention) rate at general elections has varied between 16% and 28%. Non-voting may be as much a political act as voting. Certainly, the effect of a significant proportion of abstainers may be very important for the outcome of a general election; as is the 'floating vote'. 'Floating' voters are those who are not committed to a particular party and who therefore may change their party allegiance from one general election to another. They may also include those who switch between voting and not voting. If the changing patterns of voting behaviour revealed at recent general elections reflect a decline in party loyalty, then the floating vote may be increasing. Alternatively, they could indicate a re-alignment of party preferences. In this case, future voting behaviour may once again settle down to a more consistent pattern with a lower level of floaters. It is as yet too early to say.

The first extract that follows looks at non-voting. The floating vote is then examined.

The rate of abstention will always seem higher than it really is because it is worked out according to the electoral register which soon becomes out of date. The register is put together in October and operates for a twelve-month period from the following February. During that time a proportion of the electorate will have died or left the country. Electors who can't vote because they are ill, away on business, or have moved to another constituency can apply for a postal vote. But many don't. These categories – those who should no longer be on the register and those prevented from voting – probably account for about one-third of the recorded abstention rate.

This leaves a 'real' rate of abstention of at least 13%. These are people who could vote but don't. They can be divided into **positive** (or active) abstainers and **negative** (or passive) abstainers. Positive non-voters may abstain because they are not attracted to the parties or the candidates. They may include some people in safe-seat constituencies who think there is no need to cast their vote. However, although the

Negative and positive abstainers.

overall turnout is higher in marginal than in safe seats, the difference is only small. Other positive abstainers may refuse to vote as a protest against the electoral system. Very few people have any say in the choice of candidates to stand at elections, for example. Supporters of minority parties, such as the Communists, get little opportunity to express their support as these parties put up few candidates.

The negative abstainers, on the other hand, are those who are not interested at all in politics. According to Blondel, they tend to be among the least politically-informed electors and often have no opinion on political issues.

(adapted from **Voters, Parties and Leaders** by J. Blondel, Penguin, Harmondsworth, 1969, pp. 52–6)

1. a What is the difference between an 'active' and a 'passive' abstainer? (3)
   b What **other** factors can reduce the recorded percentage turnout at an election? (3)

Is there such a creature as the 'floating voter'? It would probably be better if the term had never been invented. In the first place it must be remembered that the electorate itself is constantly changing as some people die and others come of voting age. This alone could gradually alter the political balance in the country. But the term 'floating voter' also suggests that the electorate can be conveniently divided into two categories: on the one hand the faithful supporter of one of the major parties, on the other earnest individuals seeking after truth. All survey evidence, however, suggests the contrary.

In fact, we can identify no fewer than four types of non-constant electors (the 'floaters'):

1. those whose involvement with the party of their choice is low and who therefore hesitate between voting and abstention;
2. those who experiment with alternative allegiances but generally return to the party of their first choice at election time;
3. those who support a minor party but may be deprived of a candidate of their highest preference;
4. those who experience a genuine conversion and transfer their allegiance.

These four types between them amount to a substantial minority among the electorate. And the total is certainly greater than the number who 'float' in any one election.

(from **Political Representation and Elections in Britain** by Peter G.J. Pulzer, Allen & Unwin, London 1975, pp. 123–5)

2. Why does the writer think it might be preferable if the term 'floating voter' "had never been invented"? (3)
3. Which of the four categories of 'non-constant' voters do you think would be least likely to remain a floater at future elections? (3)

Over two million voters appear to have forgotten that they voted for the Alliance at the 1983 election and believe that they voted Labour, according to the results of the Guardian-Marplan opinion polls. The polls show that as the length of time since the election increases, fewer voters remember voting Alliance.

Which party did you vote for in the last election?

	1985 Feb.	1984 Dec.	1984 Oct.	1984 Aug.	1984 Jun.	1984 Apr.	1984 Feb.	1983 Dec.	1983 Oct.	1983 Aug.	Actual result June, 1983 election
Conservative	45	45	47	41	44	46	44	44	47	44	44
Labour	36	35	36	38	36	34	36	34	31	31	28
Alliance	18	18	16	20	19	19	19	22	21	24	26

Voters who take little or no interest in politics between elections simply forget about the Alliance. They forget that they voted Alliance last time and they forget about the Alliance when asked how they intend to vote.

If this is so, it is both good and bad news for the Alliance. It is bad that so many voters seem to have forgotten of their existence, despite all their attempts to win a larger share of publicity. It is good if it means that the Alliance has a reservoir of potential support that has just temporarily forgotten of its existence but may come back in the heightened political awareness of an election or a by-election campaign.

On the other hand, it seems to indicate that the bulk of Labour voters who switched to the Alliance during the 1983 election campaign, have reverted to their traditional Labour loyalty. A single vote for the Alliance may have been put out of mind and a lifetime of Labour voting has reasserted itself, even to the extent that they believe they voted Labour when they did not. But these voters will clearly be difficult for Labour to hold as an election approaches and their political consciousness is reawakened.

(from 'Why the Alliance voters labour to forget . . .' by Martin Linton in **The Guardian** February 22, 1985, with minor additions)

4. Explain how the evidence in the table suggests that some Alliance voters believed they voted Labour in the 1983 election.

(2)

5. Using the concept of the 'floating vote', explain in what ways
   a the Labour party   (3)
   b the Alliance parties   (3)
   could be encouraged by the findings of the opinion polls reported in the passage above.

Section 4 Political Communication

Section 3 looked at some of the factors influencing party choice. Decisions may sometimes be made on the basis of what is known about particular issues or policies or they may depend on broader images that are held about political parties, politicians, and of politics in general. Either way, most people get the bulk of their information about politics directly or indirectly through the mass media. The mass media include television, radio, newspapers and magazines. They all communicate ideas, views, opinions and facts to the public. They are **mass** media because they are capable of putting over the same information to large sections of the population at the same time; they can reach a **mass** 'audience'. The mass media therefore have the potential to play an enormous role in helping to shape people's ideas and in forming their political attitudes. With a few minor exceptions, they are also systems of one-way communication. Journalists, editors, programme-makers and, on occasions, politicians can convey information to millions of readers, viewers and listeners.

This section examines the role of newspapers and television in British politics. It looks at how they obtain and present ideas and news and at how much power and influence they have. In the final three passages it also examines the other side of the political communication process: how opinions and views can be conveyed **from** the public **to** those in positions of power and influence.

1 The press

Nearly all the national daily newspapers in Britain favour the Conservative Party – particularly during election campaigns. At other times the strength of their support may vary. Some of the popular papers such as the **Daily Express** and the **Daily Mail** usually remain strongly committed to a Conservative line in their political comment. Others – the **Financial Times**, for example – may be

Thursday, June 9, 1983

Thursday, June 9, 1983

(from **The General Election of 1983** by D. Butler and D. Kavanagh, Macmillan, London, 1984)

more willing to criticize particular policies or activities. The **Daily Mirror** is the only large-selling daily newspaper to side with the Labour Party although its support is often lukewarm and not uncritical. The **Guardian** does not claim to commit itself to any party, but it is frequently seen as more sympathetic to the Alliance parties than to the others. The following information compares the sales of the national dailies and then provides some examples of how political matters are presented in the press.

Party preferences and circulations of daily newspapers, 1983

Paper	Average daily sales (millions)	General party preference
Sun	4.2	Conservative
Daily Mirror	3.3	Labour
Daily Express	1.8	Conservative
Daily Mail	1.8	Conservative
Daily Star	1.3	Conservative
Daily Telegraph	1.3	Conservative
Guardian	0.4	Alliance (?)
The Times	0.3	Conservative
Financial Times	0.2	Conservative

1. a Construct a bar chart which shows the circulation of each of the national daily newspapers in the table **and** their party political standpoints.   (4)
   b Roughly what proportion of the total daily sales are of papers likely to support the Conservative Party?   (2)

Opposite are two headlines to the same item of news. The Liberals had won a by-election in the Brecon and Radnor constituency. Their candidate gained 559 votes more than the Labour candidate. Although the Conservatives had won the seat with a majority of 8,784 at the 1983 general election, this time they came third – more than 3,000 votes behind the Liberals. Labour had been tipped to win the by-election after a number of opinion polls had put them in first place. Some senior Labour members later suggested that potential Labour votes had been lost because of comments made by Arthur Scargill, president of the National Union of Mineworkers, a few days before the election.

2. Explain how the two headlines present the outcome of the by-

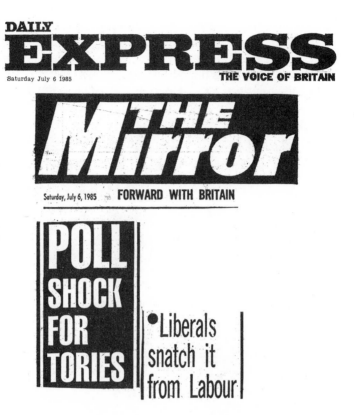

election in line with the party preferences of the newspapers concerned.   (4)

'The **Daily Mail** likes to head an illustrated report with the words: "Picture Power in the Mail". The assertion is that the "picture does the talking" in a way that mere words cannot.' The popular newspapers in particular frequently use pictures as a way of attracting the attention of the readers to reports of current events.

Caroline Rees asks if this use of pictures is done in a responsible way. She argues that Tony Benn, for example, is often shown in photographs 'looking wild-eyed as he speaks, and labelled as "loony", along with whatever it is he is speaking about.' Perhaps in an attempt to suggest that this apparent 'looniness' runs in the family, a number of pictures of Tony

Benn and his son, Hilary, were printed together in the **Daily Mirror**. At the time, Hilary Benn was a Parliamentary candidate for a London constituency. Caroline Rees describes how an unfavourable image was created by using direct flash lighting and by taking the photographs from below. The words and the caption: 'Like father...like son' are then added to complete the image.

Peter Tatchell, Labour candidate at a by-election in 1982, claims that sections of the press helped to promote a campaign to personally discredit him. Caroline Rees argues that this campaign also reflected newspaper prejudice against homosexuals. Tatchell claimed that a photograph of him, published in the **News of the World**, had been retouched to give the impression that he was wearing eye-liner and lipstick. He argued that this was a 'calculated and deliberate attempt to present me in an effeminate and derogatory manner.' The newspaper did not deny that the photograph had been retouched but rejected the suggestion that it had been done deliberately to produce the effect that Peter Tatchell claimed.

GAY ROW ROCKS LABOUR

THE Labour Party was plagued with fresh turmoil yesterday in a row over demands for freedom for homosexuals.

The far Left accused party leader Michael Foot of butchering a plan to sweep away restrictions on the activities of "gays."

The row erupted as left-wing candidate Peter Tatchell was attacked by members of his Bermondsey party over allegations that he went to a bizarre Gay Olympics sports meeting in America.

Mr Tatchell — who denied the claim — is a key figure in a massive campaign to make homosexual rights a dominant issue at this week's Labour Conference in Blackpool.

He and Greater London council leader, Ken Livingstone will be among speakers at a rally on Tuesday to demand a special debate.

BRANDED

The aims of the camp....

By GORDON LEAK

Freedom plan was butchered say the lefties

ducted of all members of the Labour National Exe-

TATCHELL: "Olympics" row   LIVINGSTONE: Supporter

Pictures may also be used to ridicule or discredit certain stands on political issues. For example, the women peace campaigners at Greenham Common have consistently been presented as 'freaks'.

The way the picture overleaf is used helps to reduce the impact of the anti-nuclear weapons argument. It implies that **all** the women at Greenham Common are dressed similarly, and that what they are doing is in some way not 'normal'.

The selection and use of pictures in newspapers is very important. Together with the headlines, it is the pictures that are seen first. Caroline Rees therefore asks, 'If newspapers

NOW FOR A FASHION NOTE FROM GREENHAM COMMON

By DAVID DAWSON

ANY old iron? It's all the rage down Greenham Common way. The women campaigners at the Berkshire peace camp are heavily into metal.
This protester has adorned her summer outfit of T-shirt and shorts with safety pins through the nose and cheek.

The women at Greenham Common have been branded by the male-dominated press, and others, as 'freaks' since they set up camp. The implication here is that *all* the women dress like this one, and that women are somehow not 'normal' unless playing out the roles men choose for them. In this way, pictures are used to undermine the argument against nuclear weapons

Safety pin-up—an iron lady of Greenham   Picture: DA'

mislead or distort with these, then what faith can be placed in the content of the story that goes with them?'

(adapted from 'The abuse of picture power' by Caroline Rees, **New Statesman**, 28 September, 1984, pp. 8–9)

3. Briefly explain the writer's concern about the use of photographs in newspapers. (3)
4. How might newspaper editors defend the use of pictures to accompany political stories? (3)

The following extract is from a newspaper account of Government proposals (issued in the form of a 'White Paper') concerning changes to the law on public order. The Home Secretary – the Government Minister responsible for public order – was, at the time of the proposals, Leon Brittan.

> Mr. Brittan's White Paper on Public Order is not a very remarkable document, but... such changes as it proposes to the law are in general sensible. It recommends that in future all those organizing marches and processions... should be obliged to give the police at least seven days notice of their intentions, so that, if necessary, conditions can be imposed in the interest of public order... Well-intentioned demonstrators already give such notice, but it would be no bad thing if those who do not were subject to a fine. Static demonstrations (unruly football crowds, massive and aggressive picketing and provocative public meetings outside embassies, for example) can be as dangerous as mobile militancy. They also, therefore, should be subject when necessary to conditions imposed by the police on size and location; but it would not be practicable, the White Paper argues, to impose on the organizers of such assemblies the duty of notification. In practice, therefore, the police would often have to impose their own conditions on the spot.... There is also a wise suggestion that the police and the Home Secretary should in future be able to ban a specific march without banning all demonstrations in the same area at the same time.

(from 'Public order', **The Daily Telegraph**, May 17, 1985, p. 16)

5. a Give **two** examples from the extract of factual reporting of the public order proposals. (2)
   b Give **two** comments from the extract which are expressions of opinion about the proposals. (2)

2 Television

Unlike the press, television (and radio) is supposed to be politically neutral. The BBC's Charter, granted in 1926, makes this clear, and a similar requirement is imposed on the commercial television companies under the 1954 Television Act. The time allocated to party political broadcasts is strictly controlled, but the television channels are also obliged to give fair and balanced coverage in their reporting of the main political parties. On other matters of political concern, such as industrial relations, they are expected to show 'due impartiality'. This means that television should not show undue bias to any particular group or argument unless it is in the 'public interest' to do so. There will obviously be disagreement, however, about what the 'public interest' extends to. There is also a growing debate about how far television is, in fact, neutral and impartial in its coverage of party politics. The following extract looks at ways in which bias can occur in television news coverage and makes recommendations to protect against it.

> 'Is TV news coverage biased? It is a crucial question when polls have regularly shown that BBC and ITV news programmes are the single most important source of information to the British population about what is happening in this country and the world.'
>
> Bias is a very complex matter. It can involve a combination of a number of things: who is chosen for interview, the way in which they are treated, the type of language used in reporting and comment, the concentration on certain views, the rejection of particular categories of news, and decisions about what is newsworthy and what is not. All of these things woven together can put over a particular impression about current events and about what is important.
>
> A single one-sided programme may be balanced by another programme biased in an opposite way. So, to investigate bias, it is necessary to take account of a range of programmes over a period of time. Television news coverage of industrial relations can be taken as an example. One view is presented far more than others. It is the view that 'excessive' wage increases cause inflation and that strikes are the main cause of Britain's economic problems. 'Trade unions are typically asked: "What are you doing to end the strike?" Management is typically asked: "How much production or exports have been lost?" The subtle innuendo is thus conveyed that trade unions cause strikes, even though disputes may well be forced by management errors.' Union representatives are

accused of 'acting irresponsibly', 'destroying the company' or 'cutting their own throats'. These types of statement are common, and they often conceal the complex issues and reasons which lie behind industrial disputes.

Television coverage of political affairs provides another example. It is through the views of the political **centre** that political matters are presented and discussed. David Owen, Shirley Williams, Ted Heath and Denis Healey are 'the good guys and girls, the "moderates". Those who take a different view are the "extremists" – the "far Right" or the "hard Left".' TV presentation of these groups tends to give the impression that they are the enemy. 'Intimidating', 'dominating' and 'bullying' are terms used to describe their actions. Politicians such as Tony Benn (on the Left of the Labour Party) and Sir Keith Joseph (on the Right of the Conservative Party) tend to be caricatured in a way that suggests they shouldn't be taken seriously. This 'personalization of politics – putting tags of approval or disapproval on **people**' – means that important political **issues** are often ignored or are treated superficially. Issues such as monetarism, socialism and nuclear disarmament are rarely seriously analysed in TV news programmes.

Michael Meacher makes a number of recommendations aimed at reducing bias on television. First, an independent body should be set up to carry out long-term research into news bias. This body should also encourage the public to comment on broadcasting standards by arranging meetings throughout the country. Secondly, there should be a clear right of reply on television for people or groups judged to have been reported in a biased or inaccurate way. Thirdly, the views of both sides in a dispute should be given 'balanced treatment and equal authority'. This would mean making television far more accessible so many more people could **themselves** put forward their views. Finally, there needs to be changes among those who occupy the positions of control in the BBC and ITV. At present there are not many black or women producers and directors. Unless this situation is improved, the interests and views of black people and women are likely to continue to receive poor television coverage. Michael Meacher argues that his suggestions are necessary democratic reforms aimed at increasing 'the free and fair

Channel 4's 'Right to Reply' provides a weekly half-hour television spot for viewers to challenge, criticize and give their views on TV programmes.

flow of information'. He recognizes, however, that attempts to introduce them would meet with 'very great resistance'.

(adapted from 'News bias' by Michael Meacher, **The Listener**, 29 July, 1982, pp. 17–18)

1. What do you understand by the term 'politically neutral'?   (1)
2. In what way is television expected to act differently from news-papers in dealing with party political matters?   (2)
3. In your own words, explain how, according to Michael Meacher, television news coverage of industrial relations is biased.   (3)
4. a In political terms, what is meant by 'left', 'centre' and 'right'?   (3)

   b How are these terms used in the extract as part of the claim that television news treatment of politics is biased?   (3)
5. a Explain the phrase 'personalization of politics'.   (2)
   b What is its connection, in the extract, with television coverage of 'political issues'?   (2)
6. Michael Meacher thinks attempts to implement his recom-mendations for reducing bias on television would encounter 'very great resistance'. Select **one** of his proposals and suggest **who** might resist it, and **why**.   (4)

3 Ownership of the media

Most of Britain's national daily and Sunday newspapers and a large proportion of local papers are owned by a handful of companies and wealthy individuals. Some of these also have shares in the commercial television and radio broadcasting companies, or in the new technology industries of cable and satellite television, as well as other branches of the entertainments industry such as cinemas, record companies and leisure centres. The extent to which owners seek to control or influence – directly or indirectly – what goes into their newspapers is a matter of debate. It probably varies, with some editors and journalists having greater independence than others. Nevertheless, it would seem unlikely that a newspaper would consistently take a general political line that went against the beliefs or wishes of its owner. The following extract looks at some of the implications of newspaper ownership and its connection with other sections of the media.

> Here is a modest proposal which, if carried out, might bring Fleet Street (the home of the national newspapers) to a standstill. Newspaper editors should be obliged to declare an interest where applicable, just as MPs and local councillors are. For example, you will occasionally find features in the **Sunday Times** these days written by Irwin Stelzer (his latest contribution was a headbanging piece about the miners' strike). All that **Sunday Times** readers are told about this gent is that he is president of National Economic Research Associates. If my modest proposal were put into effect, the paper would have to add the following line about Stelzer: 'He was until recently a business partner of Andrew Neil, who is now editor of the **Sunday Times**.'
>
> That's all. Didn't hurt all that much, did it? I'm not even arguing that Neil should be prevented from publishing Stelzer's drivel. All I'm suggesting is that the readers should be given a little more background info on the identity of the driveller.
>
> Similarly, if my proposal were accepted, Neil would still be free to fill his pages with articles about the joys of the 'wired-up society', telling us how cable and satellite TV will bring peace and prosperity to the world. But each news report, feature or editorial on the subject would carry a little passage

at the end (or the start): 'Rupert Murdoch, the owner of this newspaper, also owns Sky Channel, a cable and satellite operation which stands to make pots of money if the "wired-up society" becomes a reality.' The same inscription could be attached to all the reports which **The Times** has carried as part of its current vendetta against the BBC.

The Murdoch papers have not been the only ones to attack the BBC. The chase has been joined by the **Daily Star** and the **Express** papers, which just happen to be owned by Fleet Holdings, which just happen to be the biggest shareholder in TV-am, which just happens to stand to benefit if the BBC chops **Breakfast Time**.

And then there's Cap'n Bob Maxwell, the owner of the **Daily Mirror**. The **Mirror** has recently joined the campaign against the BBC. It has also taken to publishing starry-eyed pieces about cable TV. Needless to say, Rediffusion Cablevision, one of Britain's biggest cable firms, is owned by Maxwell.

But the real trouble with Maxwell is that, unlike Murdoch, he doesn't confine his interests to newspapers and television. There are few pies in which he doesn't have a podgy finger: he is a politician, printer, publisher, soccer boss and much else. Men such as Maxwell and Tiny Rowland, whose company Lonrho owns the **Observer**, may therefore be a greater threat to the press than someone like Murdoch, because their interests know no boundaries.

Of course my proposal would not change that: Rowland would still be free to interfere with the paper. But it would at least stop the straightforward deception of readers which now goes on.

(from 'Hidden fingers in every pie' by Francis Wheen, **New Statesman**, 29 March, 1985, p. 18, with minor additions)

1. At the time when the passage was written,
   a who was the editor of the Sunday Times?   (1)
   b which companies or individuals owned the following news-papers: **Daily Mirror, Observer, Daily Star, Sunday Times**?   (2)
2. a How would TV-am benefit if 'Breakfast Time' were to be withdrawn from television?   (2)
   b Explain the connection between the **Daily Star**, the **Express** newspapers and 'TV-am'.   (2)

Robert Maxwell, owner of Mirror Newspapers.

3. Why are some people concerned about the concentration of ownership of the mass media? (3)

4. a What does the writer mean by 'declare an interest'?   (2)
   b Why does he suggest this?   (3)
5. Suggest how the concept of a 'free press' could be used to both **defend** and **attack** the ability of owners to influence the content and general viewpoint of their newspapers?   (5)

4 The political impact of the media

To expect the press to support the Labour Party is rather like expecting turkeys to vote for Christmas.

To what extent should the mass media be regarded as major agencies of political socialization? Previous passages in this section have examined the press, television, and media ownership. But are people more likely to vote Tory just because of the Conservative bias in the British press? How far does television influence the formation of people's political views? Does the fact that the ownership of newspapers is concentrated in a few hands restrict the flow of political communication? It is difficult – perhaps impossible – to obtain hard or conclusive evidence on these matters because so many other factors can be involved. But they do raise fundamental questions about democracy. Are the media in Britain part of a democratic political system or do they work against it? The following extract presents some opposing views.

During the 1959 general election campaign the Television Research Unit studied how television coverage of the campaign affected the way people said they were going to vote. It concluded that although television could make people more informed about political issues, it did not appear to affect voting behaviour. But a study of the 1964 election suggested that television had helped the Liberal Party to increase its support during the campaign.

Media coverage of the formation of the Social Democratic Party in 1981, and its Alliance with the Liberals, is thought to have assisted the growing following for the Alliance in the early 1980s. Some people believe that the SDP was in effect **created** by the media. Compared with coverage of other minority parties, the Alliance parties seemed to receive a far greater amount of attention from the media. For example,

A creation of the media?

110 minor parties put up candidates in the 1979 election. Some of these, such as the Doglovers' Party and the Silly Party were not meant to be taken particularly seriously. But others were. The Ecology Party (now the Green Party), the Communist Party and the Workers' Revolutionary Party were some of the minority parties at the election, but none of them was afforded anything like the television exposure which the SDP and the Liberals received during and after 1981.

However, others suggest that the media do not so much **create** opinion as **reinforce** it. John Whale claims that if newspapers are mainly conservative this is only because most of their readers are. If a lot of people wanted to change the way society is organized, then they would buy papers such as the **Morning Star**, a communist newspaper. But they don't – the **Morning Star** has a very low circulation. It is also suggested that the press is bound to have a Conservative bias so long as its ownership remains in private hands. It is the Conservative Party which supports private ownership whereas Labour is the party associated with public ownership. Therefore, 'to expect the Press to support the Labour Party is rather like expecting turkeys to vote for Christmas.' Nevertheless, Conservative election victories are not inevitable. Labour did win six elections in the thirty years following the Second World War.

Graham Murdock and Peter Golding claim that the concentration in ownership of the media is a threat to democracy. It restricts the range of views which are communicated. Some groups, such as the poor, do not have the power to get their views across. **Private** ownership also means that newspapers and independent television and radio exist primarily to make a profit rather than as a public service. It means, too, that they are not accountable to the public for what they do. John Whale, however, believes that the alternative, a state-owned newspaper for example, would result in even greater restrictions on reporting.

Some people believe that 'news' can be **made** by the media themselves. They can 'set up' certain events. They can encourage 'copycat' occurrences by the way they cover other events. The reporting of inner-city riots in 1981 and 1985, for example, is thought by some to have had this effect. Others deny that the media have this power, but nonetheless claim that they can increase or decrease the importance of events and can help shape the way we see things. 'Politics', for instance, is an activity that extends far beyond Parliament. Yet, according to Colin Seymour-Ure, the media tend to restrict the reporting of politics to a 'Westminster' view. On the other hand, 'an unexpected or urgent event can be turned into a crisis by the intensity of media coverage'. The Falklands War of 1982 can be seen as an example of this, and the media's role during this episode provoked considerable debate. A BBC **Panorama** programme on the war was criticized by the Prime Minister for its 'neutral' stance. The journalists involved defended the programme by saying it was not their job to act as propagandists for the Government. Even so, disinformation was communicated unknowingly by the press from statements made by the Ministry of Defence. Ministry officials later admitted to 'news management' but rejected the claim that the Ministry had lied to the media.

In general, there are two main views about the political impact of the mass media. One view is that the mass media contribute to democracy by communicating a wide range of opinions and ideas to the public. The opposing view sees the media as restricting democracy through 'their power to manipulate the way people think about politics'. It is argued that some sections of opinion are vastly over-represented in the media at the expense of others.

(adapted from **Politics and the Mass Media** (Politics PAL Brief Two) by L. Robins, Great Glen, Leicestershire, undated)

1. a In what sense are the media alleged to have 'created' the Social Democratic Party? (2)
   b What evidence is used to support the argument that the media reflect, rather than create, public opinion? (2)
2. a List **three** arguments used to support the view that the way the media is owned 'represents a threat to democracy'. (3)
   b How can this view be challenged? (3)
3. Give one example each of how the media might
   a reduce (2)
   b increase (2)
   the importance of political events.
4. What do you understand by the terms 'propaganda' and 'disinformation'? (2)
5. The last paragraph of the extract summarizes two different views of the relationship between the mass media and democracy. Giving reasons, state which, if either, you agree with. (4)

5 The Parliamentary Lobby

Whatever the impact on people's views and on the political system, most people depend on the mass media for their knowledge of what is going on in the world outside of their own personal experience. But how do those working in the media – the journalists and reporters – get **their** information? A good deal of what goes on in government in Britain is classified as secret. Many official documents remain secret for thirty years until they (or, at least, some) are released for public inspection. But there are ways in which some information is obtainable by journalists. The first extract describes one of these procedures – the 'Parliamentary Lobby' system. The term stems from the Members' Lobby in the House of Commons where certain journalists are permitted. These Lobby journalists are provided with official or sensitive information which they are allowed to print in the newspapers without disclosing its source. The second passage critically examines the Lobby, relating it to questions about the role of newspapers in a democratic political system.

A fascinating exercise on any Friday morning when Parliament is sitting is to collect together all the national newspapers to compare the stories of their political correspondents and editors. The chances are that some phrase, some idea, will crop up several times. There will be noticeable recurring code words such as 'sources close to the Prime Minister', 'it is said in Whitehall', 'a senior government source said . . .'

The reason for this is simple. On Thursdays at 4.15 pm in a room in the Palace of Westminster, the existence of which is supposed to be a secret, an organization called the Parliamentary Lobby gathers to be briefed, first by the Prime Minister's press secretary, then by the Leader of the House of Commons, then by the Leader of the Opposition. Their words, by convention, are 'not for attribution'. This means the Prime Minister can float ideas, denigrate her colleagues, but all through the mouth of her press officer and all in a form which is totally deniable.

The Parliamentary Lobby – a 150-strong group of political specialists mostly based at Westminster – is an information cartel, useful to journalists and useful to the government. It represents one of the little-known ways in which the 'news' that appears in the papers is, in fact, structured and far from random.

(from 'Society Today' p. ii, in **New Society**, 17 November, 1983)

'The citizen as voter, consumer or student of a Politics course is very much the prisoner of the output of political journalism.' Scholars and academics who interpret and write about political affairs rely very much on newspapers for their information. They therefore depend on the quality and accuracy of what comes out of the Parliamentary Lobby – what the lobby correspondents write in the papers.

The Lobby, however, has its critics. Peter Hennessy claims that it produces a level of political reporting that is well below the standard that ought to exist in a democracy. He argues that it fails to provide an adequate daily information service about political affairs. The Lobby system allows the Prime Minister to dictate what should be the main items of political discussion each week.

The shortcomings of the Lobby system can be seen by comparing the official documents of events of the past (released thirty years later) with what the papers said at the time. The differences between the two versions can then be examined. Hennessy says that anyone interested can do their own 'what the papers never said' exercise. All you need is 'a pair of readers' tickets, a pencil and pad and a simple method. Pick your topic; read the press at the British Library's Newspaper section in Colindale; consult the official files at Kew and draw your own conclusions.' Anyone doing this will probably find a big difference between the way the story was reported in the newspapers and what was really happening 'in the heart of private government'.

It ought to be the aim of newspapers to try to ensure that these differences are reduced. Although the situation is not helped by the tight secrecy which surrounds government in this country, it is mainly up to the newspapers themselves to make things better. Newspapers should not just see themselves as existing to make a profit. They are essential for a healthy democacy. Democratic debate depends largely on the quality of information contained in newspapers. The press, therefore, must become less concerned with political gossip and personalities and be more committed to reporting the facts behind real events and issues. It must be prepared to investigate what is going on within the most powerful institutions in the country – government, industry, the unions and the professions. Newspapers should rely less on the versions of political events supplied to them by government press officers or public relations officials, and on statements made by Ministers in Parliament.

To help bring about these changes, newspaper editors should withdraw all their journalists from the Parliamentary Lobby. Instead, journalists should develop a 'new network of informants' – people who know about the real, hidden workings of government. This would free newspapers from their reliance on information obtained through the Lobby system and open up public debate on subjects other than those which the Government and Opposition want to see discussed. The result could mean that 'for the first time in British history', people who are 'prepared to read, listen and watch enough', would be able to cast their votes 'on the basis of a rational, informed choice.'

(adapted from **What the Papers Never Said** by Peter Hennessy, Portcullis Press, London, 1985)

1. a What is the 'Parliamentary Lobby?'   (2)
   b In what ways could it be 'useful' to journalists **and** to govern-
      ment?   (4)
2. Explain what Peter Hennessy, in the second extract, means by
   the citizen being 'the prisoner of the output of political
   journalism'.   (2)
3. a How is the Lobby system criticized?   (2)
   b What technique does the writer suggest for testing the draw-
      backs of the Lobby system?   (2)
4. a Identify **two** suggestions for improving political reporting.   (2)
   b What recommendation is made to bring about these
      improvements?   (2)
5. Explain why effective newspaper reporting about the work of
   government is seen as essential to a democracy.   (4)

6 Opinion polls (1)

A survey on tinned pears or suntan lotions will take 35 to 40 minutes; yet a widely publicized poll on realignments in British politics may take just four or five minutes. 'Opinion poll' is often only another name for a cheap-jack survey. (Conrad Jameson)

So far, the passages in this section have dealt with aspects of the political communication process whereby the public are presented

'I'm a "don't know". "Don't know" whether to smash your face in or not.'

(adapted from a cartoon by Edward McLachlan in **Private Eye**)

with information and views. The other side of this process – although nowhere near as common – involves ways in which people's views are made known to those in power. One such way is the opinion poll.

Public opinion polls set out to discover people's views by putting questions to what is hoped is a representative sample of the population or of a section of it. Large corporations or business firms may use them to obtain some feedback on their products – chocolate bars or television programmes, for instance – or to test if their advertising campaigns have been getting across to the public. They have also increasingly become used in politics. There are a number of different types of political polls. For example, there are those which ask for people's opinions on who they think would make the best Prime Minister, or which ask people how they intend to vote at a forthcoming election. First used, during a

British general election campaign, in 1945, polls on voting intention are not, strictly speaking, **opinion** polls, but surveys on **intended behaviour**. Unlike opinion polls proper, the accuracy of the information they produce can be checked against actual election results. Nevertheless, in popular usage the term 'opinion poll' has come to include these surveys as well, and they are examined in the following passages.

More opinion polls were published during the summer of 1983 than in any previous election campaign. The following table compares the findings of the major polls with the actual election result.

Final Opinion Polls – 1983 General Election (%)

Poll	Conservative	Labour	Alliance
Audience Selection	46	23	29
Harris	47	25	26
Gallup	45.5	26.5	26
Marplan	46	26	26
NOP	47	25	26
MORI	44	28	26
Election Result	43	28	26

(from **Politics Pal** (1984 edition) compiled by L. Robins, Great Glen, Leicestershire, pp. 15–16, with minor addition)

In 1967 the Speaker's Conference on Electoral Reform suggested that the results of political opinion polls should not be published in the three days before an election. The Government at the time rejected this recommendation because it was not convinced that voters were particularly influenced by the polls. However, it is difficult to discover how much influence they do have on the way people vote. The pollsters themselves seem uncertain. The head of one professional polling organization is reported as saying: 'Yes, we have influence, but only a little bit'.

Various theories exist. Do the polls influence the level of abstention, for example? If the polls seem to be indicating a substantial win for one party, for instance, will some people not bother to vote because they see the result as a 'foregone conclusion'? It could just as easily be argued, though, that the polls encourage a higher turnout by stimulating people's interest in the election. A common suggestion is that the polls have a 'bandwagon' effect. Voters may climb on the bandwagon of the party which the polls show is most likely to win an election. On the other hand, the opposite might occur: voters may decide to switch their support to a party that appears from the polls to be doing less well. This is known as the 'boomerang' effect. However, if one or the other of these effects occurred regularly, the polls would be consistently wrong. This has not been the case in terms of the polls' results about the two main parties; although – at least until recently – the proportions of the vote obtained by the smaller parties were sometimes underestimated.

The growth in support for the Alliance has in effect brought about national three-party politics in terms of party choice at elections. This has made the question of the power of opinion polls even more complex. Hugo Young says that some voters 'will be perplexed about what to do'. There is no problem for 'Tories in safe Tory seats, and for Labour voters in in Labour strongholds. But many other voters in those seats, and even more in less safe seats, will want to vote for the candidate who is most likely to defeat their least-favourite party. Put simply: if you want to get a marginal Tory out, should you vote Labour or Alliance? Ditto in Labour, Liberal and SDP seats.'

These are considerations of **tactical voting**. They involve voters making decisions about who to vote for on the basis of predicting which party is going to win in their constituency. But from where do voters get evidence about who is likely to win? The chances are they will take account of the **national** polls and cast their vote accordingly. But their own local situation (in their constituency) may be very different from the national picture. In such cases, national opinion polls, far from adding to democracy, may be seriously distorting the whole voting process.

(adapted from **Political Opinion Polls** by F. Teer and J. D. Spence, Hutchinson, London, 1973, pp. 129–30, 134 and 'Is it time to ban the polls?' by Hugo Young, **The Sunday Times**, November 21, 1982)

1. From the table in the first extract, state
   a which of the polls was the most accurate in predicting the outcome of the 1983 general election. (1)

     b which party's percentage of the vote was generally **underestimated** and which **overestimated** in the polls. (2)

2. During the 1983 election campaign the Alliance parties were criticized for using telephone polls. These polls indicated that their support was greater than it actually turned out to be. Why are telephone polls unlikely to provide an accurate picture of the electorate's voting intentions? (2)

3.

Party	Polls %	Election result %
X	35	31
Y	40	46
Z	22	20

    Does this table suggest a 'bandwagon' or a 'boomerang' effect? Explain your answer. (3)

4. a What is 'tactical voting'? (1)

    b What part might the polls play in encouraging tactical voting? (3)

5. a Prepare a case for the banning of polls on voting intention in the period immediately before an election. (4)

    b Prepare a case against this suggestion. (4)

7 Opinion polls (2)

Opinion polls are defended on the grounds that they aid democracy. Publication of their findings keeps people informed on the opinions of others and they provide some opportunity for the expression of public views between elections. Polls designed to test opinion on particular policies may be useful to the government in finding out people's responses to them. Nevertheless, opinion polls also receive criticism. The following extract and the questions which follow suggest why this is so and deal with some of the ways, other than their effects on voting behaviour, in which the polls may be influential in politics.

Polls no doubt play a part in influencing a Prime Minister's choice of election date. The 1964 general election was delayed until the last possible moment. The Prime Minister, Sir Alec Douglas-Home, would have been aware of the findings of earlier polls indicating that the Conservatives had a poor chance of winning. In 1970 the Labour Party had been planning for an election in October. Poll results favourable to

Labour may have contributed to Prime Minister Harold Wilson's decision to hold an earlier election (in the June), although he has denied this. (In both these cases the parties in power lost.)

Governments are obviously influenced by public opinion in general, and polls are one way in which they are kept informed on the climate of opinion on particular issues. But this does not necessarily mean that a Government will base its policies and decisions on information from opinion polls. In fact the available evidence suggests that polls have little influence on Government policy-making. The political parties, however, may well use them to help decide how best to **present** their policies and how to conduct their election campaigns.

A further effect of opinion polls has been on the way politics is reported in the media. The widespread use of political opinion polling has changed the way election campaigns, for example, are treated in the newspapers. The press cannot write authoritatively about public opinion without taking account of available opinion poll findings. The polls have also influenced newspaper forecasts of the outcome of elections as they provide journalists and editors with some sort of evidence on which to base their predictions.

(adapted from **Political Opinion Polls** by F. Teer and J. D. Spence, Hutchinson, London, 1973, pp. 136–46)

1. a From the extract identify **three** areas of politics in which opinion polls may have some influence. (3)

   b Using material from the extract, say which of these areas you consider to be **most** affected and which **least** affected by the polls. (4)

2. Study the two statements below and then answer the questions which follow.

> Polls have changed the face of British politics ... by improving the communication process between government and governed to produce a more informed and intelligent approach to political discussion. (Teer & Spence, p. 146)
> They prove nothing ... Morally speaking, opinion polls are always an embarrassment. Touted as representing public opinion, they in fact represent only private or mass opinion:

opinion taken in the dark of the doorway rather than in the open light of the forum; opinion that chokes off the opportunity to hear out arguments pro and con, to consult a neighbour, to read up, to ask a question, to answer back; opinion so half-hearted it is hard to take seriously. (Conrad Jameson, 'Who needs polls?', **New Statesman**, 6 February, 1981, pp. 13–14)

a Which of the two statements regards opinion polls in a more favourable light? (1)

b Explain the distinction made in the second statement between 'public opinion' and 'private or mass opinion'. (4)

3. Drawing on the extract above and the previous passages (Section 4.6), discuss the view that political opinion polls hinder, rather than aid, democracy. (8)

8 Referenda

Opinion polls may give those asked some opportunity to express their views on a very limited range of questions. Unlike voting, however, the expression of these opinions has no direct result. Therefore, as well as electing representatives to make decisions on behalf of the people (a form of **indirect** democracy), should electors be given the chance to vote on particular **issues**? This is what happens in a referendum. If the government agrees to abide by the result, a referendum might be seen as an exercise in **direct** democracy.

The first ever national referendum in Britain was held in 1975 to decide whether Britain should remain in the EEC (European Economic Community). The result was a two-to-one majority in favour of staying in. In 1979, referenda were held in Scotland and Wales on the question of separate governing assemblies for these countries. In neither case did the vote in favour reach the required level of 40% of registered electors. The following passage examines the arguments for and against the use of referenda in Britain.

The result of the referendum over Britain's continued membership of the EEC produced a clear result. Both major parties had been divided within their own ranks on the question. It was left to the electorate to make the decision. Because of the referendum more people probably learned something about the issues involved than if Parliament had made the choice. These arguments provide the basic democratic case in favour of referenda. The British party system provides a further argument. Many people are tired of the old party divisions and confrontations. The referendum might be seen as an alternative. It could be used to decide a whole range of issues and thereby help to break down or pass over the traditional party divisions.

Opponents of referenda have a strong case, however. They believe that the electorate as a whole is not suited to making decisions on complex policy questions. Matters irrelevant to the one being decided may be dragged in and confuse the issue. It may often not be possible to reduce the issue to a single, straightforward question appropriate for the ballot paper, particularly if it is to require a simple 'yes' or 'no' answer. In any case, does democracy require the direct form of government that referenda involve? Some would argue that it is more important to have a government which is **representative** and **responsible**. At times it may be necessary for a government to go against public opinion. All the evidence suggests, for example, that the death penalty does not usually act as a deterrent. Yet, judging by the findings of numerous opinion polls, a referendum on the reintroduction of capital punishment would undoubtedly produce a majority in favour. It can be argued that it is Parliament's job to vote on particular issues and Parliament should therefore be trusted to make the right decisions. Referenda would also take away responsibility from Government Ministers whose task it is to form policy and to see that it is carried out once Parliament has approved it. After the decision of the EEC referendum, some Ministers were then expected to carry out a major policy to which they had previously expressed total opposition.

Some of the arguments against the use of national referenda may not apply to local ones. Local referenda may be appropriate for getting answers to straightforward questions such as: 'Do you want a village hall?' 'Should bus fares for the elderly be subsidized?' 'Should public houses be shut on Sundays?' Indeed, referenda carried out by voting machine are used regularly for some local issues in certain American states. Electronic referenda could be a future

development in Britain. This would involve an automated voting system. Through the public telecommunications system, a viewdata terminal in each household could be connected to a central electoral computer. Voters could then take part directly and immediately in the decision-making process. Technologically, the possibilities are even there to do away with the Parliamentary system of representative democracy and to substitute this electronic form of 'direct democracy'.

(adapted from **Introduction to British Politics** by P.J. Madgwick, Hutchinson, London, 1984, pp. 432–4 and **Society and the New Technology** by Kenneth Ruthven, Cambridge University Press, Cambridge, 1983, p. 59)

1. Identify **two** arguments in favour of referenda.   (4)
2. Identify **two** arguments against referenda.   (4)
3. Why might local referenda be thought more appropriate than national ones?   (2)

4. Give one comment from the passage which illustrates that referenda are a form of direct democracy. (2)
5. a Why might it be thought desirable for a government, on occasions, to go against popular opinion? (2)
   b In addition to the example given in the passage, suggest an issue where this might be appropriate. (2)
6. What objections could be raised to replacing the present Parliamentary system of representative democracy by electronic referenda? (4)

Section 5 Political Parties

Section 4 examined various channels of political communication. Political parties – as well as other organized groups (often referred to as 'pressure groups' – see Section 6) – are also part of this process. Parties provide a two-way link between the rulers and the ruled. Ideas and policies can be made known to the electorate and parties provide ways for supporters to express their views. They offer an opportunity for individuals to participate in politics.

This section begins with an examination of how the party system developed in Britain and how it operates today. It continues by looking at what parties actually do and how they are organized to carry out their tasks. Comparisons of aims and policies show what the main parties stand for and where they each fit into the party system as a whole. Finally, there are brief descriptions of some of the smaller parties.

1 Development of the party system

A distinction should be made between parties **inside** and **outside** Parliament. In Britain parties developed first in Parliament, although for a long time they did not really form a party **system**. They existed as rather loose groupings of MPs who represented similar interests or shared certain ideas. It was not until well into the nineteenth century that **mass** political parties, with organizations and members outside Parliament, began to develop, as the following passage shows.

> Until the electoral system began to be reformed in the 1830s, political parties existed only in Parliament. The main division was between the Whigs (Liberals) and the Tories. The 1832 Reform Act extended the franchise. This led to the development of local registration societies to help organize the new

voters. It also encouraged the creation of the Tory Carlton Club and, for the Whigs, the Reform Club. They were set up to help arrange election activity at national level. The Tory Party became known as the Conservative Party following an election address by its leader, Sir Robert Peel, in 1834. He stated that Tory policy was to 'conserve' all that was good in existing institutions. In the 1840s, there was a split in this party. A number of Conservatives joined the opposition which eventually became the present Liberal Party. But it was not until the 1867 Reform Act, when working class males in the towns gained the vote, that the types of political parties known today began to emerge in the British political system.

Yet neither of the two Parliamentary parties could realistically claim to represent the working class. By the late nineteenth century, various organizations in the country associated with the Labour movement had developed. In 1900 the TUC (Trades Union Congress) called a meeting to discuss how these bodies could best be represented in Parliament. This resulted in the forming of the Labour Representation Committee, and twenty-nine MPs were elected at the 1906 general election. They called themselves the Labour Party and by 1922 had replaced the Liberals as one of the two major parties. Although it formed governments for brief spells during the 1920s and early 1930s, it was not until 1945

Labour Cabinet, 1945.

that a Labour Government with an overall majority of seats came to power.

Other, minor, parties have also developed at various times this century, and, in 1981, a number of Labour MPs broke away from the party and formed the Social Democratic Party. The SDP made an agreement with the Liberal Party to fight the 1983 general election jointly, and this 'alliance' has continued.

(adapted from **British Political Parties** by Alan R. Ball, Macmillan, London and Basingstoke, 1981, pp. 1–2; **British Government and Politics** by R. M. Punnett, Heinemann, London, 1976, pp. 107–8 and **British Government and Politics** by F. Randall, MacDonald and Evans, Plymouth, 1981, pp. 71–5)

1. a What do the initials SDP and TUC stand for?   (2)
   b Which of these is **not** a political party?   (1)
2. Who were
   a the Whigs   (2)
   b the Tories   (2)
3. What were the functions of
   a the Carlton and Reform clubs   (2)
   b the local registration societies?   (2)
4. How was the development of parties outside Parliament connected with reforms of the electoral system?   (4)
5. a In what sense is the Labour Party historically a working class party?   (2)
   b Despite the existence of Labour Governments before the Second World War, they were unable to make major economic and social changes until after 1945. From the evidence in the passage, why do you think this was?   (3)

2 The two (or more?) party system

At least until the mid-1970s, it was often said that Britain had a two-party system. Since 1945, either the Conservative Party has been in power with Labour in opposition, or vice versa. The results of the 1983 general election indicated the emergence of a third force in the party system: the Liberal-SDP Alliance. The Alliance received almost as many votes as Labour (see Section 2.4). Does this mean that Britain no longer has a two-party system?

The answer partly depends on whether the question refers to

the situation inside or outside Parliament. In terms of the choice of parties that people can vote for, or become members of, there is a multi-party system. In addition to the Conservative, Labour and Alliance parties, many other parties put up candidates in elections. Some of these such as the Scottish Nationalist Party, Plaid Cymru, and the parties in Northern Ireland – are regionally based. Others – for example, the Communist Party and the Ecology Party (known since 1985 as the Green Party) – do not restrict themselves to particular parts of the country, although the number of candidates they field is usually small.

There is also a number of political parties represented within Parliament. However, the House of Commons is dominated by two. Following the 1983 election 93% of MPs belonged to either the Conservative or Labour parties. Although the Alliance parties received a quarter of the total vote, between them they occupied only 23 of the 650 seats. In terms of government, rather than electoral choice, therefore, there still seemed to be a two-party system. The Conservatives continued to form the Government, Labour remained the official opposition. After the October, 1974 election, the situation had been the other way around. The Labour Party had formed the Government and the Conservatives were in opposition. In 1977, Labour, no longer able to maintain its overall majority in the House of Commons, entered into a pact with the Liberal Party. The Liberals agreed to support the Labour Government on condition that they were consulted on some policy matters. However, unlike a coalition, the pact did not involve any Liberal MPs taking places in the Government. The two-party system therefore remained.

But although the present electoral system encourages a two-party system, there is nothing inevitable about it. It is estimated, for example, that if the Alliance obtained over 30% of the total vote in a future general election its share of seats in the House of Commons could increase dramatically. A three-way split, with no party having anywhere near an overall majority, might then result. In this event, a genuine coalition, or some other arrangement between two or more parties, could emerge in order for a government to be formed. Such departures would not be new in British politics. During this century coalitions have existed in 1916–1922, 1931–40, and 1940–45. Between 1910 and 1931 there were also three periods when the Government had to rely on support from a third party.

It remains to be seen whether any similar arrangements will emerge in the future, but recent developments in the party system and in voting behaviour have renewed the debate over the advantages and disadvantages of a two-party system. The first of the following two extracts presents arguments against the two-party system. The second gives the arguments in favour.

Disadvantages of a two party system

(1) The two-party system produces 'adversary' politics. One party wins the election and acquires vast powers. The opposing party's job is to criticize and to attempt to replace the winning party. This results in an unnecessary and harmful exaggeration of the differences between the parties. Rather than examining the merits of each case, policies are opposed just for the sake of opposition.

(2) As a result of this adversary system, there is a tendency for 'extremists' to gain control of the two major parties. The Conservative Party is pushed further to the 'right' and the Labour Party further to the 'left'.

(3) The two main parties do not properly represent the political views of the majority of the electorate. Opinion polls show that the electorate is always more 'moderate' than the activists in the two major parties. In any case, the public does not think of issues in terms of the 'left-right' spectrum as party members do.

(4) The two-party system results in huge swings in government policy. A new government changes or tries to undo most of the decisions made by the previous government. This can happen each time there is a change of party in power.

(5) The two-party system makes the House of Commons less important. Because the government can usually rely on its party's overall majority it can steamroller through the House of Commons almost any policy it wants to.

(6) The present system is undemocratic and unrepresentative. Governments can be formed with majorities in the House of Commons even when the winning party has not

received the majority of votes in an election. For example, the Labour Party formed the Government in March, 1974 with only 37.1% of the total vote.

(adapted from **British Political Parties** by Alan R. Ball, Macmillan, London and Basingstoke, 1981, pp. 247–9)

Advantages of a two-party system

(1) The two-party system presents the voters with a simple and clear choice between two rivals – 'for' or 'against'.

(2) Both major parties have a right and a left wing. Each party therefore contains quite widely differing views. There are trade unionists in the Conservative Party and professionals and industrialists in the Labour Party. Each party contains a variety of social and religious groups. It is difficult for other parties to develop distinctive policies which are different from those of the main parties.

(3) The two-party system produces stable and strong government. A government is able to carry out the promises made to the electorate during the election campaign. The system is therefore democratic. The elector knows what he or she is voting for and can then check the actions of a government against its election pledges. This may not be possible with a coalition government formed after an election.

(4) The seating arrangements in the House of Commons and its 'for' and 'against' voting policies are geared towards a two-party system of Government and Opposition. It encourages good debate. The strengths and weaknesses of governments can be fully aired in view of all MPs, the press, and the public.

(5) Both parties have efficient political organizations and both have declared policies. If a Government fails, the other major party is ready to take over.

(6) The two-party system works.

(adapted from **British Constitution Made Simple** by Colin F. Padfield, Heinemann, London, 1981, pp. 39–40)

Three teams, one game. Would it work?

1. a What do you understand by the term 'adversary politics'?   (2)
   b Which of the arguments in the second extract could be used
      to defend this type of politics?   (2)
2. How could the cartoon be used to illustrate some of the
   advantages of a two-party system?   (2)
3. Which of the arguments against a two-party system do you consider to be the strongest? Give reasons.   (3)
4. What kind of evidence could be used to test the final comment
   of the second extract – 'The two-party system works'?   (2)
5. a Why can't the 1977 pact between Labour and Liberals be
      called a coalition?   (2)
   b The third comment in the second extract implies that a
      coalition government may not be as democratic as a one-party
      government. Explain this argument.   (4)

c Which of the comments in the second extract illustrates the claim that each political party is itself a kind of coalition?   (3)

3 The role of parties

Earlier sections have described how, at a general election, voters choose between candidates to elect an MP for their constituency. But it was also shown that in practice most people are voting for a party which they hope will form the next government. This gives the electorate some control – however small – over the type of policies that a government may follow. For if parties did not exist, there could be no guarantee that the policies put forward by any one successful candidate could be carried out. The other 649 MPs might disagree. By identifying with particular parties, candidates are in effect informing the electors of where they stand on a range of issues. The voters are therefore being offered different sets of policies from which to make their choice. But the activities of political parties are not restricted to election times or to Parliament. This is made clear in the following extract which looks at the **functions** of parties – at what they **do**.

A number of political functions are performed by political parties in Britain. They perform one primary function and several secondary ones. All assist the working of the political system. The main objective of political parties is to gain or retain power. Their primary function therefore, as Robert Mackenzie recognized, is to maintain competing teams of leaders in the House of Commons so that the electorate can choose between them.

All parties perform other functions, too. First, they encourage public interest and participation in politics. They provide a means by which individuals and groups can take an active political role nationally or locally. Secondly, they can pull together the views and interests of a wide range of groups and organizations. Thirdly, they provide frameworks within which people can discuss and criticize political issues. This is particularly so in the Labour, Liberal and Social Democratic parties because they all believe that their members should have considerable influence upon the process of party policy-making. The Conservatives, on the other hand, allow only a very limited role for party activists in this field. Finally, political parties also attempt to recruit members and raise money. They select candidates and organize local and national political campaigns. In the Labour Party much of the money comes from trade unions affiliated to it. In the Conservative Party much of the money comes from donations from industry and commerce. All parties also rely on the efforts of their supporters to raise money locally.

(adapted from **Mastering British Politics** by F. N. Forman, Macmillan, London, 1985, pp. 57–9)

1. Identify **two** activities in which local party members can be involved. (2)
2. What is the main difference between the Labour and Conservative parties in their sources of finance? (2)
3. Parties 'pull together the views and interests of a wide range of groups and organizations'.
   a Briefly explain what this means. (2)
   b What is the advantage of this function? (2)
4. Why do you think it is difficult – and unusual – for independent candidates (candidates not connected with any political party) to get elected to Parliament? (4)
5. a Why do political parties exist? (2)
   b Examine the view that parties are essential to a democratic political system. (6)

4 Party organizations

In order to carry out their functions, political parties have to be organized. It has been estimated that the four main parties in Britain have a total membership of about two million*. Even though many members take no active role in their parties, a con-

---

* 'The parties in Parliament' by Henry Drucker in **Developments in British Politics** edited by Henry Drucker, Patrick Dunleavy, Andrew Gamble and Gillian Peele, Macmillan, Basingstoke and London, 1984, pp. 67–8.
The figure quoted does not include the four million who are members of the Labour Party through their trade unions. The Conservative Party claims by far the largest number of individual members.

siderable amount of organization is still required. There are important differences in the organizations of the main parties, but they all aim to provide links between their national leaders, their MPs, and their local members at 'grassroots' level.

Basic organizational structure of political parties

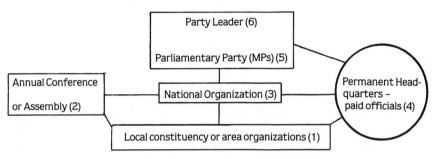

(The numbers in the diagram correspond to those in the following comments)

At the local level (1) there are organizations, composed of individual members, such as the local Conservative Constituency Associations. The Constituency Labour Parties have representatives from local socialist and trade union organizations as well as individual members. The local organization of the SDP is based on a system of Area Parties which usually consist of two or more constituencies. The contributions to national politics made by the local organizations of the main parties will normally include raising money, selecting candidates for elections, and organizing election activity. They will also send representatives or delegates to the annual conferences or assemblies (2).

The importance of the national conferences varies. Decisions of the Labour Party Conference, for example, can become official party policy which the leadership is expected to abide by. In the Conservative Party, on the other hand, Conference can express opinions on policy but does not make it. Each party also has a national organization (3), most of whose members are generally elected, which will meet more frequently than the conference. In the Liberal Party, the 'National Executive' has responsibilities for directing, co-ordinating and implementing policy. The Conservative 'Central Council of the National Union', and particularly its Executive Committee, co-ordinates the activities of the

The 1985 Labour Party Conference.

local constituency associations. In the Labour Party, a similar role is performed by the very influential 'National Executive Committee' (NEC) which also recommends policy to Conference, works closely with the party in Parliament, and supervises the party headquarters. All the main parties employ paid officials to carry out the day-to-day running of their permanent offices (4) in London.

Within Parliament (5), each of the parties forms its own committees on various subjects and branches of policy. In addition, Labour MPs belong to the 'Parliamentary Labour Party' (PLP), and similar bodies exist in the Liberal and Social Democratic parties. The nearest equivalent in the Conservative Party is the '1922 Committee' to which all Tory back-bench MPs (those who do not have specific jobs in the Government or Opposition) belong. Each party also has an elected leader (6). Although the position of the leader differs among the main parties, it is the holder of this job who would normally become Prime Minister following his or her party's victory at a general election.

Most political parties will supply diagrams or charts describing the overall structure of their organizations. These are often quite

British Political Parties: Who Controls What?

	Leader	Leading spokespersons	Party headquarters	Election manifesto	Party policy
Labour	Elected by an 'electoral college' of trade unions, constituency organizations and Labour MPs	Appointed to specific jobs by leader from a group largely elected by the Parliamentary Labour Party	Controlled by National Executive Committee which is elected by annual Conference	Cabinet/Shadow Cabinet and National Executive Committee	PLP (MPs) expected to follow broad lines of policy decided by Conference. NEC influential in recommending policy
Conservative	Elected by Conservative MPs	Appointed by leader	Controlled by leader	Issued by leader who consults Cabinet/ Shadow Cabinet	Leadership in Parliament draws up policy
Liberal	Elected by party members	Appointed by leader	Controlled by National Executive which is elected by annual assembly	Issued by leader who consults via 'Standing Committee' [The Liberal/SDP Alliance produced a joint election manifesto for the 1983 general election]	Resolutions passed by Assembly and Council are official party policy. In practice, leader does not always follow such decisions
SDP	Leader (Parliamentary leader) and President both elected by party members. Leader is first nominated by SDP MPs	Appointed by leader	Controlled by National Committee	Policy sub-committee of National Committee, chaired by leader, responsible for preparing election programmes	Council for Social Democracy responsible for adopting policy but Parliamentary Committee of SDP MPs not bound by it

(adapted and updated from 'Unloved Parties' in **The Economist**, 16 February, 1980, p. 76)

complex and, in any case, represent only the formal or official relationships between the different organizational levels of the parties. A clearer picture may be gained through discovering who is responsible for important decisions such as choosing the leader, preparing the election manifestos and making party policy. The table on page 95 compares the main parties on such questions. However, even this cannot fully describe the variations in degrees of influence and control that can occur in practice. The location of power within parties will also depend on many other factors. These include the personal style of the leader, the amount of support from members and from the public, and the actions of influential groups inside and outside the party.

1. Identify the three main 'levels' of party organization. (3)
2. Who is responsible for policy decisions in
   a   the Conservative Party (2)
   b   the Labour Party? (2)
3. Identify **three** factors which make the NEC of the Labour Party 'very influential'. (3)
4. From the information in the table, state which party leader appears to have the most power. Give reasons for your answer. (4)
5. Which party do you consider the most democratic in its form of organization? Give reasons for your answer. (6)

5 Selection of candidates

Independent MPs are rare. In nearly all constituencies the winning candidate is a member of a political party. For many years the vast majority of MPs have been either Conservative or Labour. Furthermore, many of these occupy safe seats. Particularly in these constituencies, therefore, the important choice is made not so much by the voters on election day, but by those who selected the winning candidate to stand for election in the first place. In the Conservative and Labour parties, candidates are chosen by the local constituency organizations, although the parties at national level may be able to exercise some influence. As the following extract shows, the process of choosing a candidate differs between the two main parties, although similar stages are involved. Names are put forward (nomination state); some of those nominated are interviewed and a choice made (selection stage); and then there are procedures for confirming the decision (ratification). In the Liberal Party the candidate is also chosen at constituency level from a short-list of approved candidates (whilst selection is made at 'area' level in the SDP).

Procedures for selecting Parliamentary candidates in the Labour and Conservative Parties

LABOUR	CONSERVATIVE
Nomination	
Names can be put forward by the local ward or Executive Committee or affiliated organizations (but not by individuals). NEC approves nominations.	Nominations can be made by the constituency association or its committees, or by individuals (including the candidate him/herself). The national Standing Advisory Committee on Candidates has to approve the nominations. The Central Office can also submit names.
Selection	
The Local Executive Committee draws up a short-list. The NEC can add to the short-list (but rarely does) and is represented throughout this stage. Shortlisted candidates are interviewed by the local General Management Committee. Choice is made by ballot following speeches and questions.	A small selection committee draws up a short-list. Candidates are interviewed by the local Executive Council. Choice is made by ballot following speeches and questions.
Ratification	
Final approval is given by the NEC.	Final approval is given at a general meeting of the constituency association.
Financial Matters	
Organizations that can sponsor candidates (usually trade unions) may contribute up to 80% of the maximum allowed expenditure for the election campaign. They may also contribute to the funds of the constituency party. There are strict limits to how much the candidate can contribute.	Candidates are no longer asked about their financial standing. There are also strict limitations on their contributions to party funds.

(adapted from **Introduction to British Politics** by P.J. Madgwick, Hutchinson, London, 1984, pp. 276–7)

1. Why do you think candidates are restricted in the amounts of money they can contribute to party funds? (2)
2. For **each** of the three stages in their candidate selection procedures (nomination, selection, ratification), give **one** difference between the Conservative Party and the Labour Party. (6)
3. Which of the two parties appears to permit more national control in the selection of candidates? Explain your answer. (4)
4. a In safe seats, 'selecting the candidate means selecting a Member of Parliament' (P. J. Madgwick, p. 276). Explain. (2)
   b The 'selectorate' is the name sometimes used to refer to the relatively small groups of people responsible for choosing Parliamentary candidates. Examine the suggestion that the 'selectorates' in the Conservative and Labour parties should be widened to include all local party members. (6)

6 Principles

In 1945 the Labour Party won a general election with an overall majority of 146 seats in the House of Commons. The Labour Government of 1945–50 was therefore able to implement policies that were in line with its fundamental principles of securing more social and economic equality. It brought a number of previously privately owned industries – such as coal, electricity, gas and the railways – into public ownership through nationalization. It also introduced a series of new laws which together formed the modern Welfare State. These included the setting up of the National Health Service and a comprehensive national insurance scheme to protect individuals against loss of earnings through sickness, unemployment and retirement.

Labour won a further election in 1950, but from 1951 to 1964, the Conservative Party formed the Government. In a period of growing economic prosperity the Conservatives did not seek to undo all the changes made by Labour in the years immediately following the Second World War. In fact the period extending to the mid-1970s can be seen as one in which both the major parties seemed to be drawing more closely together. The Conservatives appeared to have accepted the basic principles of the Welfare State. Labour seemed to accept the idea of a 'mixed economy' –

that some industries should be state-controlled while others should remain in the hands of private firms and companies. Any disagreements between the parties were thought to be largely matters of degree or detail.

Since that time, however, and particularly since the Conservative Party returned to power in 1979, the two main parties have moved further apart. The Conservatives have shifted further to the 'right'. Their aim has been to reduce the role of government in the economic and social affairs of the country. To this end they have privatized (sold to private investors) a number of state-owned industries such as British Aerospace and British Telecom. They have reduced some of the services provided under the Welfare State and have further proposals to radically alter the system of state benefits such as pensions. Meanwhile the Labour party has moved further to the 'left', compared with its position in the 1960s and 1970s. Some party members see this as merely a return to a political position closer to its basic principles of socialism. Others were less happy. In 1981, a number of Labour MPs left the party and – together with one Conservative MP – formed the new Social Democratic Party. The SDP and the Liberal Party are seen by many as parties of the 'centre'. As was shown in earlier sections, these two parties formed an electoral alliance to contest the 1983 general election.

Section 5.7 will examine the policies and political positions of the parties in more detail. The following extracts represent statements of principles, or basic beliefs and aims, put out by the parties themselves.

Conservative Party

Personal freedom, individuality, choice and opportunity are the bases of Conservative philosophy. We believe in the rule of law and the duty of the Government to uphold it. We are loyal to the Constitution which guarantees equality before the law for all. Conservatives care for people in need, particularly children, the elderly and the disabled. We see free enterprise – rewarding effort, skill and initiative – as the best way of creating an economy which can grow and so support improvement in social and other services. The Conservative Party is a national Party. It represents all the people of Britain without regard for creed, sex, race or background. The ability to deter

Britain's enemies and, if attacked, to defend ourselves, is a basic necessity if our other aims are to be achieved.

(from **Conservative Principles and Policies**, a Conservative Party Central Office information leaflet)

Labour Party

The Labour Party stands for social justice, for a society in which the claims of those in hardship or distress come first; where the wealth produced by all is fairly shared by all. (The Aims of the Labour Party Annual Conference 1960.)

The Labour Party believes passionately in the true dignity of human beings. From this flows the demand for the greatest opportunities and the highest standards of educational and physical development to be made available to all children; for proper care and security for people who are unable to provide for themselves through no fault of their own; for fair rewards for those who work by hand or by brain; for good recreational and cultural facilities and for enough houses to provide the opportunity for a secure and happy home life. Labour also believes that social justice and freedom are essential ingredients of society, and that its principles are not only morally and socially right, but economically essential.

Labour's belief in the dignity of human life knows no frontiers. It embraces all mankind. From it stems the desire to raise the standards of life of all impoverished and under-privileged people and to promote understanding and peace.

(from **What the Labour Party is About**, a Labour Party leaflet)

Liberal/SDP Alliance

We share a common concern about Britain's political and economic future. Our class-based party system, in which the Conservatives favour the board rooms while the Labour Party favours the trade unions, has deepened the divisions between our people. Social Democrats and Liberals alike seek a Government which will put the national interest ahead of vested interests. Our two parties have therefore come together to create a sense of common purpose.

We are committed to obtaining proportional representation at the earliest opportunity. Our shared priorities for government are to provide more jobs and secure more stable prices.

A 1931 election poster depicting Labour's view of the effects of the Government's pay and dole cuts on the poor and unemployed.

A lasting prosperity also demands the conservation of resources and the protection of the environment. We need a more balanced economy which encourages enterprise and innovation in both the private and the public sectors, and a spirit of co-operation. Only in this way can we create a fair society which provides properly for the old and the disadvantaged, and which responds compassionately to the needs of minorities.

We pledge ourselves to work within the wider international community for multilateral disarmament and for a more equitable distribution of the world's resources.

(from **A Fresh Start for Britain: Statement of Principles** by a joint working party of Liberals and Social Democrats, Poland Street Publications, London, 1981)

1. Give two examples of major political changes made by the Labour Government immediately after the Second World War. (2)
2. Explain what you understand by the terms 'nationalization' and 'privatization', and say which political party is associated with each. (4)
3. 'Consensus politics' refers to the situation where there is widespread agreement among the main parties on central political issues.
   a Which period since 1945 most resembles a situation of consensus politics? (1)
   b Give **two** examples of political issues where such a consensus appeared to have been reached. (4)
4. Which party do you think would be most closely associated with each of the following (in each case, explain your answer by reference to the three extracts on the parties' principles):
   a reform of the electoral system (3)
   b greater government spending on defence (3)
   c equality (3)

7 Policies

Parties may make statements of their principles but how do these become translated into more specific **policies**? Particularly at election times, parties have to work out plans for what they intend to do should they form the next government. At these times, the parties produce their election **manifestos** – their policy programmes. The chart which follows this passage compares some of the central policies expressed in the Conservative, Labour and Alliance manifestos for the 1983 general election.

It should not be thought, however, that there is agreement on every issue **within** each party. All political parties contain people with quite a wide variety of views on particular matters. Both the Conservative Party and the Labour Party have been split internally on the question of Britain's membership of the EEC, for example. Groups within parties are formed from those who share similar views on one particular issue or on a range of issues. These are sometimes referred to as 'ginger groups'. They include, for instance, 'Tribune', a group towards the left of the Labour Party, and the right-wing 'Monday Club' in the Conservative Party. It is common – especially in the media – to view political parties, and the groups and individuals within them, on a line, or spectrum, from 'left-wing' to 'right-wing', as in the following diagram.

(diagram adapted from **British Politics Today** by Bill Jones and Dennis Kavanagh, Manchester University Press, Manchester, 1983, p. 52)

The Labour Party is viewed on the 'left', politically, and the Conservative Party on the 'right'. But the diagram is also designed to show that each of these two parties itself has a 'right-wing' and a 'left-wing'. In the Conservative Party this distinction is often expressed as a division between 'wets' and 'dries'. The 'wets', for example, include those Conservatives who are critical of some of Margaret Thatcher's economic policies and would like to see more attention paid to the social services and 'welfare' policies. Within the Labour Party the left-wing is generally more committed to policies such as unilateral nuclear disarmament (Britain disarming on its own) and high taxes on the rich, than is the party's right-wing. The diagram also suggests that the right-wing of the Labour Party and the left-wing (or wets) of the Conservative Party may hold **some** views in common. These views may also be similar to those held by the Liberal and Social Democratic parties. To this extent they are all seen to occupy the political 'centre'. On defence policy, for instance, right-wing Labour supporters, Tory wets and the leaderships of the SDP/Liberal Alliance all favour **multi**lateral nuclear disarmament (all countries disarming together).

1. What is an election manifesto?   (1)
2. What was the main difference between the Conservative Party and the Labour Party on economic policy at the time of the 1983 election? (refer to chart on facing page.)   (2)
3. By using the information in the chart, show which party seems most committed to
   a home ownership   (3)
   b private health services   (3)
   c worker participation in industry   (3)
   d unilateral nuclear disarmament   (3)
4. In 1985, a new ginger group within the Conservative Party was formed. It called itself 'Conservative Centre Forward'. Its chief spokesman, Francis Pym, claimed that the group supported the objectives of the Conservative Government but believed that many of the policies designed to achieve the objectives were not working. The group therefore suggests that the policies should be changed. In particular, it wants the Government to do more to make industry more competitive, to increase public sector investment (such as housing and transport), and to try to develop a partnership between the unions, industry and the Government itself.

(adapted from 'Yes, Prime Minister, there are alternative Tory policies' by Francis Pym, **Daily Telegraph**, May 14, 1985, p. 20)

   a What evidence is there in this extract to suggest that the Centre Forward group agrees with Conservative principles but disagrees with the Government's policies?   (2)
   b Where would you place Conservative Centre Forward on the political 'spectrum'? (see diagram on p. 103)   (3)

Comparison of 1983 Election Manifestos

	Conservative	Labour	Alliance
The Economy and Unemployment	Reducing inflation is top priority. Control of public spending, borrowing and the supply of money. Encouragement of free enterprise to revive the economy.	Mass unemployment the central problem to tackle. Expansion of the economy through increased public spending on transport, housing, energy conservation, the social services and new technology. Increased spending to be paid for by borrowing and reducing expenditure on nuclear weapons.	Reducing unemployment is first priority. Economic growth to be achieved by increased public borrowing. New jobs to be provided by improvements to housing and the environment. Youth Training Scheme to be extended to all 16–17 year olds.
Defence	Britain's own independent nuclear weapons to be maintained. Negotiations to reduce nuclear weapons supported, but Cruise missiles to be deployed in Britain if Russians do not agree to remove their SS20 warheads.	No new nuclear bases or weapons in Britain and removal of existing ones. Against Cruise missiles and Trident. Support for NATO to be maintained but proportion of nation's resources devoted to defence to be reduced.	Participation in NATO central to Britain's defence policy. Strengthening of NATO's conventional forces. Strong support for multilateral disarmament. Trident to be cancelled.
Trade Unions and Industrial Relations	Trade union members to be given right to hold ballots to elect their leaders and to decide whether unions should have party political funds. The right of unions to call strikes without a secret ballot to be curbed.	Trade unions and Government to work out together how incomes, etc. should be distributed. Discussions with TUC on possibility of a legally enforced minimum wage.	An Industrial Democracy Act to be introduced to enable employees to participate in the running of their firms. Compulsory secret ballots to elect union leaders.
Housing	Extension of a 'home-owning democracy'.	Immediate 50% increase in local council spending on housing. Enforced council house sales to end.	Increased investment in housing. The right to buy council houses to be kept.
The National Health Service	A continued commitment to ensure that 'patients receive the best possible value for money' spent on the Health Service. Further reductions in costs of administering the Health Service. Growth in private health insurance to be encouraged.	Health service spending to be increased by 30% per year. Health charges to be phased out. Some government control of the pharmaceutical industry to ensure that available drugs are 'safe, effective and economic'.	A steady increase in money for the Health Service. Private health services would not be banned but neither would they receive government assistance.
The EEC	No withdrawal from the EEC.	Britain to withdraw from the EEC.	'Wholly committed' to staying in the EEC.
Northern Ireland	No major changes without 'the consent of the majority' of the Northern Ireland population. Law and order the highest priority.	Long-term aim of a unified Ireland through consent. A 'massive injection of resources' to 'rebuild the economy'.	A non-sectarian approach to Northern Ireland's problems to be encouraged. Attempt to replace direct rule from Westminster.

(adapted from **Election '83** by F. I. Magee, Longman, York, 1984, pp. 4–7)

8 Other parties

This section of the book has concentrated on the Conservative, Labour and Alliance parties, because, among them, they attract the vast majority of votes at election time. Nearly all MPs representing British constituencies are members of one or other of these parties. But there are other political parties in the UK. Some are represented in Parliament, others are not. The first of the following extracts lists some of these smaller parties. The remaining passages present the aims of two of them, Plaid Cymru and the SNP.

The **Scottish National Party** (SNP) was founded in 1934. It believes in the democratic right of the Scottish people to control their own affairs through an elected Scottish Parliament. In the October 1974 election, the SNP won 11 seats, but in both the 1979 and 1983 elections it won only 2 seats.

Plaid Cymru: the Welsh National Party. Its aim is to secure an independent democratic Welsh socialist state. A number of Welsh constituencies have returned Plaid Cymru MPs in recent years.

Ulster Unionists. There are various Ulster Unionist parties all of which are pledged to keep Northern Ireland as part of the United Kingdom. They are supported by the Protestants in Northern Ireland.

The **SDLP** (Social Democratic and Labour Party). This is the chief party which opposes the Unionists in Northern Ireland. It draws its support from the Catholic minority and from socialists in Northern Ireland. There are various other political groups opposed to the Unionists, including **Sinn Fein**, the political wing of the IRA.

Other parties which have put up candidates at recent general elections include left-wing parties, such as the **Workers' Revolutionary Party** and the **Communist Party**, and extreme right-wing parties, such as the **National Front**. At the 1979 general election, the National Front put up 303 candidates, but they attracted only 190,747 votes and none of them was elected.

(from **Britain's Government (Checkpoints Series No 24)** by John L. Foster, Edward Arnold, London, 1984, p. 11)

Plaid Cymru – its Welsh name means 'the party of Wales' – was founded in 1925 to secure self-government for Wales. Plaid Cymru aims at achieving Wales' right to govern itself by winning the support of a majority of her people. It rejects violence and believes in a peaceful road to Welsh freedom – by fighting elections and also campaigning to improve the lives of ordinary people in Wales today.

Plaid Cymru has three basic objectives:
1. To secure self-government for Wales through the establishment of a democratic socialist state;
2. To safeguard and promote the culture, language, environment, traditions and the economic life of Wales through the establishment of a decentralist socialist state;
3. To secure for Wales the right to become a member of the United Nations Organisation.

(from **Plaid Cymru Aims**, a Plaid Cymru pamphlet)

Scottish National Party. Our aim ... independence.

Independence means the establishment of a Scottish Parliament, elected by proportional representation, with control over all Scottish affairs. Scotland's Constitution will guard against any infringement of human rights. It will outlaw discrimination on grounds such as sex, religion or race, and will include guarantees on access to government information. A Scottish Government will be democratically accountable to the Scottish people.

'We in the SNP are not nationalists because we are proud of our country and want to conserve it the way it is. We are nationalists because we are ashamed of our country and want to improve it.' (Gordon Wilson MP, SNP Chairman)

(from **Introducing the SNP**, a Scottish National Party leaflet)

1. From the first extract, identify **three** regionally-based parties and **three** non-regionally-based parties. (2)
2. What aims are shared by
   a Plaid Cymru and the SNP? (2)
   b the SNP and the Liberal/SDP Alliance? (2)
3. To which of the main political parties does Plaid Cymru appear closest in terms of its aims? Explain your answer. (3)

4. Re-draw the diagram from Section 5.7 which shows the 'left, centre, right' political spectrum, extending the line at both ends. Show where you would place the following parties on the spectrum:
   a National Front   (2)
   b Communist Party   (2)
   c Workers' Revolutionary Party   (2)
   d Plaid Cymru   (2)
5. None of the smaller parties can hope to form the government on its own. Why, then, do they put forward candidates at election time?   (3)

Section 6 Pressure Groups

The main political parties are not as popular as they used to be. There has been a decline in voting support for the Labour and Conservative parties as the Liberals, the SDP and other smaller parties have increased their vote. A decline in the **membership** of the Labour and Conservative parties since the 1950s, however, has not been matched by a similar rise in the number of members of the smaller parties. It could be that many politically active people are switching their form of participation in politics from parties to pressure groups.

Pressure groups are also sometimes referred to as 'interest' or 'lobby' groups. They are groups of people who have some interest in common which they wish to protect or an aim which they seek to pursue. They try to influence those in society with the power to make decisions. The actions and campaigns of pressure groups will therefore often be aimed, directly or indirectly, at government – either nationally or locally.

The first passage in this section provides a comparison between pressure groups and political parties. This is followed by a description of the methods and tactics used by pressure groups. The connection between lobby groups and Parliament, and the role of trade unions and business organizations in influencing government policy, are examined. Further passages deal with the questions of pressure group power and their contribution to democratic politics. Finally, there is an examination of 'protest groups' and how they differ from other pressure groups.

1 Pressure groups and parties

Pressure groups, as well as parties, are 'political' in that they are concerned with influencing people and decisions. They both rely to a large extent on subscriptions from their members to finance their activities. But there are important differences between

them as the following extract shows. The passage begins by dis-
tinguishing between two major types of pressure group.

Pressure groups use political action to try to bring about
changes which they see as desirable, or to prevent changes
they consider undesirable. Two major examples are business
groups and the trade unions. These are important **interest** (or
sectional) pressure groups. The task of sectional groups is to
protect the interests of their members. The National Union of
Students and the British Dental Association are organizations
of this type. The other main type of pressure group is the
promotional group. These groups attempt to promote a
particular **cause**. Examples include Shelter (who work on
behalf of the homeless) and the Child Poverty Action Group.

Unlike the major political parties, pressure groups do not
seek to exercise power directly – they do not try to form a
government. They do not usually put up candidates at
elections. On occasions it has been suggested that some trade
union leaders have as much political power as the Prime
Minister. However, this overlooks the fact that no pressure
group leader, whilst acting in that capacity, is seeking to
occupy any position in the Government. Another difference is
that pressure groups are usually concerned with only one
issue (housing or child poverty, for example) or with
protecting the interests of only one group (for instance,
students or dentists). Political parties, on the other hand, are
expected to develop and pursue policies on a wide range of
issues. Furthermore, although pressure groups do attempt to
influence the political process, this is not necessarily the main
concern of their members. The motoring organizations such
as the AA and the RAC, for example, attempt to influence
government policies on the construction and maintenance of
roads, on petrol and vehicle taxes, and so on. But as far as
most of their members are concerned, the main function of
the motoring organizations is to provide breakdown and
other services.

Nevertheless, there are some similarities between pressure
groups and parties. Both types of organization will have
leaders who are supposed to represent the interests or ideas
of their members in some form. Both enable people to
participate in political affairs and both act as channels of

political communication. Many pressure groups also have links with parties. The Labour Party has always been closely connected with the trade union movement. Similarly, there are often close relationships between pressure groups representing business interests and the Conservative Party. However, these similarities and connections should not hide the main difference between them: 'parties aim to exercise political power directly whereas pressure groups do not'.

(adapted from **Parties and Pressure Groups** by W. N. Coxall, Longman, Harlow, 1981, pp. 10–12)

1. a Distinguish between **sectional** and **promotional** pressure groups. (2)
   b The following are brief descriptions of four pressure groups operating in Britain. In each case, state whether the organization is a **sectional** or **promotional** pressure group. Give brief reasons for your answers.
   'The **Chemical Industries Association** is an employers' organization. It is the overall representative body for the industry.' It aims 'to help create a business environment in which member companies can prosper'.
   '**Friends of the Earth** are supporters of a campaigning organization promoting policies to protect the natural environment.'
   '**Schools Against the Bomb** is an organization of school students throughout Britain. It is a national campaign against nuclear arms.'
   'The **Transport and General Workers Union** is concerned with the interests and protection of its members. It brings together workers from a wide range of grades and trades into one big union.'
   (The quotes are taken from information leaflets of the organizations concerned.) (6)
2. Identify **three** similarities between pressure groups and political parties. (3)
3. a Identify **three** differences between pressure groups and parties. (6)
   b Which is emphasized in the extract as the major difference? (1)
4. Pressure groups 'act as channels of political communication'. What does this mean? (2)

2 Methods

Various types of activity have been employed by pressure groups attempting to achieve their aims. They range from violent methods such as terrorism or hijacking to writing letters to newspapers or organizing petitions. The following passage examines some of the methods commonly adopted.

If a pressure group wants to inform or persuade the public it might use posters, leaflets and other forms of propaganda to publicize its cause. If it wants to show the Government that it has widespread support, it may organize mass meetings or demonstrations. Demonstrations can also be useful in boosting the morale of the group's supporters. Some groups may become more effective by working closely with a political party or through lobbying individual MPs (see 6.3). Others may be successful in bringing about the changes they want, or preventing those they don't, by exerting pressure in less open ways. These groups will have direct access to the decision-makers themselves – usually Government Ministers or senior civil servants.

The method, or combination of methods, which is chosen will depend on a number of factors. They may include the resources available (money and people, for example), the size of the organization, and the nature of the aim being pursued. Friends of the Earth, for instance, concentrate on different targets according to the particular campaign. A spokesman for this group has said: 'In our campaign against nuclear power, for example, it is important to go for public opinion rather than MPs or civil servants. Unless public concern can be felt, we will not make much progress because there is a strong nuclear lobby we have to counter.' Tactics may also vary at different times of the same campaign. Frank Field, the former director of the Child Poverty Action Group, has said: 'At certain stages one goes for civil servants, at other stages for MPs. But the essential job is to create a favourable climate of opinion.'

Getting the mass media involved can be essential in influencing public opinion in general. But the media can also be important in other ways. Frank Field claims: 'The media really are the blood supply for pressure groups. If ministers

DYING FOR YOUR VOTE

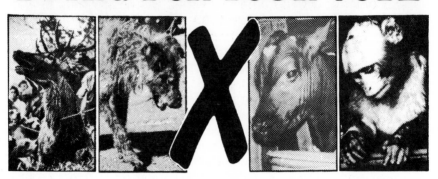

ONLY PARLIAMENT CAN STOP THIS CRUELTY

At the next General Election we will be asking the three main parties to make specific manifesto commitments to:

Prohibit The suffering caused by factory farming.

Outlaw Painful experiments on animals.

Abolish Bloodsports and other cruelties to wild animals.

Ban The abuse of pets and other companion animals.

2 or 3 million votes will tip the balance and decide who will win the next General Election. We know there are millions of people who hate cruelty to animals and we intend to mobilise that support.
If you are prepared, just this once, to use your vote for animals please complete the coupon below and send it to us now. Prior to the next Election we will advise you how best to use your vote for animals. ✂

Register of electors

Send to:
A.P.A. 91B Southwark Bridge Road, London SE1 1SG.

I will be 18 or over at the next Election and I will use my vote to help animals.

Signature _____

Name (Block Capitals) _____

Address (Block Capitals) _____

_____

Please attach a separate sheet for your friends or family.

Please enclose a first class stamp for our postal communication prior to the Election. We urgently need financial support to continue this campaign and any contribution you are able to make will be gratefully received.

A.P.A. is the Animal Protection Alliance which includes leading animal welfare societies.
Secretary: Richard Course

and civil servants have read about a group in **The Times**, then they know they are likely to get questions in Parliament about it and they become interested.' But he adds that he was 'very careful about where to place publicity. If I wanted to influence ministers or civil servants I wrote to **The Times**. If I wanted to influence trade unionists on their way to a Labour Party liaison meeting I went for **The Guardian**.'

For many pressure groups, lobbying MPs at Westminster is seen as an important activity. A group might encourage an MP to try to get Parliament to pass a new law on the group's behalf. The political affairs controller of the Royal Society for the Prevention of Cruelty to Animals, for example, is a former lobby journalist. She spends a lot of her time working with MPs at Westminster.

However, the major decisions are often made in the Government Departments of Whitehall, rather than in Parliament. Many pressure groups therefore try to direct their activities at Ministers and at the top civil servants employed in the Departments. In fact the Government relies on certain pressure groups for the information necessary to form policies and make new laws. **Which** groups are consulted, though, seems to be decided by the civil servants. Furthermore, the contacts between pressure groups and civil servants generally take place behind closed doors. The public, the media, and even Parliament do not usually get to know the details of these meetings. It is obvious, however, that some groups are far more influential than others. The National Farmers' Union is often regarded as a very privileged pressure group. The NFU represents Britain's farmers and has members on the many agricultural advisory committees which exist. The Government relies on these committees for developing and implementing its policies on agriculture, and NFU members can provide relevant knowledge and expertise. Geoffrey Alderman argues: 'It is no exaggeration to say that, without the willing co-operation of the National Farmers' Union, the implementation, and, most probably, the formulation of agricultural policy in Britain would simply not be possible.' Other groups, too, are regularly consulted by Government Departments on particular policies. The Law Society, concerning the regulation of solicitors, and the British Medical Association, about matters affecting family doctors, are two examples.

Those pressure groups which can assist Governments – by supplying information and expert advice – clearly have much easier access to Ministers and civil servants than do other groups. Groups with little to offer will have to resort to other methods. Sometimes, the **only** major option available is to try to influence the public in some way in the hope that the decision-makers will, in turn, take notice of public opinion. In these cases, the range of alternatives open to pressure groups will be limited (demonstrations, marches, posters, etc.). On the other hand, some pressure groups may be able to operate on a variety of levels and through a number of techniques of persuasion.

But whatever the methods employed, Geoffrey Alderman has some advice for people wishing to influence Government thinking. He suggests that, if possible, they should try to work through an organization that is already well-established and accepted. Forming a new pressure group is an extremely difficult and time-consuming business.

(adapted from **Pressure Groups and Government in Britain** by Geoffrey Alderman, Longman, Harlow, 1984, pp. 76–100 and 'Lobbying of MPs at Westminster seen as main activity', **The Times**, April 8, 1980)

1. Identify four types of activity which may be used by pressure groups.   (2)
2. a Why do many pressure groups try to form links with civil servants?   (2)
   b Give, and explain, an example from the passage where influencing public opinion is seen as a more appropriate strategy.   (3)
3. Giving reasons, say which of the four pressure groups listed in Question 1(b) of Section 6.1 would be
   a most likely to have close contacts with a Labour Government   (2)
   b most likely to have close contacts with a Conservative Government   (2)
   c least likely to have direct access to Ministers or civil servants   (2)
4. In 1985, the Live Aid Concert at Wembley raised many millions of pounds to help feed the vast number of people starving in parts

of Africa. During the concert, a member of U2 said: 'It should be the job of Governments. If they don't do it, we should. But we should also tell the Government that they should.' Explain how Live Aid can be seen not only as a charity but as a pressure group.   (3)

5. What difficulties would be involved in forming a pressure group?   (4)

3 Pressure groups in Parliament

The process of attempting to influence decision-making, especially decisions about the making of new laws (legislation), is sometimes referred to as 'lobbying'. The lobbying of MPs by pressure groups has increased considerably in recent years. It has also become more organized. As the following extracts show, this has caused some concern, and in 1984 a House of Commons committee began to investigate lobbying.

Parliament is to begin an inquiry this week into political lobbying and the involvement of MPs as paid advisers to pressure groups. The Select Committee on Members' Interests will focus on whether the voluntary code for MPs disclosing outside income and interests is working efficiently and whether the growing behind-the-scenes activities of specialized parliamentary lobbyists need to be controlled.

There are thought to be between 25 and 30 parliamentary lobbyists working regularly in the House of Commons. Most of them wine and dine MPs, arrange foreign trips and set up briefings for Members in the hope of influencing legislation affecting their clients. In addition some MPs are employed as consultants to firms or pressure groups. When MPs speak for these groups in debate, they must declare their interest, but they are not obliged to reveal any fees or favours they receive.

Little is known about parliamentary lobbyists, but pressure groups and big companies are increasingly turning to them to put their case in Parliament. GEC Marconi and British Aerospace employed a firm of lobbyists to lobby for a £250m missile order. The fear is that lobbyists may be exerting undue pressure on MPs. The former Labour MP for Keighley, Bob Cryer, complained that the Commons dining-rooms were being abused by lobbyists entertaining MPs. Both Labour and Tory MPs criticized the number of lobbyists who duplicated as researchers to MPs. Unlike their counterparts in America, lobbyists in Britain are not obliged to join a public register, nor do they have an established code of conduct requiring them to disclose clients, fees and connections with MPs.

(from 'Parliament to probe MPs' outside links' by Lionel Barber, **Sunday Times** February 19, 1984)

The fastest growth business at Westminster is political influence. The boom is indicated by the estimate of one leading practitioner that the total fees of more than 40 companies directly engaged in the art of lobbying increased by 50 per cent last year. Sharing in this bonanza are some 20 MPs who are directors of public relations firms and more than 100 Members who act as private consultants to individual companies. This week, the Select Committee on Members' Interests will press for fuller disclosure by MPs who operate on behalf of public relations companies, by making them list the names of all their direct clients. But it has shied away from recommending a Register of Lobbyists which would oblige those who seek to influence Parliament to disclose publicly what they are up to and who they are paying. It is expected to deal with abuses such as the employees of lobbying companies who masquerade as MPs' research assistants.

The Select Committee's report is likely to come as a disappointment to those who believe that the growing pressures on Parliament need to be much more tightly regulated. At present MPs register their paid directorships, paid employments, major stakes in companies and other parliamentary perks such as sponsored overseas trips. But these voluntary declarations are in such a vague form that it is usually impossible to gauge the extent of the interest. The Institute of Public Relations called for much fuller disclosure in its evidence to the Select Committee. It said that MPs should be asked to list how much they are paid, by whom and for what service. If MPs were obliged to disclose, then outside observers and indeed their constituents would be able to form a much fairer view about whether such links are defensible.

(from 'Probe fails to check bonanza in lobbying at Westminster' by Adam Raphael, **The Observer** June 9, 1985, p. 5)

1. Give a specific example from the first extract of the activities of parliamentary lobbyists.   (1)
2. What evidence is provided in the second extract to support the claim that parliamentary lobbying is rapidly expanding?   (2)
3. a Who carried out the inquiry referred to in the extracts?   (2)
   b What were the two main aspects which the inquiry was set up to investigate?   (2)
   c Roughly how long did it take to carry out the investigation and publish the report?   (2)
4. a Identify **two** recommendations that the report was expected to make.   (2)
   b Why, for some people, would these measures not go far enough?   (3)
5. What are the dangers and benefits of parliamentary lobbying?
                                                                      (6)

4 Trade unions and business organizations

Trade unions are formed to protect the interests of workers in particular industries or types of work. The main task of the NUM (National Union of Mineworkers), for example, is to protect the pay, conditions of work and jobs of Britain's coal miners. Members of NALGO (National and Local Government Officers' Association) expect their union to carry out a similar function for them. Business pressure groups take a variety of forms. Many are employers' associations set up to further the interests of employers in certain types of industries. The Chemical Industries Association and the National Farmers' Union, both referred to earlier in this Section, are examples of organizations representing employers. Many business organizations are themselves members of the Confederation of British Industry (CBI). The CBI seeks to promote the interests of business as a whole. A similar body on the union side is the Trades Union Congress (TUC). These two organizations act as pressure groups in that they attempt to influence government policy in ways that will benefit their member organizations.

It is often said that trade unions and groups representing large businesses are the most powerful pressure groups in Britain. However, their interests are often different and even opposed. Some people believe that the influence of big business is balanced by the power of organized labour (the trade unions). Others claim that, in general, big business has more power because of the type of economy which exists in Britain. The British economy, like most others in the Western world, is based on private enterprise and the pursuit of profit. Even though Governments attempt to regulate the workings of the economy in various ways, private business – including the large multi-national or transnational corporations – are to a large extent left to their own devices. Decisions about where to invest, what to produce and how to produce are not generally made by Governments, but by business people and business corporations.

Even so, business decisions may well be affected by the economic policies of different Governments. And the influence on Governments of trade unions on the one hand and business organizations on the other can vary according to the party in power. Trade unions enjoy close relations with the Labour Party. Some Labour MPs are sponsored by particular unions. Many Conservative MPs have close links with business organizations. Some are themselves directors or employees of private companies. Both unions and business groups can therefore exert some pressure at the Parliamentary level. But this will not automatically result in policies favourable to one side or the other. More important will be the possible links with Government Ministers, their Departments, and even the Prime Minister. Through bodies such as NEDC (the National Economic Development Council) business leaders and unions can have direct contact with the Government. For a time in the early 1980s, the TUC pulled out of NEDC meetings. This was a protest against moves by the Conservative Government to force certain changes to the unions. In 1979, the Conservatives had replaced Labour as the governing party. There then followed a period of marked decline in the power of the trade union movement, as the following extract describes.

The trade unions have experienced a sharp decline in influence. Only a few years ago they were thought by many people to be one of the most powerful forces in the country. In **The Times** (1.9.82) John Hoskyns traced their changed fortune, 'today, union prestige and authority have declined beyond recognition. They are more disliked, less feared, less respected.' The result of the 1983 general election was a big blow to the trade union movement because it meant another 4 or 5 years in the political wilderness. Earlier governments, particularly Labour ones, had involved the trade unions in decision-making on economic policy. Also, governments would intervene in major strikes to try and reach a quick settlement. Union leaders would be called to Number Ten, and beer and sandwiches were said to be served whilst nego-tiations took place. Today the phrase 'beer and sandwiches' is used to represent the days when governments and unions worked together closely. The highest level of cooperation between government and unions was the 'Social Contract' agreed between Harold Wilson's Labour Government and the union leadership. In sharp contrast Mrs Thatcher's Govern-ments have refused to intervene directly in industrial disputes, nor is it thought that the unions have a useful role to play in helping to make economic policy. John Smith,

Labour's Employment spokesman, has commented, 'What has happened under the Conservatives is that the trade unions have been shut out of Whitehall completely.'

Mrs Thatcher came to power in 1979 pledged to reform trade unions. High unemployment weakened the unions just at the time when they needed strength to resist the Government. In 1979 the total membership of all unions in the TUC was over 12 million – today it is 9.7 million, which is less than half the workforce.

(from **Politics Pal** by L. Robins, Great Glen, Leicestershire, 1983, p. 18 and 1985, p. 17)

A series of new laws between 1980 and 1984 weakened the position of the unions. The banning of unions from the Government Communications Headquarters at Cheltenham, and the defeat of the miners' strike in 1985, seemed to reduce the confidence of the union movement even further. However, there were then signs that many people thought the Government had gone too far in its attacks on the unions. Some trade unions have a political fund from which money is given to the Labour Party. The 1984 Trade Union Act forced these unions to hold a vote amongst their memberships on whether these political funds should continue. Probably to the surprise of the Government, union members in many cases voted overwhelmingly to keep the funds.

No such requirement to hold a ballot applies to companies, or their pressure groups, who contribute financially to the Conservative Party. Groups representing business interests would normally expect a Conservative Government to be more sympathetic to their aims. But even the influential National Farmers' Union (see Section 6.2) has not always got its way in recent years. This has been due partly to splits and disagreements within the organization and partly to the fact that it now 'has to compete with European farmers in influencing the Common Agricultural Policy of the EEC' (**Politics Pal** p. 18). The CBI has on occasions been critical of the Government which has often ignored its advice. However, any decline in power of the CBI has been balanced by the increase in influence of another business pressure group, the right-wing Institute of Directors. This organization is headed by Sir John Hoskyns, a former adviser to Margaret Thatcher.

Protest in Downing Street against the banning of trade unions at the Government Communications Headquarters, Cheltenham.

1. a Are the TUC and CBI **sectional** or **promotional** pressure groups? (1)
   b What are the main functions of these two groups? (2)
2. a Why do you think business groups and trade unions are considered to be the most powerful pressure groups? (2)
   b Explain how high rates of unemployment can reduce the power of trade unions. (3)
   c Identify two other factors that have weakened the unions in recent years. (2)
   d Identify two ways in which the relationship between the Government and the trade unions changed after 1979. (4)
   e What evidence is provided to suggest that pressure groups representing business interests are not always successful in influencing the policies of a Conservative Government? (2)
3. a Why are business groups more closely associated with the Conservative Party and trade unions with the Labour Party? (2)
   b Giving reasons, say whether you think pressure groups should be allowed to give money to political parties. (2)

5 Pressure group power

Here are some of the stories, concerning pressure groups, reported in **The Times** during the period October 1981 to January 1982. On 21 October **The Times** reported a speech by Dr John Havard, secretary of the British Medical Association, who claimed that the law allowed 'fanatical and moralistic' pressure groups to hound doctors in the courts. Some days later, during the trial at Leicester Crown Court of Dr Leonard Arthur (accused and subsequently acquitted of attempting to murder a baby), Sir Douglas Black, President of the Royal College of Physicians, declared from the witness box that organizations such as 'LIFE' and 'EXIT' were 'helping to destroy the confidence of doctors and nurses' (**The Times**, 31 Oct.). EXIT is an organization set up to promote voluntary euthanasia. LIFE, organized originally to fight the 1967 Abortion Act, has more recently campaigned on the issue of 'mercy killings'; according to **The Times** (6 Nov.) it was the chairman of LIFE who had reported Dr Arthur to the police.

But, having recorded the British Medical Association as **objecting** to the activities of pressure groups, **The Times** carried a report (11 Dec.) that the Association was itself refusing to co-operate with an inquiry by the Department of Health into the cost and efficiency of family practitioner services. A few days later the Motor Agents' Association advised its petrol-retailer members to ignore a government ruling that the practice of surcharging customers who bought petrol by credit cards should end. And early in the new year **The Times** (14 Jan.) reported that after two months of bargaining the Society of London Art Dealers had con-descended to make available to the Office of Fair Trading its evidence on the so-called 'buyer's premium' charged by auctioneers. The Office was thus enabled to proceed with an investigation into whether the auction houses of Sotheby's and Christies had colluded (got together in secret) over the introduction of the premium and whether these firms were therefore in breach of fair trading practices.

The above examples have not been selected at random. They have been chosen to demonstrate (1) that modern British pressure groups can be very powerful; (2) that public policy is often dictated or strongly influenced by the inter-action of different groups; (3) that good government demands the co-operation of pressure groups. It is not only the 'big battalions' of industry and the trade union movement which are able to exercise a veto over (reject) the intentions of government and Parliament.

(from **Pressure Groups and Government in Great Britain** by Geoffrey Alderman, Longman, Harlow, 1984, pp. 124–5, with minor additions)

Nevertheless, some pressure groups are obviously more power-ful than others. The more powerful groups are frequently those least heard about publicly. Their direct contact with the top decision-makers means that they have to rely less on the media and public opinion to put across their case. On the other hand, those groups in the weakest position are often almost totally dependent on publicity. Their pressure and influence can only be indirect. They will sometimes be the 'noisiest' or most noticeable pressure groups because of the limited range of methods at their

What You Can Do

* Campaign against the arms race by joining your local CND group (see box)
* Write to your MP—they do take notice of letters
* Discuss the arms race and the Third World with your friends and neighbours
* Get your union branch, church group or similar organisation to discuss these issues at their next meeting.

HELP CND STOP THE ARMS RACE. JOIN US.

Your support can make a difference.
☐ Yes, I want to help.
Here is my donation of £

Name _____ (BLOCK CAPITALS)

Address _____

_____

_____ Post code _____
(IMPORTANT)

☐ And, I'll join the Campaign for Nuclear Disarmament.
Adult £9 ☐, Household £12 ☐, Student £3 ☐, Unwaged & Pensioner £2 ☐, Youth CND (21 and under £1)☐ (tick one).
☐ I also want to stay informed. Sent me SANITY, CND's monthly magazine £6 ☐ (please tick)

Please find enclosed £_____ donation.
£_____ membership.
| Pub. | £_____ Sanity.

Please makes cheques or postal orders payable to CND
And send with completed form to Alison Williams
CND, 22-24 Underwood Street, London N1 7JQ
If resident in Scotland send to
Scottish CND, 420 Sauchiehall Street,
Glasgow G2

CND

CND Publications Ltd 22-24 Underwood St. London N1 7JQ

IN THE NEXT 24 HOURS, £1¼ BILLION WILL BE SPENT ON ARMAMENTS WHILE 10,000 PEOPLE WILL DIE THROUGH LACK OF FOOD.

War on Want

disposal: demonstrations, protest marches, and other forms of direct action.

Cyanide scare

TWO million cigarettes have been removed from sale after a cyanide scare. A holidaymaker who bought a packet at Gatwick airport found a handwritten message which said: 'These cigarettes have been impregnated with cyanide. Animal Rights Liberation Front.'

(Sunday Times, September 1, 1985, p. 2)

In general, the power of national pressure groups can vary according to how 'high' their direct influence can reach among:

(1) Government Ministers and Departments
(2) Parliament (MPs and parties)
(3) Public opinion.

Those able to reach (1) will often have the most power, and those restricted to (3) the least. However, there will be exceptions. Furthermore, some pressure groups may be able to operate effectively on more than one level, as previous passages have shown.

But how should the power of a pressure group be judged? One way is to examine how successful it is in achieving its aims or furthering its interests. However, such 'success' is not always easy to measure. The Campaign for Nuclear Disarmament has not been successful in abolishing nuclear weapons. But few would doubt that it has increased public awareness and concern about the dangers and effects of nuclear war. The aims of a pressure group may be only partly met in the short term, but the group's activities may still have some effect, as the following two examples indicate.

> Opposition leaders yesterday demanded that the Government match the Live Aid cash for fighting famine in Africa and accused the Prime Minister of miserly cuts in aid... Mrs. Thatcher...said she was proud of the Government's record on providing short-term famine relief to Ethiopia and Sudan... The dispute illustrated the potent effect of Live Aid last weekend on the debate on aid in the Commons, often a matter of interest to a minority of MPs... The extravaganza organized by Bob Geldof...has ensured that the Government's aid policy will be discussed more fully in public than before.
>
> (from 'Match Live Aid famine cash, PM is told' by James Naughtie, **The Guardian**, July 17, 1985)

> The Irish Republic's leading supermarket chains have agreed to phase out the sale of South African goods after negotiations...to end a 14-month strike by a group of anti-apartheid workers at a major Dublin supermarket.
>
> (reported in **The Observer**, September 15, 1985, p. 11)

On their own, the activities of Live Aid could not change the relations between rich and poor nations which result in mass starvation in parts of the world. A small group of strikers from an Irish supermarket could not end apartheid in South Africa. But these two examples can be seen as **partial** successes for groups neither of which could count on regular and direct contact with top decision-makers. Both groups altered, in however small a way, an economic situation (providing cash/boycotting goods). Both influenced the way certain issues are debated (Third World poverty/South African apartheid). And both probably helped to change or strengthen attitudes about them.

1. a From the first passage (by Geoffrey Alderman) identify two
      sectional and two **promotional** pressure groups.   (2)
   b In general, which type do you think has more power, and
      why?   (4)
2. Briefly summarize Geoffrey Alderman's assessment of the
   power of pressure groups.   (4)
3. How would you measure the power of pressure groups and
   what problems are involved in doing so?   (4)
4. Some groups have no contact with Government Ministers or top
   civil servants. In what ways might they still be effective? Use
   examples from the above passages to support your answer.   (6)

6 Pressure groups and democracy

I had tremendous help from SPUC (Society for the Protection of the Unborn Child) in terms of facts and figures and research. I simply could not have done the work myself.
(John Corrie, MP)

Professional associations like the British Medical Association and the Prison Officers' Association have the most weight in short-circuiting representative democracy.
(A former Home Office official)

(Both quotes from **The Times**, April 9, 1980)

If pressure groups can be powerful, and some have more power than others, a further question is raised. Do pressure groups aid democracy, or do they interfere with it? The following extract looks at some of the arguments involved.

It can be argued that pressure groups help to make the political system more democratic in a number of ways. Many pressure groups are able to provide detailed information on particular aspects of current or planned economic and social policy. This helps the process of government. Pressure groups can act as channels of political communication and consultation between the public and the Government. At the same time they can keep a check on Government activities. They also provide a way in which individuals can participate in politics other than (or as well as) joining political parties. Political parties may be unwilling to defend minority interests, for example those of prisoners, or to support groups not directly connected with this country, such as Blacks opposing apartheid in South Africa. Pressure groups such as PROP (Preservation of the Rights of Prisoners) and the Anti-Apartheid Movement may be able to promote causes or help defend interests to which parties may pay little attention. Finally, pressure groups can sometimes reduce party conflict by dealing direct with Ministers and civil servants.

Against these benefits, however, it can be argued that pressure groups are often unrepresentative of the majority of their members. Their leaders are sometimes appointed, rather than elected, and they do not have to explain or justify themselves to the public as a whole. Those pressure groups which are able to influence Government Ministers and senior civil servants directly, often do so in secret. Consultations take place behind closed doors. Such activities can also be said to be by-passing Parliament. And yet it is the Members of Parliament who are democratically elected to represent the public. Furthermore, because pressure groups vary in the amount of influence they have, they do not represent society equally. Some pressure groups representing business or professional interests, for example, are strong. Others – such as those representing immigrants, old-age pensioners or the unemployed – are weaker and often less well organized.

(adapted from **British Politics Today** by Bill Jones and Dennis Kavanagh, Manchester University Press, Manchester, 1983, pp. 102–3)

1. a Identify **four** arguments which support the claim that pressure groups help democracy.   (4)
   b Support **two** of these arguments with evidence from previous passages in this section.   (6)

2. a Identify **four** arguments which support the claim that pressure groups make the political system less democratic. (4)
   b Support **two** of these arguments with evidence from previous passages in this section.   (6)

7 Protest groups

The pressure groups examined in this section have each been concerned with promoting a single cause or defending a particular set of interests. But there are other political or social movements in society whose aims and membership are more general. Their concerns may cover a number of issues at the same time. They may not fall readily, therefore, into either the 'sectional' or 'promotional' categories of pressure group. The authors of the first of the two passages which follow describe them as 'protest groups'. Both extracts provide possible examples.

'Protest groups may be defined as groups that aim to bring about fundamental changes in public policy, political institutions and sometimes society itself.' They are not political parties but neither can they be classified as sectional or promotional pressure groups. Like other pressure groups, but unlike parties, they do not seek to form the government. Protest groups are different from **sectional** pressure groups because their members do not come from a particular section of society, and their organization is less formal. Their aims are more radical than **promotional** pressure groups and are not confined to single issues. Protest groups are more likely to use mass-action tactics such as demonstrations, although there is often disagreement over which methods to use. As well as aiming to change government policy, some protest groups hope to change social attitudes in general.

The women's movement might be seen as an example. It wants to see certain changes in policy which affect employment and taxation, for instance. But it also aims to change attitudes throughout society. Disagreements over tactics occur, supporters are drawn from many different sections of society, and 'membership' is not strictly defined. Not only does the women's movement attempt to alter attitudes directly, it also works with other pressure groups, where appropriate, as well as with political parties.

(adapted from 'Two new protest groups: the peace and women's movements' by Paul Byrne and Joni Lovenduski in **Developments in British Politics** edited by Henry Drucker, Patrick Dunleavy, Andrew Gamble and Gillian Peele, Macmillan, Basingstoke and London, 1984, pp. 222–4)

'I'm not political, see?' said the young man in the Amesbury car park. 'These parties, they're all the same.'

One young man with him, shocked, tried to argue the merits of the Labour Party. But he refused to be impressed and all around him, stretched out on the grassy bank, young people in their teens and early twenties nodded their agreement.

They wanted to have a festival at Stonehenge, and it was clear that 'They' were going to stop them. 'They' are the powers that be, the Establishment, the Police, the political parties who have swapped places occasionally throughout the years when these people were growing up, and as far as the people in the Amesbury car park can see, it had not made the slightest difference. We still have vivisection, right? And nuclear weapons? And there are still Hooray Henrys going about with their champagne bottles . . . there are still the rich to despise the poor, and the poor to loathe the rich. For the generation coming of age in the '80s, conventional politics have failed to change anything. Their solution is to reject conventional politics.

The group in the car park represent what is, if not a completely new phenomenon, then certainly a growing one. These young people are involved in intense political activism, but it is associated with a variety of issues rather than a coherent political grouping. They are strongly into animal rights, many being vegetarians or even vegans. They are also supporters of the peace movement and frequently involved in the actions at bases and setting up peace camps. However, as a whole, they are very definitely **not** interested in CND as an organization which seems far too middle-of-the-road for them.

(from 'Party poopers' by Polly Woolley, **New Statesman**, 7 June, 1985, pp. 16–17)

1. According to the first extract, how do 'protest groups' differ from
   a political parties   (1)
   b sectional pressure groups   (2)
   c promotional pressure groups?   (4)
2. Give **two** reasons why, in the first extract, the women's movement is used as an example of a 'protest group'.   (4)
3. a In your experience, to what extent are the political views of the group described in the second extract typical of 'people in their teens and early twenties'?   (3)
   b Can the people described in the second extract be regarded as part of a 'protest group'? Give reasons for your answer.   (3)
   c In what ways might they be seen to differ from the women's movement as described in the first extract?   (3)

Section 7 Fundamentals of British Government

The extract in Section 1.1 emphasized that politics arises out of conflict. People and groups disagree about what to do and how it should be done. All groups in society – however informal or loosely organized – have certain rules designed to regulate behaviour and manage conflict. Amongst groups of friends such rules may remain largely unspoken and hardly recognized. It is only when someone does or says something that is considered inappropriate or to be 'going too far' that others in the group may take action. For instance, the offending individual may be ignored or shunned by the rest of the group. Whatever the punishment, action has been taken because a rule has been broken.

More formal groups – such as clubs and organizations of various types – may have more definite rules and regulations. Often these are written down. Infringement of club rules could lead to expulsion from the organization.

For societies, or nation states, there will be sets of rules which are called laws. They may include basic principles about how the political system should be organized. There will also be other rules which outlaw particular acts such as murder. Laws will vary from one society to another depending on what the people (or certain groups of people) in each society consider to be important. In the societies of the Western world (such as Britain, the USA, and the countries of Western Europe) for example, a lot of emphasis is put on private property and material goods. In such countries there are likely to be many laws dealing with ownership, theft, and so on.

This section introduces some of the basic institutions and ideas that are involved in the processes whereby laws in Britain are made, administered, and enforced.

1 Three roles of government

Between 1945 and 1948 a number of new laws were introduced which formed the modern 'welfare state' in Britain. Probably the most important was the law which made possible the National Health Service. Anyone living in this country was to be able to obtain medical treatment free of charge in a hospital or by a general practitioner. It was to be paid for partly by insurance contributions made each week by people of working age and partly through general taxation. To provide the service, hospitals had to be built and equipped, doctors and nurses to be trained, and many other people employed to carry out all the other work involved in health care and treatment. Action would also need to be taken against any individuals who failed to pay their weekly insurance contributions or their taxes.

This example demonstrates that the **making** of laws forms only part of what is involved in the government of a country. Once made, a law has to be **administered** and **enforced**. The following extract describes who is responsible for carrying out each of these functions within the British system of government.

Three kinds of political power are involved in governing a country.

1. **Legislative** power. To **legislate** is to make or change laws. This task is carried out by Parliament.

2. **Executive** power. This involves implementing the law – seeing that the requirements of laws are carried out, or administered. The routine tasks are performed by government employees known as civil servants. They work in various government departments and each department is the responsibility of a Government Minister who is a politician. The most senior Government Ministers, together with the Prime Minister, form the Cabinet which has overall control of the executive function. It is also the Cabinet's job to form policy and suggest new laws.

3. **Judicial** power. This is the power to decide whether laws have been broken and, if so, to punish those held responsible. This role of law enforcement is carried out by judges and magistrates in the law courts.

If all these powers were carried out by only one person or a single group, the political system would be referred to as a dictatorship. Until the seventeenth century Britain was a dictatorship in the form of an 'absolute monarchy'. The monarch (a king or queen) could overrule any decisions made by Parliament. Ministers were merely personal advisers to the monarch. As judges were appointed and removed by the king or queen, judicial power was also effectively in the hands of the monarch. Although in practice these three powers have since largely been taken away from the personal control of the monarch, there remains a formal link between them and the Crown. This is reflected in official titles such as 'Her Majesty's Government'.

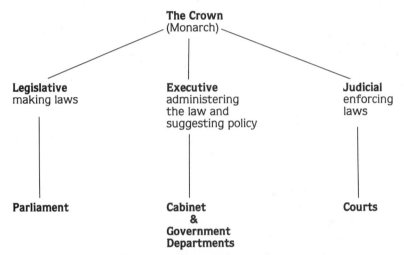

The Crown
(Monarch)

Legislative
making laws

Executive
administering
the law and
suggesting policy

Judicial
enforcing
laws

Parliament

Cabinet
&
Government
Departments

Courts

(adapted 11 ?m **Central Government and the Political System** by Keith Marder, Wheaton, Exeter, 1979, pp. 3–4)

1. In Britain, which institutions or bodies are responsible for
   a administering the law   (2)
   b changing the law   (2)
   c enforcing the law   (2)
2. In 1973 the school-leaving age was raised to 16. 'First, the age limit had to be changed by law. Secondly, preparations were necessary to provide additional school places. Thirdly, the courts now had to deal with individual cases where the law was not observed.' (Keith Marder, **Central Government and the Political System**, p. 3)
   Match the three tasks mentioned here with the following

powers: executive, judicial, legislative.   (3)
3. a What is a monarch?   (1)
   b In your own words, briefly explain the system of 'absolute
      monarchy' and say how this differs from the system of
      government in Britain today.   (5)
   c Suggest reasons why a system of absolute monarchy would
      be inappropriate for modern Britain.   (5)

2 The British constitution

The previous extract (7.1) showed that the legislative, executive
and judicial functions of government are carried out by different
institutions within the British political system. Some separation of
powers is thought necessary in a system of government to prevent
the danger of tyranny (the excessive or cruel use of power).

Tyranny could arise if all powers were concentrated in the hands of one person or group. Yet at the same time, those responsible for carrying out each of these roles need to have enough power to perform their tasks effectively. To help achieve a balance there has to be a set of basic rules according to which the system of government operates. These basic rules or principles form what is called the **constitution** of a state. The following extract examines the characteristics of the British constitution. (Later sections of the book will investigate how far a balance is, in fact, achieved. The extent to which Parliament, Cabinet and the courts are, in practice, separate, will be examined, as will the question of whether any one of them has gained more power at the expense of the others.)

The majority of the countries in the world have a **written** constitution. The basic principles about how the system of government should be organized will have been written down in a single legal document. Usually this will have been done following a sudden and complete change of the political system of the country. This happened in Russia in 1917 because of a revolution. It occurred in Germany in 1918 and 1945 after defeats in war. In India it followed the withdrawal of a foreign power (Britain) in 1947. In each of these examples, the old system of government ceased and a written constitution was prepared which laid down the basic rules for a new system.

No abrupt changes like these have occurred in Britain for three centuries. The British system of government which exists today has developed gradually. Consequently, Britain's constitution is rather unusual. It cannot be found in any single document, and this is why Britain is described as having an **unwritten** constitution.

Nevertheless, **some** of the basic principles of Britain's system of government are written down, as they are contained in certain Acts of Parliament (statute law). The European Communities Act 1972, which enabled the UK to join the EEC, is an example of a fairly recent statute law of constitutional significance. This is because it has affected Parliament's power to make and change certain laws. Other constitutional rules have come out of decisions made by judges in the law courts, and are known as 'common law'.

Finally, some principles of the constitution have arisen through custom. Certain practices have become recognized and accepted over time. These are referred to as constitutional **conventions**. It is a convention, for example, that the Queen will use her power to dissolve Parliament – and therefore bring about a general election – only if the Prime Minister specificially asks for this to be done.

Partly because the British constitution is unwritten, it can be changed fairly easily. Basic changes can be made in the same way as any other law is made – by passing an Act of Parliament. Changes can also occur over time as new conventions develop. So the British constitution is relatively **flexible** – capable of easy change. In contrast, the written constitution of the USA can only be altered by a special procedure which involves not only the legislative institutions of the US government itself but also those of each of its fifty states. As a result, the United States constitution has had only 26 alterations in the 200 years since it was written. In some countries – Australia and Switzerland are examples – constitutional amendments take place only after the public has voted to accept them through referenda.

The written constitutions of many countries contain a section which guarantees certain basic rights to the individuals living there. These may include the rights to legal equality, freedom of speech and assembly, and the right to move from one part of the country to another. The first eleven amendments to the United States constitution, for instance, together form a Bill of Rights. Not having a written constitution, Britain has no Bill of Rights of this type. It is argued that it is not necessary because there are certain rights under common law. These rights exist in a negative way: in general, individuals are allowed to do whatever they want unless there is a law which forbids it. Other people claim that this negative system is insufficient to protect the rights of minority groups such as Blacks or homosexuals. It is also argued that certain rights or freedoms have been reduced in recent years by an increase in police powers. As a consequence, a campaign for a Bill of Rights in this country has grown. However, if a Bill of Rights is to be effective, it has to be more permanent than ordinary laws. This helps to protect it from being amended every time a new party comes into

'Says nothing here about the right to work.'

power. This can present problems. For example, the United States Bill of Rights says that the 'right of the people to bear Arms shall not be infringed'. As a constitutional measure it has proved difficult to change. Pressure groups, such as the National Rifle Association have managed to prevent attempts to introduce 'gun controls' on the ground that they are 'unconstitutional'.

(adapted from **Central Government and the Political System** by Keith Marder, Wheaton, Exeter, 1979, pp. 1–3 and **Public Administration: The Political Environment** by Roger Stacey and John Oliver, MacDonald and Evans, Plymouth, 1980, pp. 37–9)

1. In what sense does Britain have an unwritten constitution?   (1)
2. Identify the three sources of the British constitution referred to in the passage.   (3)

3. a Why is the British constitution described as **flexible**?   (2)
   b Why might flexibility be considered an advantage?   (2)
   c What disadvantages might there be?   (4)
4. a During the dispute in the coal industry in 1984–5, some miners were prevented by the police from travelling to other pits. Which freedom or right, mentioned in the passage, might have been denied in such cases?   (2)
   b Examine the suggestion that Britain should have a Bill of Rights.   (6)

3 The sovereignty of Parliament

A central principle of the British constitution is the sovereignty, or supremacy, of Parliament. Parliament is the only body in the country that can make laws, according to this principle. No other person or institution can overrule or change the laws it makes. In the United States, the Supreme Court has the power to declare laws made by Congress (the law-making body) unconstitutional. This cannot happen in Britain. The courts have to enforce the laws which Parliament has made. In theory, Parliament can do anything it wants to. It could, for example, decide to hold no more elections. That such a decision would be unlikely is an indication that the principle of Parliamentary sovereignty is, in practice, restricted. The following passage examines some of these restrictions.

Parliamentary sovereignty is a legal, not a political, principle. It gives a misleading idea of where power lies in modern Britain. In reality, there are many external restraints that can limit the actions of Parliament. Powerful pressure groups may be able to frustrate attempts to introduce laws on matters that go against their interests. They may also be able to lessen the effects of laws already made by Parliament. In the early 1970s, for example, parts of the 1971 Industrial Relations Act were rendered unworkable by the refusal of the trade unions to cooperate and the reluctance of the Conservative Government to use some of the powers provided by the Act.

The supremacy of Parliament is also limited politically by the realities of foreign affairs. Britain makes treaties with other countries and is a member of international organizations such as NATO and the International Monetary Fund. In principle a future government could, through Parliament, decide to ignore such treaties or fail to abide by the rules of the international organizations. But unless it wished to withdraw from them altogether, it would not usually be politically possible to implement such decisions.

Britain's entry into the EEC is regarded by some politicians as the biggest threat to Parliamentary sovereignty in recent times. Under the terms of entry, regulations made by the European Community automatically become law in Britain. This happens whatever the British Parliament thinks about them. This certainly seems to infringe the principle of the sovereignty of Parliament. Parliament could always decide to withdraw from the EEC, but the longer it remains a member the less likely this becomes. The political and economic consequences of pulling out of Europe become more serious as time goes by.

The supremacy of Parliament is also limited by the party system. The biggest party in the House of Commons usually forms the Government. The Government can then rely on its majority support in the House of Commons to secure Parliamentary approval for its proposals. Most major policies and laws are therefore initiated by the Government, not Parliament.

(adapted from **British Constitution Made Simple** by Colin F. Padfield, Heinemann, London, 1981, pp. 21–3; **Introduction to British Government** by S. G. Richards, Macmillan, London and Basingstoke, 1984, pp. 14–15, 208–10 and **Parliamentary Government in Britain** by Michael Rush, Pitman, London, 1981, p. 15)

1. Briefly explain the principle of Parliamentary sovereignty.　(4)
2. a　How does Britain's membership of the EEC limit the principle of Parliamentary sovereignty?　(2)
　 b　Does the fact that Britain could withdraw from the EEC make this limitation less severe? Explain your answer.　(2)
3. Identify **three** other ways in which the supremacy of Parliament is restricted.　(6)
4. a　'In theory, the British Parliament ... could pass a law imposing the death penalty for car-parking offences, and

judges in the courts would have no choice but to apply that penalty as the will of Parliament.' (Keith Marder, **Parliament and Its Work**, p. 16)

Why is it extremely unlikely that Parliament would make such a law? (3)

b It is sometimes said that Parliament has **legal** sovereignty but **political** sovereignty lies with the electorate. What do you understand by this statement? (3)

4 The rule of law

Some politicians frequently warn of the dangers of a breakdown in 'the rule of law'. Some forms of trade union action attract such comments from the Right. Similar claims have been made from elsewhere on the political spectrum against proposals to increase police powers of arrest or detention. The rule of law is seen as a basic constitutional principle. Its main features are presented in the following extract.

There are three basic aspects to the rule of law. The first is that the law should apply equally to every person in society. No exemptions or special favours should be granted to those in government or other positions of power. Secondly, there should be 'freedom from arbitrary arrest and imprisonment'. This means that people should receive punishment only if they have been found guilty in a proper law court of breaking a specific law. Thirdly, the courts should not be subject to political interference when making their judgements. It is therefore considered necessary to keep the judiciary separate from the legislative and executive bodies. This is why judges cannot become members of either the House of Commons or the Government. Despite this, there is some overlap. The Lord Chancellor (who appoints judges and magistrates) is head of the judiciary. He also sits in the House of Lords (which is part of the legislative body) and is a member of the Cabinet, too. He is thus involved in all three branches of government authority.

In fact it is a Lord Chancellor, Lord Hailsham, who referred to the rule of law as a 'gigantic confidence trick'. By this he meant that if a sufficiently large number of people, or a powerful pressure group, decided not to abide by a certain law, it would not be possible to enforce the rule of law. For example, a large group of ratepayers decide not to pay their rates, or a trade union defies a law it considers to be against its members' interests. Because of the numbers involved 'it would be physically impossible to imprison them'.

(adapted from **Introduction to British Government** by S.G. Richards, Macmillan, London and Basingstoke, 1984, pp. 16–18)

1. Identify the three main principles of the rule of law. (3)
2. a In what way is the principle of the separation of powers connected to the rule of law? (3)
   b How does the position of Lord Chancellor appear to go against the principle of the separation of powers? (3)
   c What are the possible dangers of this? (3)
3. a Most people most of the time obey the law. Why do you think this is? (4)
   b What could governments do if public acceptance of the rule of law broke down? (4)
   (Section 1 may provide some ideas to help with answers to the two parts of this question.)

Section 8 Parliament

Section 7.1 stated that the power to make and change the laws of the UK is held by **Parliament**. Parliament is the **legislature**. Properly speaking, it consists of three elements: the House of Commons, the House of Lords (which together make up the Houses of Parliament) and the Crown (the monarch). This section will show that, nowadays, it is the House of Commons which is the most important of these three institutions. In fact, quite often when the word 'Parliament' or 'parliamentary' is used it is mainly the House of Commons that is being referred to.

The **Government** is something rather different, although there is a connection. A Government is usually made up of some of the MPs from the majority party in the House of Commons (plus a few members, of the same party, from the House of Lords). It will normally consist of about 100 people most of whom become Government **Ministers**. These Ministers will have **executive** duties. As well as seeing that Parliament translates the Government's proposals into laws, they are responsible for ensuring that policies are properly executed – carried out. The terms 'the Government' and 'the Executive' are therefore sometimes used interchangeably (to refer to the same thing).

So **some** MPs will also be in the Government, but most will not. Those MPs not in the Government but who belong to the party from which it is formed, normally support the Government. They can do this by voting in favour of the Government's proposals in the House of Commons or by what they say outside Parliament and in the media.

This section, then, is concerned with Parliament. The earlier passages (1–3) explain how the House of Commons is organized to carry out its functions. Its functions are then examined by looking at the part played by the Commons in making laws (4 and 5), controlling money matters (6) and in checking up on the work of the Government (7 and 8). After a look at the role of the party Whips in the Commons (9), there is an assessment of how effective the House is, and how it might be improved (10). The remaining passages examine the role of the other institutions of Parliament – the House of Lords (11 and 12) and the Monarchy (13).

Parliament and Government

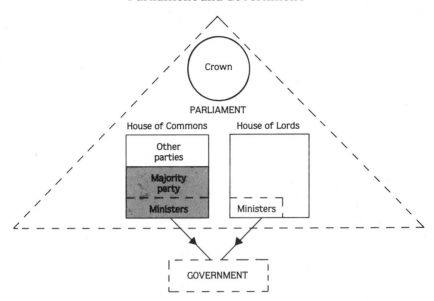

1 The organization of the House of Commons

The House of Commons is made up of 650 Members of Parliament (MPs). Each MP represents one constituency in the United Kingdom. The organization of the House of Commons, including the layout of the Chamber, is described in the following passage and diagram.

The party winning the most seats in a general election forms the Government and its leader becomes Prime Minister. In the 1979 and 1983 elections, the Conservative Party obtained the most seats. The Prime Minister chooses a team of Ministers from members of her own party in the House of Commons and the House of Lords. Together these Ministers form the **Government**.

The second largest party in the Commons at these two elections was the Labour Party. Labour MPs therefore became the official **Opposition**. The job of the opposition is 'to

From a drawing by John Mansbridge

S	Mr Speaker	T	Table of the House	SA	Serjeant at Arms
P	Press Galleries	D	Despatch Boxes	M	Members' Galleries
H	*Hansard* Reporters	Ma	Mace†	G	Visitors' Galleries
O	Government Officials' Box	L	Lines‡		
	(advisors to Ministers)	B	Bar of the House		
C	Clerks of the House*	X	Cross Benches		

*When the House goes into Committee, the Speaker leaves the Chair, and the Chairman sits in the chair of the Clerk of the House, which is the one on the left.   †When the House goes into Committee, the Mace is put 'below the Table' on brackets.   ‡Lines over which Members may not step when speaking from the front benches.

The Chamber of the House of Commons
(from **The House of Commons: A Guide for Visitors to the Galleries**, HMSO, London, 1984, p. 3)

challenge the Government, to make it explain its policies and to check that it does its work properly'. While in opposition a party will continue to plan its own policies as it may itself be called upon to form the government after the next election.

The Chamber of the House of Commons

The Leader of the Opposition would normally then become the Prime Minister.

The seating arrangements of the House of Commons Chamber emphasize the division of most Members into Government and Opposition. The diagram shows how the two sides are clearly divided. The Government sits to one side of the Table and the Opposition and smaller parties to the other. (The smaller parties do not necessarily vote with the Opposition.)

The front benches on the Government side are reserved for Cabinet Ministers and other Ministers in the Government. The same applies to the other side. On the front benches are the leading spokepersons of the Opposition – the 'Shadow Cabinet'. Each member of the Shadow Cabinet will specialize in a particular aspect of work which corresponds to that of a Government Minister. This enables the Opposition to criticize a Government Minister if they disagree with his policies. It also provides the opportunity for the Opposition spokespersons to develop the knowledge and skills they will require if their party forms the next government. Other MPs – who are not on the Opposition front benches or do not belong to the Government – are known as back-bench MPs, or 'backbenchers'.

Debates in the Chamber are chaired by the Speaker of the House of Commons (whose job is examined in the next passage – 8.2). MPs are protected by **Parliamentary privilege**. This means that they are not subject to legal action in the courts over what they say in debates in the House. They are, however, bound by the rules and discipline of the House itself, as Parliamentary privilege also means that the Commons can control its own proceedings and punish its members. At the end of a debate there may be a formal vote, called a 'Division'. Members vote by walking through one of two corridors, known as 'Division Lobbies'. They are counted as they come out of either the 'No Lobby' or 'Aye (yes) Lobby' (which one depends on whether they agree or disagree with the proposals which have been debated).

After each general election a 'new Parliament' begins. So the **life** of each Parliament can be anything up to five years. The actual time will depend on when the Prime Minister calls the next election. Each Parliament is divided into **sessions**. A Parliamentary session will normally last about a year (from November to November). There are breaks at Christmas, Easter, Spring Bank and during the Summer. When not in recess, business in the Chamber of the House begins at 2.30 p.m. on Mondays to Thursdays and at 9.30 a.m. on Fridays.

Daily timetable of the House of Commons

2.30 p.m. Prayers

2.35 p.m. **Preliminary business** – such as motions for new writs for by-elections or unopposed private bills.

2.45 p.m. 'Question Time' – questions to Ministers from MPs.

3.30 p.m. **Public business** – the main debates of the day, including those concerning proposed new laws.

10.00 p.m. **Public business ends***
Adjournment debate – on a topic raised by back-bench MPs.

10.30 p.m. House adjourns (closes for the day)

(* The House frequently fails to complete its business by 10.00 p.m. and often sits for many hours afterwards – sometimes all night.)

(adapted from **Politics and Government in Britain** by Tom Brennan, Cambridge University Press, Cambridge, 1982, p. 186; **Debates: how Parliament discusses things** (Education Sheet 2), pp. 5–7 and **The House of Commons: general information** (Education Sheet 4), pp. 2–3, 13–14, by Elizabeth Stones, Public Information Office, House of Commons, London, 1983)

1. Briefly explain what is meant by each of the following:
   a Parliamentary session (2)
   b Recess (2)
   c A Division (2)
   d Shadow Cabinet (2)
   e Parliamentary privilege (2)
2. Distinguish between
   a **Parliament** and the **Government** (4)
   b a front-bench and a back-bench MP (2)
3. Explain the role and purpose of the Opposition in the House of Commons. (4)

2 The Speaker

The proceedings of the House of Commons are presided over by the Speaker (or one of his deputies). The office of Speaker goes back over 600 years. The following passage explains the Speaker's position and functions.

Speakers are elected, by MPs, at the start of every new Parliament or when the previous Speaker dies or retires. Although the Speaker is himself an elected MP he is not permitted to speak for his constituents in the Commons. He does not take part in political debate and is expected to be impartial – to remain above party political controversy. He does not vote in the House except in the event of a tie. But even in these situations, the Speaker is not expected to vote on the merits of the issue before him. He is guided by precedent – by the decisions of Speakers in similar previous cases.

The Speaker acts as chairperson during debates in the Chamber. It is his job to see that the rules of debate are followed. It is also the Speaker who decides which MPs are to be allowed to speak. In deciding who to 'call' to speak, he needs to take account of a number of factors. The official speakers for the Government and the Opposition will be called and possibly also those for the smaller parties. Other MPs who may have a special interest in or knowledge of the subject of the debate may be selected. So, too, may Members whose constituents are particularly affected by the matter being discussed. The Speaker must also be fair to the different political parties in the House of Commons. This is especially important when deciding who to call to speak during Question Time when MPs have a chance to put questions to senior Government Ministers, including the Prime Minister. In June 1985 the Speaker, Bernard Weatherill, received a complaint that too few Labour backbenchers were being called to speak. One MP said that this had created an 'impression of bias'. The Speaker defended his actions by pointing out that there were more Conservative than Labour MPs. He did not think it biased or unfair, therefore, if he took account of the balance of numbers in the House. However, after charges that he was setting a new rule, Mr Weatherill agreed to give further thought to the question.

In attempting to preserve order in the House, the Speaker has a number of sanctions at his disposal. He can direct a Member to withdraw any remarks made in 'unparliamentary' language. A Member can be suspended from the House if he disobeys the Speaker's instructions. The Labour MP Dennis Skinner has been expelled from the House on more than one occasion in recent years. In 1980 Ian Paisley, Ulster Democratic Unionist MP, was suspended after calling the Secretary of State for Northern Ireland a 'liar'. Brian Sedgemore MP was disciplined in a similar way in November 1985. He had refused to withdraw an allegation that the Chancellor of the Exchequer had perverted the course of justice. In the event of serious general disorder in the Commons, the Speaker can suspend the proceedings. In January 1985 the Speaker suspended the sitting for 20 minutes following continued protests from a group of Labour MPs against the Government's refusal to agree to a debate on

No wonder they made him Minister of Defence.

the coal dispute. A few years earlier, the previous Speaker, George Thomas, suspended the House because of disorder following the announcement of a very close Commons victory for the Labour Government on a controversial issue. When the Speaker had announced that the Government had won by 304 votes to 303, a group of Welsh MPs, including Neil Kinnock, began to sing the Red Flag (a traditional socialist song). Some Conservatives reacted by making Hitler-type salutes. George Thomas has described how scuffles broke out. Michael Heseltine, a senior Conservative MP, grabbed the mace from the table in front of the Speaker and wielded it over his head. 'Heseltine told me later he was going to give it to Labour, but just how was never made clear. It looked to me as if he was going to crash it down on top of them. That was the moment I suspended the sitting'.

The Speaker has to interpret and enforce Standing Orders –

the rules of procedure for the House of Commons. He is frequently called upon to decide if a certain action or point is in accordance with these rules. He has to deal with applications for emergency debates and to decide whether a complaint of breach of Parliamentary privilege should be investigated further. In addition, the Speaker represents the House of Commons on ceremonial and formal occasions.

(adapted from 'Speaker promises questions review' by Julian Haviland, **The Times**, June 21, 1985, p. 1; **The Speaker of the House of Commons** (Factsheet No. 21) by C. C. Pond, Public Information Office, House of Commons, London, 1984 and **George Thomas, Mr. Speaker: The Memoirs of the Viscount Tonypandy**, Century, London, 1985, pp. 147–52, 190, 192)

1. a Identify **four** functions of the Speaker.   (4)
   b Giving reasons, say which you consider to be the most important.   (3)
2. What disadvantages are experienced by people living in the Speaker's constituency?   (2)
3. Identify **two** ways by which the Speaker can discipline a Member of Parliament.   (2)
4. a In what circumstances may the Speaker suspend a sitting of the House?   (2)
   b What would this action achieve?   (2)
5. a Why is the Speaker expected to be politically neutral?   (2)
   b Identify **three** ways which help to maintain the Speaker's neutrality in the House of Commons.   (3)

3 The control of Government business

Because it usually has a majority in the Commons, a good deal of the activity which goes on in the House is started and controlled by the Government. When a new session of Parliament is opened each year, the Queen's Speech is delivered. This speech, written by the Prime Minister, outlines the new laws which the Government hopes Parliament will pass during the year. Many of these proposals will be opposed by the opposition party in the House of Commons. But time is limited, and back-bench MPs will also want opportunities to raise issues and to introduce their own legislative proposals. There are, therefore, certain arrangements which can help the Government to get through its legislative programme, as the following passage describes.

Each week, the Chief Whips of the Government and the Opposition get together to arrange the following week's business. The Speaker is notified of the leading speakers from each party who would like to address the House during the debates. This is known as arranging things through the 'usual channels'. The weekly business is announced by the Leader of the House (a senior Cabinet member) who is also responsible for arranging the Commons' programme over the entire Parliamentary session. The **details** of proposed new laws are usually discussed in smaller committees, composed of MPs from each party, rather than in the Chamber of the House of Commons itself. This saves time. The Speaker likes to ensure that speeches in the Chamber are kept relatively short. MPs who persistently try to make long speeches may find the Speaker becomes reluctant to call them to speak. During two recent Parliamentary sessions the Speaker has been allowed to restrict speeches of certain types to ten minutes each.

Under the House's Standing Orders, the Government has a number of devices it can use to restrict debate so that decisions can be made. These include the 'simple closure' and the 'guillotine'. The **guillotine** is usually reserved for those occasions where it has not been possible to obtain agreement through the 'usual channels'. The procedure involves allocating a set period of time for debate on each of the sections, or clauses, of the proposed legislation. Once the time is exhausted, discussion ends and a vote is taken. The Government used the guillotine during the debate on its proposals to abolish the Greater London Council and six metropolitan councils. **Simple closure** is aimed at preventing 'filibustering' (where a Member speaks just to take up time with the intention of delaying or preventing a decision being reached). The MP in charge of the proposal asks that 'the question be now put'. If at least 100 Members are present, and a majority of them agree, the Speaker can decide to end the debate and put the matter to a vote.

Nevertheless, despite the existence of procedures to limit debates, long speeches do occur from time to time. In March 1985 Ivan Lawrence, a Conservative MP, created a record for the longest House of Commons speech this century. In opposing his Government's proposals on the flouridation of water, he spoke for four hours and 23 minutes.

(adapted from 'The MP who spoke for four hours' by Alan Hamilton, **The Times**, March 7, 1985, p. 1; **How Britain is Governed** by J. Harvey, Macmillan, Basingstoke and London, 1983, pp. 74–5; **The Procedural Changes agreed on 31st October 1979** (Factsheet No. 3) by C. C. Pond, Public Information Office, House of Commons, London, 1984 and **The House of Commons: general information** (Education Sheet 4) by Elizabeth Stones, Public Information Office, House of Commons, London, 1983, pp. 13–14)

1. Who is responsible for arranging the business of the House of Commons for
   a each week   (2)
   b each session?   (2)
2. a What is the 'Queen's Speech'?   (1)
   b Why is it written by the Prime Minister and not by the Queen?
                                                                         (2)
3. What is a filibuster?   (2)
4. a Distinguish between the 'guillotine' and the 'simple closure'.
                                                                         (6)
   b Why do you think the Government does not use such devices all the time?   (5)

4 Making laws (1) Types of Bill

The House of Commons performs a number of tasks. Perhaps its best known function is its contribution to the making of new laws. Section 8.5 will examine the legislative process in more detail. The following extract distinguishes between the different types of Parliamentary Bill.

No new law can be made by Parliament unless it has completed a number of stages in both the House of Commons and the House of Lords. The Queen also has to sign to show that it has been given the **Royal Assent**. Only after the Royal Assent does it become a new law or **Act of Parliament**. Before this, while it is still journeying through Parliament, it is called a **Bill**. Bills can begin in the House of Commons or the House of

Lords, so they can pass through Parliament in one of two ways.

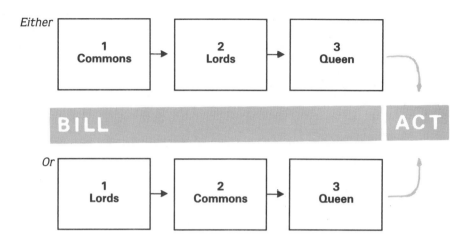

There are various different types of Bill which pass through Parliament. The two main sorts of Bill are **Public Bills** and **Private Bills**. Private Bills are only intended to affect a particular area or organization. A local council, for example, may need specific powers to carry out a special function within its area. Public Bills are intended to affect the public as a whole – such as a proposal to allow shops to open on Sundays. There are two types of Public Bill. The majority are sponsored by the **Government**. Government Bills will be piloted through Parliament by a Minister from the appropriate Government Department, for example Ministers from the Department of Education and Science would be responsible for seeing that an Education Bill became an Act of Parliament.

The other type of Public Bill, known as a **Private Members Bill**, is sponsored by an individual MP rather than by the Government. He will promote the Bill as an individual rather than as a member of a particular party and will therefore not be able to rely on the support of a majority in the House of Commons. The Murder (Abolition of the Death Penalty) Act of 1965 began as a Private Member's Bill sponsored by Sidney Silverman, a Labour MP. Many Private Members' Bills concern moral issues which may cut across party lines. Many fail to complete their journey through Parliament perhaps through lack of support or, more likely, because of shortage of time. Government business is usually given priority and Private Members' Bills can get squeezed out.

(from **How Laws are Made** (Education Sheet 3) by Elizabeth Stones, Public Information Office, House of Commons, London, 1983, pp. 4–5, with minor additions)

1. What is the difference between
   a a Bill and an Act?   (2)
   b a Public Bill and a Private Bill?   (2)
   c a Government Bill and a Private Member's Bill?   (2)
2. Government Bills are 'piloted through Parliament by a Minister'. What does this involve?   (2)
3. Give **three** reasons why Private Members' Bills are less likely to become law than Government Bills.   (6)
4. Why do you think that
   a it is Private Members' Bills, rather than Government Bills, that are generally used for legislation on moral issues?   (3)
   b Government business is normally given priority over Private Members' Bills?   (3)

5 Making laws (2) The process

The previous extract (8.4) stated that a new law has to pass through a series of stages in Parliament. These stages are described in the second passage which follows. However, a lot of preparatory work will usually need to be done before a Bill can even enter Parliament, as the first extract explains. In both passages the processes refer to Government Bills.

Before a Bill can be introduced into Parliament several things have to happen. Normally, **consultations** take place with those who are likely to be affected by the Bill. Within a Department, both the Ministers and the permanent officials, **civil servants**, will be involved in the consultation process. Sometimes the Government will set out its ideas for a Bill in a discussion document known as a **Green Paper**. Organizations can send their comments back to the Department. Often the planned contents of a Bill will be changed in the light of this new evidence. The civil servants might suggest several alternative ways in which this could be done, but the actual decision will be left to the Minister. After this discussion stage, the Department may then produce firm proposals in a **White Paper**. This will form the basis of the Bill to be introduced into Parliament. The process of putting the terms of a Bill down on paper is known as **drafting**. A small number of lawyers (who are also civil servants) are specially trained for this job. The Bill has to be exact and not leave any loopholes, unlike the sentence here, taken from an American law – 'No one shall carry any dangerous weapon upon the public highway, except for the purpose of killing a noxious animal or a policeman in the execution of his duty.'

(from **How Laws are Made** (Education Sheet 3) by Elizabeth Stones, Public Information Office, House of Commons, London, 1983, pp. 6–9)

Once the Bill has been drafted it is ready to enter Parliament and go through a number of stages (some of which are called 'readings'). Sometimes it may pass through all its stages very quickly. A Bill to ban alcoholic drinks at football matches took a matter of days. Other Bills can take many weeks or months. Parliament spent over 300 hours, over a period of many months, discussing the Bill to abolish some major local councils in England, despite the use of the guillotine. In the illustration overleaf it is assumed that the Bill is introduced first into the House of Commons.

1. Distinguish between a 'Green Paper' and a 'White Paper'. (2)
2. Briefly distinguish between the responsibilities of Ministers and civil servants in preparing a Bill for Parliament. (2)
3. Explaining your answer, say which of the two Houses of Parliament has the greater power in the passage of a Bill. (4)
4. Why do you think it is considered necessary for a Bill
   a to pass through **both** Houses of Parliament? (2)
   b to go through so many different stages in each House? (4)
5. Show how, and at which points, pressure groups could attempt to exert influence
   a during the preparation of a Bill (3)
   b during its passage through Parliament. (3)

The passage of a Bill through Parliament

HOUSE OF COMMONS

First Reading – The Bill is formally introduced to allow the opposition time to consider the Bill before the Second Reading.

Second Reading – The purposes and main principles of the Bill are debated. Non-controversial Bills may be discussed by a committee instead of the whole House.

Committee Stage – The **details** of the Bill are discussed by a Standing Committee composed of MPs from different parties roughly in proportion to their numbers in the House.

Report Stage – The House considers changes (amendments) made at the Committee Stage and may make further amendments.

Third Reading – The Bill as a whole is considered.

HOUSE OF LORDS

The Bill goes through the same five stages as in the Commons.

| If the Lords **accept** the Bill it is passed for the Royal Assent. | If the Lords **reject** the Bill it is delayed for a year. | If the Lords **amend** the Bill it goes back to the Commons, which accepts the changes OR the Lords withdraw them. |

ROYAL ASSENT
A formality. The Bill then becomes an Act of Parliament.

(adapted from **Local and Central Government** by Kathleen Allsop (revised by Tom Brennan), Hutchinson, London, 1982, p. 97 and **Guide to British Government** by C. A. Leeds, Croxton Press, Swanage, 1977, p. 25)

6 Controlling finance

In addition to its general legislative tasks, the House of Commons has certain responsibilities for checking and approving Government activity in money matters. The first passage outlines the main procedures involved. The second assesses them.

Before the Government can raise or spend money, it must have permission from Parliament. As the House of Lords has no control over financial matters it is the House of Commons which has to give this permission. The Commons contains MPs who are directly elected by the public to look after their interests. It is only right, therefore, that they, rather than Members of the House of Lords who are not elected, should agree before the public have to pay taxes.

The Commons, first of all, controls the **raising** of money. Each year, usually in March or early April, the **Chancellor of the Exchequer** presents his **Budget Statement** to the Commons.

Chancellor Nigel Lawson, Budget Day, March 19, 1985

In this, he explains how the Government intends to raise the money it needs to run the country during the following year. Some of this money will be **borrowed** by selling Government Bonds on the Stock Exchange. The other way of raising money is by **taxation**. The Budget may, therefore, contain proposals to cut or increase taxes.

Obviously it is the duty of the House of Commons, on behalf of the people, to make sure that taxes are not raised without good reason. The Budget Proposals therefore have to be examined and discussed very carefully. What actually happens is that the Budget Proposals are set out in the **Finance Bill** which will go through all its stages like any other Bill. This usually takes about four months. At the end of this time, the Finance Bill becomes the **Finance Act** – a new law permitting the Government to raise the money it needs.

The House of Commons also has to give its approval before any money can be **spent** by the Government. Each year the Government presents its **Estimates** to the House of Commons. These set out the amounts required by each Government Department. The House has to agree to these Estimates before the Departments can be given any money. Three days are now set aside for discussion of the Estimates.

The House of Commons also has a way of checking up on Government Departments afterwards, to see whether they did their housekeeping properly. This work is done by the Public Accounts Committee. This committee can examine cases of overspending by a Department and can also check whether the Government spent its money wisely. In order to carry out this work properly the Committee can see any accounts or documents which it considers necessary. It can also hold meetings where witnesses are questioned. The extract below shows how a leading official from the Department of Energy was examined in October 1979 after too much money had been paid out to North Sea oil companies.

264. We were told in July, I think, that £150,000 had been recovered. What is the figure now? – (Sir **Jack Rampton**.) The total amount of mistaken payments in an arithmetical sense is still £153,000. That is the total, and I think that virtually all of it has now been recovered.

Mr Palmer

265. I have one very simple question. Can Sir Jack tell us what exact difference the error in arithmetic made? – It is eleven million.

266. Forgive me for putting it in this way, but is it not extraordinary, dealing with large sums of money like that? A cashier in a shop is not expected to make an error in addition. Eleven millions: it is just an error in arithmetic. It seems an extraordinary mistake to make? – I do not know how, precisely, it occurred, but what happened was that there was a decimal point in the wrong place. That is what happened, but how it actually occurred I do not know.

Mr Douglas

267. Sir Jack, perhaps you could indicate for the benefit of the Committee exactly what degree of accuracy we should put on these figures now? – I have total confidence in these figures, and I think that they have been gone through with the greatest care.

(Minutes of evidence taken before the Committee of Public Accounts on 31 October 1979)

The Committee is helped in its work by over 500 auditors who all specialize in Government accounts. Once a series of investigations is complete, the Committee presents a Report to the House of Commons, which may choose to debate any-thing it considers particularly serious. These Reports are available to the public and the press. Any really bad mistake is, therefore, likely to be widely reported in the press.

(from **The House of Commons: general information** (Education Sheet 4) by Elizabeth Stones, Public Information Office, House of Commons, London, 1983, pp. 6–7)

Despite these formal arrangements, however, the House of Commons does not itself **control** finance in the sense that it makes the **decisions** on the raising and spending of money. A former Prime Minister, Harold Wilson, has stated that it is the Government, not Parliament, that has 'complete control' over expenditure. It is the Government that decides how much should be spent and what it is to be spent on. 'The same is true of taxation. No back-bench Member can propose an increased tax burden of a single penny'. This means that as long as the Government can maintain its majority in the House, the Government proposals in the Finance Bill can become law quite easily. The Chancellor of the Exchequer is often willing, however, to offer minor concessions following criticisms made in the House of Commons.

But if the House of Commons generally has no real financial control, other than formally granting permission for money to be raised and spent, its Public Accounts Committee (PAC) is taken seriously by Ministers and senior civil servants. This committee is composed of back-bench MPs from the main political parties in the House and it can question civil servants. Harold Wilson reports:

> Even the toughest, most experienced permanent secretaries [top civil servants] have expressed feelings amounting almost to terror when they face examination. They are briefed for days by their financial officers... They will have read the...auditors' notes, comments and criticisms on the particular spending programmes...and will arrive with masses of files, supported by financial advisers. I recall one permanent secretary..., a war hero, tough, experienced..., who had served a wide range of senior ministers in war and in peace, telling me that...the night before he appeared before the PAC each year he never slept a wink. Other...officers have told me the same.

(adapted from **The Governance of Britain** by Harold Wilson, Weidenfeld and Nicolson, London and Michael Joseph, London, 1976, pp. 149, 171–2, 174)

1. Identify **two** ways by which the Government can raise money. (2)
2. Explain the difference between the Budget and the Finance Act. (2)
3. a What are the Estimates? (2)
   b What say does the House of Commons have over the Estimates? (2)
4. Why does Harold Wilson consider that Parliament has no real control over taxation and expenditure? (4)
5. a What are the two functions of the Public Accounts Committee? (2)
   b The PAC can only examine Government expenditure after the money has already been spent. Drawing on the information in the two passages, discuss how far you think this limits the power of this committee. (6)

7 Examining the Government's work
(1) Debates and Question Time

Section 7.1 indicated that it is the task of the **Government** (the Executive) – particularly the Prime Minister and the Cabinet – to introduce policies and to control their implementation. Earlier passages have also emphasized that the Government can usually expect to gain Parliamentary approval for its policies because of its party's majority in the House of Commons.

Nevertheless, the House of Commons does get the chance to discuss and challenge policy proposals. It can also maintain some sort of check over the administration of policy. There are several ways in which this examination of the activities of Government can occur. They include debates and Question Time (which are considered below) and through various types of committee work (dealt with in 8.8).

The House of Commons (and the House of Lords, too) is a **debating** chamber. There are debates on Bills, as they pass through their various stages, and on statements made by Ministers. Debates are held on White Papers and on reports of Parliamentary committees. The contents of the Queen's Speech (the Address given at the opening of each Parliamentary session) are debated, and there are opportunities for MPs to ask for debates on particular topics. An MP can put down a motion for an Adjournment Debate, for example. Adjournment Debates take place during the final half-hour of each day's sitting of the House of Commons. Printed records of all Parliamentary debates are published in **Hansard** which is the official report of the House of Commons. These reports show that the standard of debate in the Commons can vary from the serious to the frivolous. On occasions tempers begin to wear thin, as the following extract (from a debate on the economy) appears to indicate.

> **Mr. D. N. Campbell-Savours** (Workington): The right hon. Gentleman will soon learn of the policies of the Opposition if he chooses to fight a by-election. He should cut out the abuse.
>
> **Mr. Rodgers:** Is the right hon. Gentleman able to say—
>
> **Mr. Campbell-Savours:** When will the right hon. Gentleman fight one?
>
> **Mr. Rodgers:** Oh, do shut up.
>
> **Mr. Campbell-Savours:** The right hon. Gentleman is indulging in personal abuse.
>
> **Mr. Rodgers:** This matter was debated—
>
> **Mr. Campbell-Savours:** The right hon. Gentleman has been

speaking for about five minutes and all that we have had from him is personal abuse. It is about time that the representatives of the Social Democratic Party in this House devoted some time to making reasonable political comments based on commonsense and stopped talking nonsense.

Further comments from Mr. Rodgers are then followed by:

Mr. John Silkin (Deptford): The right hon. Gentleman, as always, is talking nonsense, and is doing so at great and exceedingly boring length.

Mr. Tristan Garel-Jones (Watford): Answer the right hon. Member for Stockton (Mr. Rodgers).

And, following Mr. Silkin's reply . . .

Mr. Rodgers: I have never heard such gobbledegook. I do not understand it. I am prepared to give way to the right hon. Gentleman again if he wishes to explain. I do not think that the house knows what he means.

(from **Hansard** for 11 November, 1981, Volume 12 No. 6, HMSO, London, p. 316, reproduced with the permission of the Controller of Her Majesty's Stationery Office)

Question Time occupies between 45 and 55 minutes of the daily timetable of the House of Commons. Government Ministers answer questions put to them by MPs. Ministers will have been notified of the questions beforehand. This enables them to work out, with their civil servants, the best way to answer them (or, sometimes, to avoid answering them). Part of Question Time on Tuesdays and Thursdays is devoted to questions put to the Prime Minister (often by the Leader of the Opposition). Excerpts from Prime Minister's Question Time are regularly broadcast on the radio. MPs can also receive written answers to questions. The following extract suggests some of the purposes for which MPs may use Question Time.

MPs do not only ask questions merely to gain information. There are often other, easier ways of doing this such as writing to the Government Department concerned. Question Time is used for a variety of purposes. An MP may wish to draw attention to a particular grievance affecting an individual or group in society. He may wish to impress his constituents, or his constituency party, by showing them that he is taking an interest in matters that concern them. Question Time may also be used to give publicity to the aims or activities of a pressure group – perhaps one with which the MP has close connections. Quite often questions are asked in an attempt to embarrass the Government. This is often a reason behind the questions put by the Leader of the Opposition during Prime Minister's Question Time. In such cases, the answers will be designed to give away as little as possible. But a Minister, or the Prime Minister, cannot always be prepared for the **supplementary** questions which may follow the original question. The questioner is permitted to ask one supplementary question after the Minister has given his prepared answer to the original. The Speaker may then allow further 'supplementaries' from other Members.

Whatever the motives behind particular questions, Question Time is one way in which MPs can try to make the Government **accountable** to the House of Commons. Ministers are being asked to explain their actions and their policies. Question Time also helps protect against inefficiency in the work of Government Departments.

(adapted from **How Britain is Governed** by J. Harvey, Macmillan, London and Basingstoke, 1983, pp. 94–5)

1. From the list of debates (given in **Hansard** overleaf) held during one day in November 1981, give an example (by title) of the following types of debate:
   a Adjournment Debate   (1)
   b Debate on the Queen's Speech   (1)
   c Debate on a Ministerial statement   (1)
2. a How does Question Time help to make the Government more 'accountable'?   (1)
   b In February 1984, Opposition MPs complained that the Government was misusing Question Time. They claimed that the Government had been issuing 'planted' questions for its own backbenchers to ask. How can this be seen as a 'misuse' of Question Time?   (3)
3. a Identify **five** reasons why MPs may ask questions during Question Time.   (5)

Volume 12
No. 6

Wednesday
11 November 1981

HOUSE OF COMMONS
OFFICIAL REPORT

PARLIAMENTARY DEBATES

(HANSARD)

CONTENTS

LONDON
HER MAJESTY'S STATIONERY OFFICE
80p net

b Suggest which of these you think may have been the main reason in each of the following examples from Question Time in the House of Commons. (The name of the MP putting the question and the constituency he represents are given at the start of each question.) (5)

Mr. Andrew Bennett (Stockport North): To ask the Minister of Agriculture, Fisheries and Food, if he will make a statement on his policy towards the gassing of badgers.

Mr. Robert Kilroy-Silk (Ormskirk): To ask the Prime Minister, if she is satisfied with the co-ordination between the Home Department and the Department of Health and Social Security in transferring mentally disturbed persons from prisons to National Health Service hospitals.

Mr. Dennis Canavan (Falkirk West): To ask the Secretary of State for Education and Science, whether he will make a statement about the teachers' pay dispute.

Mr. Robert Robinson (Belfast East): To ask the Secretary of State for Northern Ireland how many houses owned by the Northern Ireland Housing Executive in Belfast are fitted with: (a) metal window frames, (b) PVC window frames and (c) wooden window frames.

Mr. David Alton (Liverpool, Mossley Hill): To ask the Secretary of State for Social Services, what was the total amount allocated by his Department to counter: (a) all forms of drug abuse and (b) heroin abuse in particular, in each of the last 10 years for which figures are available; and for each year how much of the total allocation was spent on: (i) publicity and advertising, (ii) funding of rehabilitation or treatment centres for drug users and (iii) grants to other organisations.

(Questions taken from **House of Commons Order Papers** for 12 November, 1981 and 21 June, 1985, reproduced with the permission of the Controller of Her Majesty's Stationery Office)

4. Harold Wilson has said:

No Prime Minister looks forward to Prime Minister's Question Time with anything but apprehension; every Prime Minister works long into the night on his answers, and on all the notes available to help him anticipate the ... supplementary questions that follow his main ... answer. (**Governance of Britain**, p. 132)

Why are supplementary questions often more difficult to answer than the original question?   (3)

8 Examining the Government's work (2) Committees

Much of the work of the Commons does not take place in the chamber of the House itself, but in its committee rooms. Committee work provides MPs with opportunities to meet in smaller groups to examine particular areas of interest or concern. Some of the main types of committee and their functions are described in the following comments.

Select committees. These are committees, composed of MPs from more than one party, which are formed to keep an eye on various aspects of the Government's work. An example of an influential select committee is the Public Accounts Committee which examines government expenditure. Select committees may also be used to inquire into a particular subject or event, such as the cir-cumstances surrounding the sinking of the Argentinian cruiser, the *General Belgrano*, during the Falklands conflict. Select committees have been a regular feature of Parliament's work for a number of years, but in 1979 a system of specialized Departmental select committees was introduced. Each of these committees can investigate the spending, administration or policy of a particular Government Department. It can then report on its investigations to the House of Commons. The committees can ask for documents to be made available and may interview Ministers and civil servants. However, the amount and quality of information they obtain may vary. In 1985 the Leader of the House of Commons, John Biffen, announced that certain details about nationalized

Departmental Select Committees of the House of Commons

Agriculture	Environment	Trade and Industry
Defence	Foreign Affairs	Transport
Education, Science and Arts	Home Affairs	Treasury and Civil Service
Employment	Scottish Affairs	Welsh Affairs
Energy	Social Services	

industries would not be released to select committees unless permission was gained from the appropriate Minister. Norman St. John Stevas – who had been responsible for setting up the departmental select committees – claimed that this would interfere with Parliament's function of checking the Executive.

The following extract examines the effectiveness of the departmental select committees.

It is unlikely that select committees will significantly alter the balance of power between the House of Commons and the Executive. Their reports are not usually given much attention and 'there is little that committees can do if Ministers and Departments decline to listen to them'. The committees do not take decisions. In general, they are likely to remain 'places in which members can be kept busy without causing too much trouble for those in Government'.

However, the establishment of departmental select committees has produced some gains. Ministers and civil servants are encouraged to explain and justify their actions and decisions. The work of the committees has also led to more information being publicly available to those who want it. Those committees involved in industrial and economic affairs can help to establish links between the worlds of politics and industry.

(adapted from 'An academic's view' by Nevil Johnson in **Commons Select Committees: Catalysts for Progress?** edited by Dermot Englefield, Longman, Harlow, 1984, pp. 60–65)

All-party subject groups. These are unofficial groups composed of backbench MPs interested in particular subjects which do not usually produce deep divisions on party lines. Among those in existence in 1984 were groups on Conservation, Disablement, Road Safety, Solvent Abuse, Association Football and the Scotch Whisky Industry. All-party groups help to draw attention to certain aspects of public affairs. On occasions they may be able to persuade Ministers to take action which will help their causes or interests.

(adapted from **All Party Subject Groups in the House of Commons** (Factsheet No. 7) by Elizabeth Osborn, Public Information Office, House of Commons, London, 1984)

Party committees. Each of the main parties in Parliament set up their own committees which attempt to keep abreast of most aspects of government activity. They provide an opportunity for backbench MPs to exert some influence on the senior members of their party (and of the Government if their party is in power).

In addition to the committees mentioned here, there are also the **standing committees** of the House of Commons which examine the details of Bills at the committee stage of the legislative process (see 8.5). The following table summarizes the main types of committee in the House of Commons.

Type of committee	Composition	Function
Standing committees	MPs of main parties	Examine the details of Bills passing through the Commons
Select committees	MPs of main parties	Scrutinize and investigate the work of Government
All-party subject groups	MPs from any party	Promote particular causes which are of interest to individual MPs
Party committees	MPs of that party	Keep check on, and try to influence, the work of the leading members of that party

1. Distinguish between the functions of
   a a party committee and an all-party subject group   (3)
   b a select committee and a standing committee   (3)
2. The following are titles of reports issued by some of the **departmental select committees** listed in the passage. In each case, state which of these committees would have produced the report.
   a The role of British aid in the economic development of Zimbabwe   (1)
   b Government's statement on the new nuclear power programme   (1)
   c Youth unemployment and training   (1)
   d Animal welfare in poultry, pig, and veal calf production.   (1)
3. a How can select committees help to check the activities of the Executive?   (4)
   b What difficulties do they experience in doing so?   (4)
4. Some politicians believe that the work of the departmental

select committees reduces the importance of the Chamber of the House of Commons. What do you understand by this criticism?   (2)

9 The Whips

The examination of the role of the House of Commons (8.4 to 8.8) could suggest that real power lies with the Government, rather than the Commons. The Government introduces, and steers through Parliament, most of the legislation. The Commons has little real control over finance. Even its attempts to check the activities of the Executive through select committees, for example, are not as effective as some would like. One of the main reasons for this subordinate role of the Commons to the Government is the party system in Parliament. A party with an overall majority can usually obtain Parliamentary approval for its Government's policies. But approval is not automatic. It requires organization. This is a function of the party Whips, as the following extract explains.

To maintain its majority in the House of Commons, the Government has to have ways of managing and controlling the MPs of its own party. Similarly, the Opposition needs to organize its own backbenchers so that it can effectively challenge the Government. Maintaining party discipline is one of the managerial tasks of the party Whips.

The Chief Whip on the Government side is of equivalent rank to a senior Minister. He has a number of Assistant Whips to help him. The Opposition also has a Chief Whip and assistants. The Government Whips try to ensure that their members always form a majority in their attendance at the House and that they vote for the Government in divisions. Each week the Whips send out printed instructions to their MPs which show when they should attend the House. Importance of attendance is indicated by the number of times an instruction is underlined. A three-line 'whip' means that attendance is essential. Two lines tell the MP that he or she must attend unless arrangements have been made under the 'pairing' system. Government and Opposition Whips can agree for a member on each side to 'pair' – to be absent at the same time. This cancels out each other's vote. A one-line whip merely 'requests' MPs to attend.

Extract from a whip

On MONDAY, 1st December, 1980, the House will meet at 2.30 p.m.
Industry Bill: 2nd Reading and related Money Resolution.
(Money Resolution EXEMPTED BUSINESS for 45 minutes)

Divisions will take place, and your attendance at 9.30 p.m. for 10.00 p.m. and until the Money Resolution is obtained is essential unless you have registered a firm pair.

On TUESDAY, 2nd December, the House will meet at 2.30 p.m.
British Telecommunications Bill: 2nd Reading and related Money Resolution. (Money Resolution EXEMPTED BUSINESS for 45 minutes)
Opposition Prayer relating to the National Health Service (Charges for Drugs and Appliances) Regulations.   (EXEMPTED BUSINESS FOR 1½ hours)

Important divisions will take place, and your attendance at 9.30 p.m. for 10.00 p.m. and until the business is concluded is essential.

Pairing gives MPs the opportunity to carry out other business. For example they may wish to visit and give talks in different parts of the country to maintain contact with party supporters outside Parliament. One MP who refuses to pair, however, has said he sees no reason why he should make it easy for a member on the other side to have a day out at Ascot.

With the large Conservative majority following the 1983 general election, pairing became less vital. But however lax or rigid party discipline may be at different times, the Whips cannot always prevent individual MPs from rebelling against the party line on particular issues. Although rarely threatened with defeat on a major issue, in recent years the Government has experienced frequent back-bench revolts with some members either abstaining or voting against the instructions of the Whips. In such cases, the Whips can threaten to withdraw the 'whip' from a rebel MP. In effect this means he would be expelled from the parliamentary party. He would

'Good idea this pairing.'

then be unlikely to be re-selected as a candidate for that party at the next election. But such action is rare. Persuasion, of varying degrees, is a more usual method of discouraging future revolts.

Much of the Whips' work, however, is not about party discipline. A regular task of the Government and Opposition Chief Whips is to arrange, through the 'usual channels', the business of the House for the following week (see 8.3). The Whips also keep a look-out in their parties for promising back-benchers suitable for promotion to more senior jobs. On the Government side, this will involve suggesting to the Prime Minister potential recruits for junior ministerial posts in the Government. Probably the main role of the Whips, though, is in acting as a two-way link between the party leaders and the backbenchers. They can keep the leaders informed of the feelings of their supporters in the House as well as presenting the wishes of the leadership to the backbenchers.

(adapted from **British Government** by Glyn Parry, Edward Arnold, London, 1979, p. 232)

1. Identify **four** functions of the party Whips. (4)
2. Why are Whips in a better position than party leaders to keep in touch with back-bench MPs? (3)
3. What special difficulties may confront a Government Whip when his party has
   a a very small majority (2)
   b a very large majority (2)
   in the House of Commons?
4. a What can a Whip do if a member disobeys his instructions? (3)
   b Suggest **three** reasons why it would normally be in an MP's own interests to follow the instructions and requests of his party Whips. (6)

10 Reform of the House of Commons

Norman St. John Stevas, a former Conservative Leader of the House of Commons, has argued that it has never been Parliament's job to **control** the Executive. Nevertheless, he – together with politicians from all parties – has expressed concern over the decline in the ability of the Commons to act as a check on the activities of Governments. The previous passage (8.9) suggested that the strength of the party system in the House of Commons, managed by the Whips, has been partly responsible for this loss of power. Bill Jones and Dennis Kavanagh (**British Politics Today** pp. 78–9) describe how other factors have also contributed to this decline. They argue, for example, that influential pressure groups have come to by-pass Parliament through their direct contacts with Ministers and civil servants. The mass media has a similar effect: 'In a one-hour interview with the Prime Minister broadcasters like Robin Day have more chance to probe and challenge than the elected chamber has in most weeks.' (Jones and Kavanagh, p. 79.) In fact the growth in the power of the Prime Minister has itself reduced the independence of backbenchers. This is because it is the Prime Minister who decides which MPs shall be 'promoted' to jobs in the Government.

There are signs, however, that the decline of the House of Commons may have been halted – or at least slowed down – in recent years. Some reforms have been made, such as the new system of departmental select committees (see 8.8). Back-bench MPs have been more prepared to take a stand against their party leadership on some issues. The Conservative Government's proposals to increase parental contributions to student grants were dropped following pressure from its own backbenchers, for example. In 1985, the massive Conservative majority in the Commons was reduced to only 17 when 78 Tory MPs either abstained or voted against an £11,000 pay rise for the Lord Chancellor.

Not all politicians want the House of Commons to have more power, particularly if this means it would have more work to do. Lord Hailsham (in the **Dilemma of Democracy**, 1978) believes that the House should do **less** work. Enoch Powell thinks that changes designed to make the House of Commons more informed, such as a greater use of committees or better research facilities, would be counter-productive. He argues that they would reduce the effectiveness of the House itself in carrying out its central task. This he sees as the job of 'ensuring that government is carried on...with the...consent of the people through their representatives'. ('Parliament and the question of reform' by Enoch Powell in **Updating British Policies** edited by Lynton Robins, The Politics Association, London, 1984, p. 10.)

Some politicians, then, consider that the main purpose of the House of Commons is to sustain the Government. Others see a wider role for it. They believe that the House should be reformed so that it can examine more effectively the policies and administration of the Executive and, where necessary, challenge the Government. This, it is claimed, is necessary 'if parliamentary democracy is to play its proper role as the main safeguard of human rights, civil liberties, free speech and social justice in our nation' ('Parliamentary reform' by Tony Benn in **Updating British Politics**, p. 11).

There is a debate, therefore, about whether the House of Commons **should** be reformed. The following extract includes some ideas on **how** it could be reformed.

In December 1966, Richard Crossman, at that time Leader of the House of Commons, spoke to the House on the question of its reform. He said that there was no point in harking back to ancient days. It must be accepted that nowadays it is the electorate, not the Commons, who make and unmake Governments. The Cabinet must run the Executive and initiate and control legislation. The party machines must manage most of the business of the House through the usual channels and organize backbenchers into disciplined political armies. This is the structure of modern political power and reform of the House of Commons should mean adapting out-of-date procedures to make it more efficient.

Crossman continued by saying that there are three questions by which the workings of the Commons should be tested. First, can the legislative process translate policies into laws quickly enough? Secondly, does the timetable leave room for debating important, topical and controversial issues? Thirdly, although legislation and administration must be firmly in **Government** hands, can the House of Commons still provide an effective check on the work of the Executive? Crossman argued that the existing procedures and any proposals for reforming the Commons should be judged by these three tests.

Since the time when Crossman made these comments, demands for reform have increased. Stronger select committees and other changes were introduced in 1979. These go some way towards meeting the demands, but many criticisms remain. These 'range from continuing disquiet about the archaic . . . nature of some traditional procedures to suggestions that MPs should be better paid, have more adequate research assistance and that Membership of the House should be a full-time commitment for all MPs in a House of Commons which meets at reasonable hours'.

Several specific suggestions have been made. One proposal is to change the legislative process by making greater use of standing committees. These committees could have increased powers, such as the power to question witnesses (which select committees have). This suggestion would help the Commons to cope with the increasing amount and complexity of legislation (as well as other business) that has occurred over the years. Some MPs, as well as others outside the House, would like to see a Freedom of Information Act introduced. The present Official Secrets Act can make it difficult for MPs to obtain the information they need to perform their legislative and investigatory roles. This Act has also caused controversy in recent years with the prosecutions of civil servants for passing 'classified' information to an MP or the press. It is argued that a Freedom of Information Act would make governments less secretive and more 'open'.

Some MPs also think that the House of Commons itself could be opened up more to the public by televising its proceedings. In July 1985 the House of Lords agreed to extend the trial period of televising its proceedings. Some people expected the House of Commons to agree to a similar experiment – particularly as the leaders of the two main parties were both thought to favour television coverage. But later that year the Commons decided by a majority of only 12 votes not to allow television cameras into the Chamber. Margaret Thatcher voted against.

Backbench MPs still press for better working facilities including the provision of improved conditions for women members. Some would also like the House of Commons to begin work earlier in the day to reduce the risk of all-night sittings. The length of the Parliamentary session could also be increased.

(adapted from **Politics and Government in Britain** by Tom Brennan, Cambridge University Press, Cambridge, 1982, pp. 227–9 (including the direct quotation) and 'Mrs. Thatcher backs TV in Commons' by Adam Raphael, **The Observer**, April 28, 1985)

1. Give **four** reasons suggested for the decline in power of the House of Commons. (4)
2. a In what sense does the electorate 'make and unmake Governments'? (2)
   b What are the 'usual channels' through which the business of the House is conducted? (2)
3. What does Richard Crossman see as the proper roles of
   a the Government (including the Cabinet)? (2)
   b the House of Commons? (3)
4. Suggest ways in which more use could be made of standing committees in the legislative process. (A re-reading of Section 8.5 could be useful here.) (3)
5. Suggest arguments for and against televising the House of Commons. (4)

11 The House of Lords (1)

The passages in this section have so far been concerned mainly with the House of Commons, or 'lower house'. The 'upper' or 'second' chamber in Parliament is the House of Lords, and the following passages examine its composition, powers and functions.

Except for the Church of England bishops who are allowed to sit in the House, members of the House of Lords are called **peers**. The majority are **hereditary peers**. They have inherited their titles and, when they die, the titles will pass to their children. The remainder are **life peers**. They have been awarded their titles for their own lifetime, but cannot pass them on at death. In June 1984, the House had a total of 1188 members (of whom 64 were women) in the following categories:

Bishops	25
Hereditary peers	795
Life peers	368

(Figures taken from **Information Sheet No. 2**, House of Lords Journal and Information Office, London, 1984, p. 1)

None of them is elected. The total includes 28 Law Lords who play a special judicial role when the House acts as the final court of appeal in the country.

Not all of those entitled to take their place in the House do so.

Some never attend. Others turn up only when the House is dealing with something that is of particular interest to them. During the 1981–2 session the average daily attendance, from a 'potentially active membership' of about 900, was 284 (House of Lords **Information Sheet No. 2**, p. 4). Many, however, do not stay long enough to vote in the Divisions. Attendance has increased since peers have been able to claim attendance allowances. Ordinary members of the House of Lords are not paid a salary.

A few days before the start of the experiment to televise the House of Lords, the journalist Simon Hoggart provided the following description of the chamber and some of its occupants.

> If the Queen were here, as she is at the annual State Opening of Parliament, she would sit on the throne. Her Church of England bishops would sit on the right, and facing them her SDP and Liberal peers. Her Government is also on the right, further back nearer the galleries, and facing them, her loyal Opposition. The cross-benchers [independents], a growing group, occasionally spill over onto the Labour seats. When broadcasting begins there will also be four cameramen, positioned around the Chamber, each clad, at their lordship's insistence, in dark suit and tie.
>
> Just in front of the throne are three woolsacks. Woolsacks were a common, comfy item of furniture in the Middle Ages, rather like Habitat bean bags. The Lord Chancellor, currently Lord Hailsham, sits on the furthest woolsack, looking like a doll perched on a sofa. Nominally he is the Speaker, but unlike Jack Weatherill in the Commons, he is not really a chairman. He 'puts the question' at the beginning of a debate, and 'takes the voices' at the end, but otherwise all he has to do is listen. Occasionally he leans over to the Liberals and mutters 'bloody fool' or 'absolute rot' while someone is speaking, but this is not a constitutional obligation. Now and again, viewers might notice his head slump forward, his eyes close, his wig twist inside out and his stick fall gently to the floor. They might imagine he is asleep, but they would be wrong. Those watching will realize that Lord Hailsham has in fact been **concentrating**. With a sudden start his eyes jerk open, the wig is replaced; and he glowers sternly at whoever is speaking.
>
> (from 'Screen test for the Lords' by Simon Hoggart, **The Observer**, January 13, 1985, pp. 45–6)

As the authority of the Commons increased following the Reform Acts of the 19th century, the power of the House of Lords declined. This century there have been several changes some of which have further reduced its powers. The **Parliament Act, 1911** removed the Lords' power over Money Bills (which give approval for raising taxes, for example – although they can still delay a Money Bill for one month). It also restricted their power to delay other legislation passed by the House of Commons to two years. This was reduced to one year by the **Parliament Act, 1949** (see Section 8.5). The **Life Peerages Act, 1958** allowed the creation of **life** peers, including women peers. This was the first time that women were permitted to become members of the House of Lords. From 1964 to 1983, successive Prime Ministers appointed **only** life peers. This practice was broken when Margaret Thatcher appointed two new hereditary peers: Lord Tonypandy (the former Speaker of the House of Commons) and Lord Whitelaw (the deputy leader of the Conservative Party). The **Peerage Act, 1963** made it possible for peers to give up their titles for their own lifetime. This frees them to become members of the House of Commons, if elected to represent a constituency in the normal way. It was this Act which paved the way for Lord Home to disclaim his title and to become elected to the Commons as Sir Alec Douglas-Home, MP. He had also become Prime Minister in 1963. Lord Stansgate renounced his title in the same year and is now better known as Tony Benn, MP. The Act also allowed women peers who had inherited their titles to sit in the House of Lords.

The following passage looks at the functions and powers of the House of Lords in more detail.

Except for its lack of control over financial matters the functions of the House of Lords appear similar to those of the Commons. It takes part in the law-making process, examines the work of government, holds debates and conducts inquiries. However, there are differences in how it carries out its tasks. These differences are partly due to the Lords having less power than the Commons.

Sections 8.4 and 8.5 explained Parliament's legislative role. Some Government Bills, usually non-controversial ones, begin their passage through Parliament in the House of Lords. But the Lords' main task in the legislative process is to review and revise Bills that have already been through the House of

Commons. It can delay a Bill for one year, but it is rare for the Lords to reject a Bill entirely. It is far more likely to make amendments where it thinks appropriate. As the Labour peers' Chief Whip, Lord Ponsonby, has said: 'We are an unelected and unrepresentative house. It is not our role to stop the house debating Bills brought in by an elected government. Our role is to amend and revise.' (quoted in the **Sunday Times**, March 4, 1984) The House of Commons can then decide either to accept the alterations (which it often does) or to reject them.

Like the House of Commons, the Lords hold debates. They may be on specific matters of policy or on topical issues of more general concern. Debating is generally more relaxed and courteous than in the Commons. The Lords have more time and party lines are not so rigidly kept to. There are party Whips, and in 1984 one Conservative member, Lord Alport, had the whip withdrawn (although there seems little point in withdrawing the whip from a member of the House of Lords). But many peers are not aligned with any party (these are the independent, or crossbench, peers) and, besides, in general debates no vote is taken.

A few members of the House of Lords will be Government Ministers. Their Parliamentary task is to explain Government policy to the Lords, and to defend it, by making statements and answering questions. They will also be responsible for steering Government Bills through the House of Lords. The Lords can also set up select committees to investigate particular subjects or problems. Unlike the House of Commons, though, it does not have a system of **departmental** select committees.

An additional function of the House of Lords – and one not performed by the Commons – is to act as an appeal court within the judicial system. In this capacity only the Law Lords take part. They are, or will have been, senior judges in the legal system of the country. The House of Lords is the highest court of appeal which means its decisions on points of law are always final.

(adapted from 'The House of Lords: recent developments' by Peter G. Richards, **Teaching Politics** Volume 14 No. 2, May, 1985, pp. 181–191 and **The House of Lords** (Education Sheet 5) by Elizabeth Stones, Public Information Office, London, 1983)

1. When were women first allowed to become members of the House of Lords? (1)
2. What is
   a a crossbencher? (1)
   b a Law Lord? (1)
3. Who formally presides over debates in the House of Lords? (1)
4. Why should the difference between the number of hereditary peers and the number of life peers have been reduced between 1963 and 1983? (2)
5. Explain how the restrictions on the length of time for which a Bill can be delayed represent a major limitation on the power of the House of Lords. (2)
6. Having the party whip withdrawn is much less serious for a peer than for a Member of the House of Commons. Why? (3)
7. a Identify **three** functions of the House of Lords. (3)
   b How do each of these differ from the Commons in the way they are carried out? (6)

12 The House of Lords (2) Abolition or reform?

For many years the House of Lords has been criticized. it was said to be undemocratic. It was a left-over from earlier times. It had a permanent Tory majority which was a threat to a Labour Government. The Lords' power of delay could prevent a Labour Government from completing its legislative programme during its final year of office (i.e. before a general election).

Recently, however, the position of the House of Lords has been changing quite dramatically. It has defeated the Government in votes far more frequently than the Commons has. In fact, with the large Conservative majority in the Commons following the 1983 election, the House of Lords has been called a more effective 'opposition' than the official Opposition in the Commons.

Traditionally, a Conservative Government can expect a trouble-free time in the upper house. On paper, the 400 Tory peers easily outnumber Labour's 130 and the Alliance's 80. But in practice, total attendance by peers rarely exceeds 250. The Government relies on the key votes of crossbench

peers to get its programme through. But there are growing
signs that both the independents and a sizeable group of
Tory rebels are in a mood to carry out systematic legislative
ambushes.

During the 1983–4 session, for example, the Lords managed
to revise a number of Government Bills. They secured a
provision in the Telecommunications Bill for stiff penalties for
unauthorized phone-tapping, and they amended the Police
and Criminal Evidence Bill. In the following session, the
Government dropped its Bill to give parents the choice of
whether or not to allow their children to be caned in schools.
The withdrawal of the proposal came after a Lords' amend-
ment to ban corporal punishment in schools altogether. In the
same session, the House of Lords defeated the Government
on a number of clauses of the Bill to abolish the Greater
London Council (GLC) and six other councils. Seventy-six of the
Lords' ninety-eight amendments to this Bill were later
accepted by the Government. Although most of those
accepted involved only minor alterations, two were
considered to represent significant changes to the
Government's original proposals.

In fact it has been opposition to Government plans
affecting local councils – particularly Labour-controlled
councils – that has placed some Labour politicians in a
dilemma. Proposals to abolish the House of Lords have
appeared in a number of Labour manifestos since 1935. The
Labour Party is opposed to the existence of a House which is
not accountable to the electorate and which is based on
heredity and patronage (in this case the power of the Prime
Minister to create new peers). Yet it was the House of Lords
which was prepared to mount a challenge to the Government's GLC proposals. It operated a greater check on the
activities of Government than the Opposition in the
Commons, hampered by the large Conservative majority, was
able to do. Because of this, some politicians on the Labour left
have been having second thoughts about abolishing the
Lords.

The House of Lords is also seen to have other advantages. It
can deal with business for which the Commons has little time.
It plays an important role in dealing with private Bills and in
keeping an eye on EEC activities. The House is also able to

draw the Government's attention to potential difficulties in proposed legislation. This provides an opportunity for the Government to re-think its proposals where necessary.

(adapted from 'Labour protests as guillotine falls on bill to abolish GLC' by Alan Jarvis, **The Guardian**, July 9, 1985, p. 27; 'Tory rebellion in the Lords' by Martin Kettle, **Sunday Times**, March 4, 1984, p. 5 – from which the direct quotation in the passage is taken – and 'The House of Lords: recent developments' by Peter G. Richards, **Teaching Politics** Volume 14 No. 2, May, 1985, pp. 181–191)

1. The House of Lords could **asbolished**, **reformed**, or **kept as it is**. Say which of these you would favour, and why. (10)

Despite the changing position of the House of Lords, there are still calls for its abolition. Its recent increase in influence may only be temporary. Its undemocratic composition and representation of privilege is offensive to many people. Others believe that a second chamber is necessary. They think that some of the present functions should be kept, but accept the need for changes – particularly in its composition. Attempts to introduce significant reforms have been made, but have failed. In 1969 reform proposals were in effect defeated by an 'alliance' of the Conservative right and the Labour left in the Commons. Those on the right believed the proposals would limit the Lords' powers too much. The left thought that the reformed House would have too much power and would have preferred it to be abolished altogether. In fact, one of the problems facing reformers is that if the second House is made as democratic as the Commons, there would be demands for it to be given equal powers. As Simon Hoggart has remarked, '...reform of the Lords would automatically mean strengthening the authority of the Lords, and the Commons won't wear that'. (**The Observer**, January 13, 1985, p. 46)

Because it is difficult to get agreement on what should happen to the House of Lords, its abolition or reform in the near future seems unlikely. But the issue will still be discussed. The following passage outlines some of the ways in which the second chamber could be reformed.

In 1918 the Bryce Conference recommended reforming the upper House. It said that most of its members should be elected by the House of Commons. It also thought it desirable to avoid a permanent political bias towards any one party.

In the 1968–9 session, the Labour Government introduced a Bill to reform the House of Lords. The idea was to have a two-tier structure. Existing hereditary peers were to be allowed to keep their places in the House and to speak in debates. But only 'created' peers (mainly the life peers) would have the right to vote as well. At the time this would have reduced the number of voting peers to about 230. Of these it was intended that the Government should have a small majority over the other parties, but not when the crossbenchers were included. A retirement age of 72 was proposed. The power to delay Bills was to be reduced to six months.

A committee of Tory peers, chaired by Lord Home, made further suggestions in 1978 for reform of the House of Lords. It recommended that two-thirds of the members should be elected on a regional basis by proportional representation. The remainder would be appointed on the advice of the Prime Minister.

Other reform proposals have been put forward over the years. A more recent suggestion in the **Sunday Times** has been for an upper House composed of those defeated candidates at a general election who had reached a set proportion of the votes in their constituencies.

(first three paragraphs adapted from **Governing Britain** by A. H. Hanson and M. Walles, Fontana, 1984, pp. 99, 103–6)

2. Assume that there is to be a reformed second chamber. What recommendations would you make for its composition, functions and powers?   (10)

13 The monarchy

A monarchy is a form of government with one person as head of state – a king or queen. The position is usually hereditary, passed down through a family line, as in Britain. The system of absolute monarchy which lasted in this country until the seventeenth century, was described in Section 7.1. Legislative, executive and judicial powers were all exercised or controlled by the monarch. Since that time, these powers have passed to the Houses of Parliament, the Cabinet and Prime Minister, and the law courts. It was shown, however, that the Crown maintains a formal, constitutional link with each of these institutions. Royal Assent is required before Bills can become law. The Queen opens and closes Parliamentary sessions. Formally it is the Queen who approves appointments to top positions in the executive and judiciary. Under the Royal Prerogative the Crown can make treaties with other countries and even declare war. In practice the monarch is 'advised' in all these matters by the Prime Minister and other Government Ministers, and it is generally assumed that the monarch today is a **symbolic** head of state only.

The Queen's functions are largely ceremonial and this could account for the undoubted popularity of the royal family in Britain. **Republicanism** does not seem to be widespread in this country. In a republic, such as the USA or France, the head of state is often elected. He or she does not occupy the position on the basis of heredity. A republican is therefore someone who would support the abolition of the monarchy. Republicans in Britain view the monarchy as an outdated symbol of inequality and of upper class power and domination. The costs of supporting a royal family are seen as an unjustifiable expense to the taxpayer. There is also the argument that through constant media attention the activities of 'the royals' present a diversion from the more serious problems of government and society generally. The monarchy is defended on the grounds of tradition and on the social and economic benefits it is said to bring. For example, it is claimed that the costs of keeping a royal family are recovered through the tourism it generates. It is also argued that the Queen's foreign visits help to maintain good relations with other countries, especially those of the Commonwealth.

Nevertheless, there are fears that possible future developments could involve the Crown in rather more than the ceremonial and formal duties of today. Examples are considered in the following extract.

The 1983 Labour Party manifesto confirmed its policy

commitment to abolish the House of Lords. Imagine that Labour had won the election and the Government had managed to get an abolition Bill through the Commons and (probably after a delay) the House of Lords, too. Would the Queen be justified in refusing the Royal Assent to the Bill? Lord Crowther-Hunt believes she would. What would be the position on a Bill to abolish the monarchy itself? Such a Bill would be unlikely. Even within the Labour Party republicanism is not a central issue.

However, there could be situations in which the Queen, perhaps even against her own wishes, might be drawn into politics in a public way. For example, the Crown does have the direct and personal power to refuse to dissolve Parliament before the maximum five year period between elections has passed. It is also the monarch who invites a particular politician to form a Government. Conventionally, the invitation automatically goes to the leader of the majority party in the Commons following a general election. But what if the centre parties – probably the Liberals and the SDP – dramatically increased their numbers of seats. A coalition Government would be a distinct possibility. In such a case the choice of leader – and therefore also of the parties from which the Government would be drawn – may not be obvious. This could give the Crown a more decisive role in the making of a Government.

The Labour Party does not have a definite policy stance on the political position of the monarchy. However, Tony Benn has suggested that the Queen's powers relating to the dissolution of Parliament and choice of Prime Minister could be transferred to the Speaker of the House of Commons. The Speaker, he argues, is more directly answerable to the Commons. He is also expected to be neutral – to stand apart from the political parties.

(adapted from **Introduction to British Politics** by John Dearlove and Peter Saunders, Polity Press, Cambridge and Basil Blackwell, Oxford, 1984, pp. 88, 105)

1. What is the difference between a monarchy and a republic?   (2)
2. Distinguish between the Queen's constitutional and ceremonial roles and give an example of each.   (4)

3. What do you understand by the phrase '**symbolic** head of state'?

(4)

4. Discuss the suggestion that the monarchy should be abolished.

(10)

Section 9 Members of Parliament

Those entitled to sit in the House of Commons or the House of Lords are all members of **Parliament**, but the label **MP (Member of Parliament)** is applied only to the 650 elected representatives in the Commons. This section examines the role of the individual MP – especially the back-bench MP – inside and outside Parliament.

1 An MP's job (1)

Some idea of the activities of an MP in Parliament can be gained from Section 8 (particularly 8.4 to 8.8) which examined the work of the House of Commons. A back-bench MP will be expected to support the front-bench of his party by voting at the end of debates and at the different stages of Bills going through the Commons. He might also speak in debates on particular issues. An MP may be involved in committee work – perhaps on one of the standing committees or on a select committee. Committees often meet in the mornings before the day's business in the chamber of the House begins. There are also opportunities for individual MPs to raise issues of special interest or concern to them. These include motions for adjournment debates or other debates permitted under the rules of the House. In July 1985, for example, the Labour MP Jack Ashley gained the support of over 100 MPs for a debate on compensation for children who have suffered brain damage through vaccination. An MP may be able to introduce a Private Member's Bill, perhaps on behalf of a pressure group.

But an MP is also a representative of a constituency. Part of his time will be spent dealing with letters and inquiries from his constituents. These will include complaints about alleged unfair treatment or inefficiency by government officials. They may concern, for example, disputes about income tax or social security payments, worries about redevelopment plans, complaints about the postal service or problems over housing. Some of these grievances will involve other bodies – such as local councils – rather than central (national) Government, but an MP may still be able to help by contacting the organization concerned. During a Parliamentary session, some MPs find that this constituency work can take up most of their mornings. Most MPs also hold regular weekend 'surgeries' in their constituencies – perhaps fortnightly or monthly. At these surgeries individual constituents or local pressure groups get the chance to discuss grievances or problems with their MP directly.

Some of the inquiries or complaints from constituents, whether by post or in person, can be dealt with fairly quickly. A letter from the MP to the appropriate Government Department, local council or other organization may help to get the problem dealt with sooner than it might have been. Letters from MPs are usually taken seriously even when they concern something over which they have no direct influence. Other inquiries can involve the MP in a good deal of research or time spent following up the problem. If response to the MP's initial approach is unsatisfactory he might take further action. He may table a question for Question Time in the Commons or try to get the matter debated in the House. Some problems might be settled more informally through personal contact with a Minister. The Parliamentary Commissioner for Administration (the 'Ombudsman') can investigate certain complaints on behalf of an MP (see Section 11.7). An MP is usually in a better position than an individual constituent to secure publicity about a grievance. He may therefore encourage the media to take an interest in the case. They will not always do so, but the chances may be greater if the MP can also enlist the support of an appropriate pressure group.

Merely because an MP takes an interest in a constituent's problem or complaint, however, there can be no guarantee of a satisfactory outcome. Back-bench MPs are not members of the Government. Their power is limited. Although they receive allowances for research and secretarial assistance, the amount of help available to most backbenchers is not extensive. But they can often be useful in making the necessary contacts and in speeding up the investigation of a complaint. Some MPs regard their role of protecting the rights of individual constituents as their most important duty. They often gain the reputation of being 'good constituency Members'. Other MPs may be less enthusiastic or have less time. They may be more interested in national issues or in party work where they may feel able to exert more influence or power. Some may be more concerned to pursue their own political careers in other ways than constituency work. There are MPs who commit themselves full-time to their work but many have ouside business interests. The law and journalism are popular additional jobs. An increasing number are acting as paid 'consultants' to various business organizations. Front-bench Members will find much of their time taken up with matters of government or opposition. Although they may have less time for constituency work, their influence will generally be greater.

1. List the ways in which an MP can investigate a grievance on behalf of a constituent
   a in Parliament   (3)
   b outside Parliament   (3)
2. Why will constituents not always get their problems satis-factorily resolved after contacting their MP?   (4)
3. Would you prefer your MP to be (a) a backbencher who spends a lot of time in his constituency, (b) a Cabinet Minister, or (c) a nationally well-known figure in his party? Give reasons for your answer by examining each alternative.   (10)

2 An MP's job (2)

The following two extracts look at the job of an MP from rather different angles. The first is a report on a typical Parliamentary day of one MP. The second deals mainly with the financial rewards of MPs – both inside and outside Parliament.

> The House of Commons has been described as the most exclusive club in London, and after spending a day there with John Whitfield, MP for Dewsbury, I am inclined to agree.
> We arrived at the House at 10.00 a.m. and went straight to the members' Post Office. His mail was an average batch, about 30 letters varying from circulars to requests for advice or help from his constituents. The post bag is an invaluable link between MPs and the people whom they represent.

Most of John Whitfield's mornings at the House are spent replying to letters; some replies demanding considerable research. Before becoming an MP he was a solicitor and has some knowledge of how information can be found. One obvious source of information for MPs is the Commons Library which includes copies of past debates, legislation and other parliamentary matters. On the day I was with him, John Whitfield was tabling a Parliamentary Question asking for a written reply from the Home Secretary clarifying his position with regard to prison sentences for child murders. After John Whitfield had completed the draft of his question we went down to the Tables Office where the question was checked and recorded. He then went to the Whip's office to see how he had to vote that day and when.

In the Chamber of the House at 2.30 p.m. prayers were said, and at 2.35 the business of the day began. The first hour of the session is Question Time. But the main interest on that afternoon centred on the debate on the US invasion of Grenada. By 3.45 the House was packed. John Whitfield sat thoughtfully through two speeches, and then, like many other MPs, left the House. The job of an MP involves much more than sitting in the House of Commons. That afternoon, John Whitfield had been invited to attend a presentation by the Health and Safety Commission of their noise awareness campaign. This type of presentation is a regular feature of Parliament. Not only does it give MPs the chance to meet each other but also keeps them in touch with pressure groups outside Parliament. In the case of the Health and Safety Commission's presentation, this was in some way a lobby as they are hoping to have legislation passed which will reduce the maximum level of permissible noise in workplaces.

At 6.50 p.m. the division bell sounded. It was time for MPs to vote on the motion. We were now well into the evening, and the next item on the agenda was Civil Defence. The Government had issued a three line whip, so all Conservative MPs had to be present to vote at the end of the debate. Following this was a motion regarding oil taxation. There was a two line whip and so Government members with a firm pair were excused.

(from 'Day in the life' by John Barrett, **Over 16** Volume 1, January, 1984, pp. 12–13)

An MP is on £16,904 a year*. Most middle managers are not in with a chance to go on fact-finding trips of heavily-beached countries or to jot down their weekly thoughts for a newspaper. A Member of the House of Commons is. 'You've got to make your career in three ways,' a former Labour MP told me: 'By reaching the Cabinet, or by saying, "I'm going to screw this place for every outside consultancy going," or by deciding to do a good job as a local MP.' As it happened, he now does none of these things, having been slung out by the Tory landslide without a penny saved.

The most junior of the ruling party's Whips finds himself on over £25,000, which adds more than a little to the pleasures of being in government. Neil Kinnock, as Leader of the Opposition, receives over £40,000, while the big boys in the Cabinet come, if you deduct the price of a moderate meal for two, up to a respectable £45 grand. At Number One stands the Prime Minister, with a socking £53,600 plus tied cottage in Downing Street. She chooses to take a voluntary cut down to Cabinet Minister level, an example to us all. Denis's pension must help to keep her above Supplementary Benefits level. (Incidentally, these figures are made up of two elements: £11,709 for answering letters from constituents and other local duties, and a varying amount for ruling, or misruling, the nation.)

There are some Members of Parliament for whom the PM's full salary is peanuts – and many for whom the Backbencher's pay is a pittance; 80% of Tories are believed to double it at least. Journalism can provide steady employment as Joe Ashton, Labour Member for Bassetlaw could tell you, though he probably won't. He writes a Wot-I-Fink column twice a week in **The Star**. Envious Labour MPs put his fee today at £250 a piece. But it is mainly the Tories who are the big earners. An MP is a good type for a firm to have on a retainer. It is unlikely that the election address of Sir Ian Percival goes like this: 'If elected, I promise to devote myself to Gam (Bermuda) Ltd., of which I am a director, and Cay-Ber Management Ltd., a local Bermuda corporation which also has the benefit of my direcorship. I undertake to apply myself rigorously to my legal employment as a Recorder, and you can

(* MP's salaries were due to increase to £17,702 in 1986 and £18,500 in 1987.)

count on me to keep hard at it as a barrister, without interfering with my position as a member of the law firm of Sidley & Austin, in Chicago actually. My farms of approximately 100 acres in Kent will not be neglected, believe me. Now then, did somebody mention Southport?' Only his constituents living there.

Cecil Parkinson is another for whom the statutory £16,904 is not the largest sum to feature in the accounts of his household(s). A director of Babcock International, Tarmac, Save & Prosper, Sears Holdings and Jarvis (Harpenden) Holdings, he still trails behind James Prior, who is Chairman of GEC, and a director of Barclays Bank and of Sainsbury's. Talking of Sainsbury's, a member of that family, the Hon. Timothy, is also Member for Hove. According to Andrew Roth, compiler of **Parliamentary Profiles**, 'Tim Sainsbury admits to being a multi-millionaire. He has a 124 million-pound stake in the family firm, and his income in 1983 alone was £1.8 million.'

(from 'Nice little earners: politicians' by Jonathan Sale, **Punch**, May 8, 1985, pp. 34–7)

1. Which of the two extracts on MPs would you describe as mainly
   a uncritical   (1)
   b satirical   (1)
2. a Draw up a timetable, based on the first extract, of a typical day for a back-bench MP in Parliament.   (5)
   b What other activities might he or she be involved in?   (3)
3. Are MPs worth their salary? Give reasons for your answer.   (5)
4. Discuss the suggestion that being a Member of Parliament should be a full-time occupation.   (5)

3 Social background

There would not be much point in discovering the average shoe size of MPs or comparing the height–weight ratios of Labour and Conservative Members. The **social** characteristics of MPs, on the other hand, may well be more relevant. What sort of education did they receive? What jobs have they done? What are their social class backgrounds? How many are women? Are the different ethnic groups in the population represented in Parliament? The following passage provides some evidence about the social composition of the House of Commons.

Seventy-nine per cent of all MPs in the house of Commons following the 1983 general election had had some form of higher or further education. Thirty-six per cent had been to Cambridge or Oxford university. Sixty per cent of all Conservative MPs had been educated at private schools compared with 16% of Labour Members and 23% of those from the smaller parties. In terms of their previous jobs, only 4% of Conservative MPs were working class compared with 43% of Labour MPs. Some occupations are over-represented. There are many lawyers, consultants and company directors among Conservative Members. Teaching and journalism appear frequently in the previous jobs of Labour MPs.

Some groups are not directly represented in the Commons at all – notably Blacks and Asians. Others are severely under-represented. Less than 4% of MPs are women. The following table shows the number of women MPs after each general election since women first gained the vote.

Women MPs

1918	1	1955	24
1922	2	1959	25
1923	8	1964	29
1924	4	1966	26
1929	14	1970	26
1931	15	1974 (Feb)	23
1935	9	1974 (Oct)	27
1945	24	1979	19
1950	21	1983	23
1951	17		

(Numbers may vary between general elections because of by-election changes)

The 1979 general election produced the first woman Prime Minister in Britain. It also resulted in the smallest number of women MPs elected for 28 years. Why are there so few women MPs? It is too simple to say that not enough put them-selves forward. Traditional attitudes about the 'proper' roles of men and women in society are slow to change. They can affect women's ideas about themselves and men's beliefs

Diane Abbott could become one of the first black Members of Parliament. In 1985 she was chosen as prospective Labour Party candidate for the safe Labour seat of Hackney North and Stoke Newington.

about the capabilities of women. It is still generally thought that it is women who should be mainly responsible for bringing up children. Combining a paid occupation with child-care is always difficult, but perhaps especially so for an MP. It is probably no coincidence that only two of the 27 women MPs elected in October, 1974 had children under 10 years old. Women probably experience more difficulties in getting selected as Parliamentary candidates. This may partly be due to the belief of selection committees that women candidates are not popular with voters. Where a woman **is** selected, it is rarely in a safe-seat.

Among the small numbers of women who have become MPs since 1918, very few have had jobs in the Cabinet. Karen Hunt states: 'Women who do succeed are therefore seen as exceptions or as Margaret Thatcher is often described – "the best man for the job".' But Hunt also adds: 'There's more to politics than MPs.' She shows how, historically, women have always been politically active in various forms of pressure group or protest movement. The Women's Peace Camp at Greenham Common and Women Against Pit Closures are two significant recent examples.

(adapted from **British Political Facts 1900–1979** by David Butler and Anne Sloman, Macmillan, London and Basingstoke, 1980, p. 230; **Dod's Parliamentary Companion 1985**, Dod's Parliamentary Companion Ltd., Hailsham, 1985; **Mastering British Politics** by F. N. Forman, Macmillan, Basingstoke and London, 1985, pp. 26–7, 154 and 'Women and politics' by Karen Hunt in **Political Issues in Britain Today** edited by Bill Jones, Manchester University Press, Manchester, 1985, pp. 184–197)

1. From the evidence provided, construct a table comparing the percentages of Conservative and Labour MPs in terms of their occupational class background and their schooling.   (4)
2. Expanding on the information in the passage, suggest ways in which the political socialization of men and women can help explain the under-representation of women in the House of Commons.   (8)
3. 'The social composition of the House of Commons does not need to be representative of the electorate in order to represent its interests.' Explain and discuss this argument.   (8)

4 Conflicting loyalties

MPs may not be representative of the electorate in terms of their social characteristics and background. They are, however, elected to represent the interests of their constituents. But the political parties also expect their MPs to support them in Parliament. What if an MP's party and constituency interests conflict? Which should come first? Are there other groups or principles which may compete for an MP's allegiance? The following extract explores the problem of conflicting loyalties.

The winning candidate at an election becomes the MP for a particular constituency. He is then expected to represent all his constituents and not just those who voted for him. But how does he do this? Edmund Burke was an MP in the eighteenth century. His election address to the voters of his Bristol constituency in 1774 became famous because of the distinction he made between a **representative** and a **delegate**. A delegate was a person elected by the people to express their views directly and accurately. A representative, on the other hand, is elected to stand for, and speak on behalf of, the people. This does not involve acting merely as a messenger for his constituents. An MP, as a representative, should use his own judgement to decide what is in the best interests of the people. And this applies not only to the interests of his own constituents, but to the country as a whole. Burke proclaimed:

> Parliament... is an... assembly of one nation, with one interest, that of the whole. You choose a member indeed; but when you have chosen him, he is not a member of Bristol, but... a member of Parliament.

However, to expect MPs to exercise their own judgements in this fashion today is to ignore the importance of political parties. Writing in the 1960s, Richard Crossman argued:

> The prime responsibility of the member is no longer to his conscience or to the elector, but to his party. Without accepting the discipline of the party he cannot be elected, and if he defies that discipline, he risks political death... Party loyalty has become the prime political virtue of an MP, and the test of that loyalty is his willingness to support the official leadership when he knows it to be wrong.

A.H. Hanson and Malcolm Walles claim that Burke's argument is no longer relevant. They say it is not their judgement that MPs owe the electorate, but their loyalty to their party. It is only this way that Parliament can get anywhere near to carrying out the 'wishes of the electorate'. If each of the 650 MPs were left to make his own judgement on every issue, it would be difficult to see how the country could continue to be governed. Parties make government possible and they provide voters with a choice. The electorate also knows who to blame or praise for the actions of Governments. This should help to make Governments more **responsible**.

Nevertheless, as previous passages have shown, MPs do not always toe the party line. On occasions an MP may vote against his party, abstain, or at least voice his doubts over a

specific policy. He or she may do this for one or more of a number of reasons. He may judge a policy to be against the interests of the country or of his own constituents. The proposed course of action may be contrary to the interests or cause of a pressure group with which the MP is connected. He might also find himself unable to support his party on a matter of conscience or because his own interests may conflict with it.

(adapted from **Basic Political Concepts** by Alan Renwick and Ian Swinburn, Hutchinson, London, 1980, pp. 92–101)

1. Identify **six** allegiances which may compete for an MP's loyalty. (3)
2. Can loyalty to party be justified as the main duty of an MP? Explain your answer. (5)

3. For each of the three examples which follow, state the possible conflicts of loyalty involved, and – explaining your answer – suggest what the MP should do.

  a An MP is opposed to defence policies involving nuclear weapons. Her party supports the development of a new factory to make components for nuclear missiles. The factory is due to be built in the MP's constituency, providing hundreds of new jobs in an area of high unemployment.   (4)

  b An MP is a vegetarian. He represents a rural community in which many of his constituents make a living from agriculture. A delegation of local farmers urges him to press for greater EEC assistance to expand pig farming in the area.   (4)

  c During the course of a Parliament, an MP leaves his party and takes the whip of an opposing party. His local constituency party say that he should resign his seat and fight a by-election, arguing that he had been selected as a candidate for their party which he has now left. The MP claims there is no need to do this as he was elected to represent **all** of his constituents which he can continue to do irrespective of which party he now supports.   (4)

Section 10 The Prime Minister and the Cabinet

Sections 8 and 9 were concerned with Parliament – the **legislature**, or legislative body. This section and the one which follows will examine the **executive**. It is the executive – the government – which is responsible for administering the law and developing policies for the running of the country. The Government consists of the Prime Minister, Cabinet Ministers, Ministers not in the Cabinet, Junior Ministers (Parliamentary Secretaries) and Government Whips. It is composed of **politicians** – usually about 100 in total (see p. 144). Government Ministers are assisted by civil servants who are **permanent officials** (in Britain the officials are not changed when the party forming the government changes).

At the head of the executive are the **Prime Minister** and the **Cabinet**. This section deals with the relationships between them by examining their roles, powers and organization. Unlike the work of Parliament, it is difficult to obtain detailed information about the operations of the Prime Minister and the Cabinet. Records of Cabinet meetings are not made publicly available. The provisions of the Official Secrets Act can be used to restrict information on almost any aspect of the Prime Minister's work. 'Not surprisingly,' writes Anthony King, 'many of the most interesting things written about the prime ministership have been written by people who have worked in Number 10 or else have served in the cabinet.' (**The British Prime Minister**, 1985, pp. 2–3). This is reflected in the passages in this section which include extracts from the writings of a previous Prime Minister and former Cabinet Ministers.

1 The Prime Minister's job

When the Conservative Party won the 1979 general election its leader, Margaret Thatcher, became Prime Minister. She was the

Prime Ministers since 1945 Election

Period	PM	Party	Age at start of job	Education	Reason for leaving job
1945–51	Clement Attlee	Labour	62	Haileybury public school / Oxford University	Party defeated in general election
1951–55	Winston Churchill	Conservative	76*	Harrow public school / Oxford University	Retired
1955–57	Anthony Eden	Conservative	57	Eton public school / Oxford University	Illness
1957–63	Harold MacMillan	Conservative	62	Eton public school / Oxford University	Illness
1963–64	Sir Alec Douglas-Home	Conservative	60	Eton public school / Oxford University	Party defeated in general election
1964–70	Harold Wilson	Labour	48	Wirral Grammar School / Oxford University	Party defeated in general election
1970–74	Edward Heath	Conservative	53	Chatham House Grammar School / Oxford University	Party defeated in general election
1974–76	Harold Wilson	Labour	57	See above	Retired
1976–79	James Callaghan	Labour	64	Portsmouth Northern Secondary School	Party defeated in general election
1979–	Margaret Thatcher	Conservative	53	Grantham High School / Oxford University	

* Had previously been PM

ninth person to hold the job since Winston Churchill's war-time coalition ended in May 1945. The table lists details of all the Prime Ministers since the general election of July 1945.

Unlike most Ministers in the Cabinet, the Prime Minister does not have his or her own Government Department to run. (Government Departments deal with particular branches of Government work such as foreign affairs or trade and industry.) But there is a 'Prime Minister's Office' which consists of groups of people who assist, advise and make arrangements for the Prime Minister. It includes a Private Office which deals, for example, with the PM's official engagements, and a Political Office which maintains contact between the PM and her party and constituency. Some Prime Ministers also have their own personal advisers, from outside the civil service, on particular aspects of Government work. Quite early in her first Government, Mrs. Thatcher, for example, appointed Professor Alan Walters as her personal adviser on economic policy. The PM's work also involves close contact with the Cabinet Office (see 10.7).

Each Prime Minister will have his or her own particular ways of organizing the job. In the following extract, Harold Wilson – Prime Minister for two periods in the 1960s and 1970s – writes about his.

Most days, after reading the morning press, I would be at my desk in Downing Street at 9.30 a.m. I would have a quick check with Private Office to learn of any overnight developments or crises and would make dispositions for the work of the day.

On Thursdays, and sometimes Tuesdays, there is a Cabinet, usually lasting the greater part of the morning. On other days there will be Cabinet committees to chair. There may be speeches to prepare, an ambassador or high commissioner to call or a visiting president or prime minister or colleagues to see. The leader of the House or chief whip might call to discuss overnight parliamentary developments or prospects for the day or longer ahead. Boxes [of urgent Government papers] would normally have been done the previous night, as would parliamentary Questions on Monday and Wednesday nights.

Late morning I would meet with my Political Office for up-to-date political issues, arrangements for political meetings in the country or messages from party headquarters. At 1.45 or later I would have a quick lunch at the House, almost always at the table where the whips and senior ministers gather. Informal government business would continue throughout lunch and over coffee. I might ask two or three back-benchers or junior ministers to join us for coffee. After that I would usually go to the tea-room for informal chats with back-benchers or ministers, and then to the afternoon's work.

On Question days I would return to my room at the House to prepare for the 3.15 p.m. ordeal. Usually, after that, I would return to No. 10 for a routine similar to that of the morning.

The pattern of the day's activities could be rudely disturbed not only by a sudden crisis (including, twice in 1974–6, a hijacking), but also by overseas visits or by state visits or head of government visits from foreign or Commonwealth countries.

The best impression of the pattern of the prime minister's day or week is to analyse his diary for a given period. An analysis of these for the last three months of 1975 leads to the following tabulation:

Audiences of the Queen	8
Cabinet meetings	11
Cabinet committees	24
Other ministerial meetings	43
State visits	1
Other head of government visits	5
Other foreign VIP visits	8
Visits abroad	2
Visits to Northern Ireland	1
Meetings with industry, prominent industrialists, etc.	28
Official meetings	27
Ministerial speeches	17
Political speeches	9
Visits within Britain	13
Official lunches and dinners	20
Political meetings – no speech	11
TV or radio broadcasts	8 (excluding party conference)

Each day sees a number of often unprogrammed meetings with ministers. Most days the prime minister will see the foreign and commonwealth secretary and the chancellor. Other ministers usually called by appointment, or one or two would stop to raise some matter after Cabinet or a Cabinet committee. Still more frequent – several each day – were meetings with the staff of Private Office and with the secretary of the Cabinet.

Formal deputations would come from the principal national organizations: the Confederation of British Industry, the Trades Union Congress, the National Farmers' Union and many others. Sometimes the prime minister takes the initiative to invite representatives of an important group of people to come for an informal evening meeting or dinner.

(from **The Governance of Britain** by Harold Wilson, Weidenfeld & Nicholson and Michael Joseph, London, 1976, pp. 83–7)

1. Which post-war Prime Minister attended neither a public school nor a university? (2)
2. Who has been the longest-serving Prime Minister since the Second World War? (2)
3. a What is the difference between the Prime Minister's Private Office and his Political Office? (2)
   b Why do you think such a distinction is maintained? (2)
4. According to the extract, in what ways did Harold Wilson keep in touch with
   a Cabinet Ministers? (5)
   b Back-bench MPs of his own party? (3)
   c Major pressure groups? (2)
   d Government leaders from other countries? (2)

2 Prime Ministerial power

Another way of looking at the job of Prime Minister is to examine the powers that go with it. As earlier sections have shown, it is the Government, rather than Parliament, that has real control over legislation, policy and finance. And it was long recognized that the centre of government power was to be found in the Cabinet – the team of senior Government Ministers chosen by the Prime Minister. However, since the 1960s there has been a growing argument that Britain's system of 'Cabinet government' has been developing into 'Prime Ministerial government'. Prime Ministers have become more closely involved in foreign and economic affairs.

Publicly, parties and Governments, and their policies, have increasingly become identified with their leaders – as in phrases such as 'the Thatcher Government' and 'Thatcherism'. It is claimed that the vast powers available to a Prime Minister are a threat to democracy. Too much power, it is suggested, now lies in the hands of just one person. This is the view taken by Tony Benn in the first extract which follows. He describes the range of powers of a modern Prime Minister. The second passage takes issue with this view. It outlines a number of ways in which Prime Ministerial powers are, in practice, restricted.

The powers now exercised by a British Prime Minister are so great as to encroach on the legitimate rights of the electorate. They undermine the essential role of Parliament and they usurp [take over] some of the functions of collective Cabinet decision-making. Altogether, the present centralization of power into the hands of one person amounts to a system of personal rule in the very heart of our parliamentary democracy.

The most decisive power exercised by the Prime Minister derives from the fact that, constitutionally, the Crown entrusts the task of forming an administration to an individual, who is then solely responsible for nominating the Cabinet and all other Ministers. He or she can, therefore, appoint and dismiss Ministers with no constitutional requirement to have these changes approved by Parliament. By the use, or threat of use, of that power, all the others I shall describe fall into his or her hands alone, to use as he or she thinks best.

The Prime Minister has the power to create peers. Then there are all the other honours in the Prime Minister's power such as baronetcies and knighthoods. The Prime Minister expects to be consulted, personally, on appointments of all chairmen of nationalized industries. The scale of all this personal patronage is breathtaking – no medieval monarch could approach it; nor could an American President. There is more. Prime Ministers also appoint permanent secretaries [top civil servants], ambassadors, chiefs of staff, the heads of the security services, MI5 and MI6. The Prime Minister also plays a part in choosing archbishops, bishops and judges.

The second greatest power, after patronage, lies in the

complete personal control of the conduct of government business as it is carried out by Ministers and officials. The Prime Minister determines which items of business are to be discussed in Cabinet and which are to be excluded. He or she has the power to set up Cabinet committees, appoint their members and keep their existence secret from the public, from Parliament, and even from other members of the Cabinet. The Prime Minister has the power to circulate, or to withold, Cabinet committee papers from other Cabinet members who do not serve on that committee. The Prime Minister is thus able to bring forward policies he favours, and to stop those he opposes.

A Prime Minister is also in a unique position to control the flow of information about the work of government. Alone among Ministers he or she has the power to inform Parliament or the public directly on any matter relating to the Government's policy or activity. The Prime Minister's personal responsibility for the security services also entitles him or her to have any person – including Ministers – put under surveillance; and to withold knowledge both of the fact of surveillance, and its outcome, from anyone he or she chooses.

The Prime Minister can advise, and normally expect to secure, a dissolution of Parliament before the end of its natural life-span. And simply by tendering his or her own resignation to the sovereign, he or she can terminate the life of the whole Government. But the Prime Minister's real power flows from his or her ability to threaten to resign or to dissolve Parliament if the Cabinet will not support him or her.

The powers enjoyed by the Prime Minister, then, are very wide indeed and can be used to exclude Parliament and the public from the knowledge necessary for them to operate effectively. /

(Extracts from 'Curbing the power of PMs' by Tony Benn, **The Observer**, 15 July, 1979, p. 10, with minor additions)

Modern Prime Ministers do have a wide range of powers. They can appoint, reshuffle and dismiss Ministers. They can control Government business. They have enormous powers of patronage./ But Tony Benn's analysis plays down the **constraints** which exist on a Prime Minister's power.

Some of these constraints come from a Prime Minister's Cabinet colleagues and some from his party in general. A Prime Minister cannot afford to isolate himself from other senior Cabinet members – especially those who may be after his job. The vast and complex nature of the job means that a Prime Minister will have to share the burden of decision-making. The existence of Cabinet committees can be a further restriction on Prime Ministerial power as many decisions are taken there. Prime Ministers cannot afford to persistently ignore their own backbenchers. Their loyalty is required to secure Parliamentary approval for the Government's policies. To a lesser extent, a Prime Minister will also have to take some account of the party outside Parliament. This is likely to be a bigger constraint on Labour, rather than Conservative, Prime Ministers, however.

The ability of a Prime Minister to control the flow of government information can also be exaggerated. Although all Prime Ministers attempt to do this, 'leaks' from the Cabinet or from Government Departments are not uncommon. It is often difficult to keep awkward decisions secret, as the events following the sinking of the *General Belgrano* during the Falklands War showed.

(adapted from **Introduction to British Politics** by P.J. Madgwick, Hutchinson, 1984, p. 72 and 'The threat to democracy – Number 10' by Adam Raphael, **The Observer**, 15 July, 1979)

1. What are 'powers of patronage'? (2)
2. Outline the powers of the Prime Minister in relation to
   a the Cabinet and its committees (4)
   b Parliament (2)
3. What does Tony Benn regard as the main source of a Prime Minister's powers, and why? (2)
4. Explain how, according to the second passage, Prime Ministerial powers are restricted by
   a the Cabinet and its committees (3)
   b Parliament (2)
5. What are Cabinet 'leaks' and how might they limit the power of a Prime Minister? (3)
6. Why is a Labour Prime Minister more likely to be constrained by his party outside Parliament than is a Conservative PM? (2)

3 Prime Ministerial styles

Relative to other politicians, Mrs. Thatcher is insensitive, confrontationist, stubborn, abrasive and authoritarian... but at least we have all had notice of her intentions.
(Bill Jones)

Mrs. Thatcher could put a poodle in the cabinet, and live to tell the tale.
(Hugo Young)

The extent to which outside constraints limit the power of a Prime Minister will depend to some extent on the individual occupying the job. Each Prime Minister will bring his or her own style to the job which will have some effect on how government power is exercised and distributed. The following extracts all concentrate on Margaret Thatcher's Prime Ministerial style, although the earlier passages make some comparisons with previous PMs. The first and final extracts are written by a professor of Government. The second passage is by a political journalist. The third is from a politician who has been a member of Conservative Governments under four Prime Ministers and who was dismissed from Margaret Thatcher's Cabinet in 1983.

Heath's cabinet was so united that it did not require leadership... Wilson was usually content to count heads round the cabinet table. Callaghan in his cabinet took the occasional initiative... but generally concerned himself... with keeping his colleagues out of trouble and refereeing cabinet disputes....

Most prime ministers tend to play a waiting game in cabinet and cabinet committees. They encourage the minister or ministers most centrally concerned with an issue to introduce the discussion and then intervene themselves only at a fairly late stage. The aim is to see whether a consensus [a general agreement] emerges around the table. If one does, that settles the matter unless the prime minister has some particular reason for expressing a contrary view. If no consensus emerges,... then the prime minister may well come in and try to steer the final decision in one direction or another... Thatcher, by all accounts, operates in a totally different manner. She states her views at the outset, or lets them be known. Often she thinks aloud. She interrupts ministers with whom she disagrees and insists on standing and fighting her corner. Unlike most prime ministers, she does not merely chair cabinet discussions; she is an active participant in them. More often than not she dominates them.

(from 'Margaret Thatcher; the style of a prime minister' by Anthony King, pp. 115–7 in **The British Prime Minister** edited by Anthony King, Macmillan, Basingstoke and London, 1985)

How does she differ... from her predecessors? First, she has the power of conviction. She knows, irresistably, what she wants to do. Second, she has the power of energy. She has the power over jobs and much else, because she cares to exercise it. Other prime ministers were quite happy to let all civil service promotions and other public jobs be decided by... the supreme mandarins [*the very top civil servants*]. Third, she has the power of solidarity – solidarity on her terms... The Thatcher cabinet is composed of... competent placemen gratefully taking any lead the prime minister cares to give them, alongside a few one-time dissenters who do their best to keep out of her way... Mrs Thatcher could put a poodle in the cabinet, and live to tell the tale.

(from 'Another job for her boys' by Hugo Young, **Sunday Times**, January 2, 1983)

Margaret Thatcher... likes everything to be clear-cut: absolutely in favour of one thing, absolutely against another... To be loyal means one hundred per cent acceptance of Government thinking: any dissent, or even the admittance of doubt, is treachery and treason... Margaret Thatcher still asks people the question, 'Are you one of us?' by which she means, 'Are you completely free of any doubt as to the utter rightness of everything we are doing?'

The Government's style of operation has steadily become less flexible and more centralized. This process stems from the Prime Minister's tendency to think that she is always right. In turn, this leads her to believe that she can always do things better than other people, which then encourages her to do everything herself. The two consequences of this are, first, that central government now exercises direct control over more and more aspects of our lives and, second, that within the Government the Prime Minister exercises direct control over more and more Departments. Both developments conflict with the Government's stated beliefs in individual freedom and the danger of state intervention... The Prime Minister... would ideally like to run the major Departments herself and tries her best to do so... Margaret Thatcher may have a retentive grasp of detail, but she cannot know enough to dictate the policy of each Department, as she has gradually discovered. Her response has been to expand the Downing Street staff to include experts in every major area, thus establishing a government within a government. In most cases, people have been chosen who reinforce her point of view rather than challenge it...

This drift towards centralization also affects the management of news. All Governments want a favourable Press and they go to considerable lengths to achieve one, but this Government goes further than most. Increasingly, Ministerial and Departmental Press releases are channelled through Downing Street and suppressed or modified as necessary. The notorious leaks have emanated as much from Downing Street as from anywhere else. The Press receives a very good service from Number 10, which is perhaps why much of it is so uncritical.

(from **The Politics of Consent** by Francis Pym, Hamish Hamilton, London, 1984, pp. 2, 16–18, with minor addition)

Has Thatcher... fundamentally changed the office of prime minister? Up to a point the answer... is 'no'... The job itself has not greatly changed. But... the repertory of available prime ministerial styles has been extended... It is open to a determined prime minister to take more and more decisions and to defy other members of the cabinet to say that he or she has no right to take these decisions. This is precisely what Thatcher has been doing, in extending her surveillance of senior civil service appointments, in working increasingly through small groups of ministers rather than through the cabinet and cabinet committees, in making it clear to her colleagues that she expects to be consulted about virtually the whole range of ministerial activity. She has been pushing out the frontiers of her authority . . .

(from 'Margaret Thatcher: the style of a prime minister' by Anthony King, pp. 136–7 in **The British Prime Minister** edited by Anthony King, Macmillan, Basingstoke and London, 1985)

1. In your own words, describe how – according to Anthony King – Margaret Thatcher's role in Cabinet differs from that of earlier Prime Ministers. (4)
2. How might a Prime Minister attempt to secure loyalty from his or her Cabinet colleagues? (3)
3. a From the final extract, identify **three** ways in which it is claimed that Margaret Thatcher has extended the authority of the Prime Minister's role. (3)
   b From the other extracts, identify evidence for **two** of these. (6)
4. How might intentional 'leaks' to the press from Downing Street help to strengthen the position of the Prime Minister? (4)

4 Forming a Cabinet

One of the first tasks of a new Prime Minister is to form a Cabinet. The Cabinet usually consists of about 20 senior politicians, most of whom will also be responsible for particular Government Departments. Some members of the Cabinet will be selected from the House of Lords, but in modern times most will be MPs. From time to time the Prime Minister may change or 'reshuffle' his or her Cabinet. This may be necessary because of a death, illness or resignation. Alternatively, a reshuffle may be a political move to alter the balance of views connected with different sections or wings of the party. Margaret Thatcher gradually reduced the number of the original 'wets' in her Cabinet. Politicians who strongly supported her economic policies were appointed to the key economic posts in the Cabinet. At the same time her appointments and dismissals were carefully planned and timed to prevent alternative power bases from developing which might have threatened her own position. The tables on pages 214–5 show the composition of Margaret Thatcher's first Cabinet and her cabinet six years later. A number of other changes had been made in the intervening period.

Margaret Thatcher's first Cabinet formed after the 1979 election.

Margaret Thatcher's Cabinet following the general election of May, 1979

Prime Minister	Margaret Thatcher
Home Secretary	William Whitelaw
Lord Chancellor	Lord Hailsham
Foreign and Commonwealth Secretary	Lord Carrington
Chancellor of the Exchequer	Sir Geoffrey Howe
Industry Secretary	Sir Keith Joseph
Defence Secretary	Francis Pym
Lord President of the Council	Lord Soames
Employment Secretary	James Prior
Lord Privy Seal	Sir Ian Gilmour
Minister of Agriculture, Fisheries and Food	Peter Walker
Environment Secretary	Michael Heseltine
Secretary of State for Scotland	George Younger
Secretary of State for Wales	Nicholas Edwards
Secretary of State for Northern Ireland	Humphrey Atkins
Social Services Secretary	Patrick Jenkin
Chancellor of the Duchy of Lancaster and Leader of the House of Commons	Norman St. John Stevas
Trade Secretary	John Nott
Energy Secretary	David Howell
Education and Science Secretary	Mark Carlisle
Chief Secretary, Treasury	John Biffen
Paymaster General	Angus Maude

Margaret Thatcher's Cabinet following the September, 1985 reshuffle

Prime Minister	Margaret Thatcher
Lord President of the Council	Viscount (Lord) Whitelaw
Lord Chancellor	Lord Hailsham
Foreign and Commonwealth Secretary	Sir Geoffrey Howe
Trade and Industry Secretary	Leon Brittan
Chancellor of the Exchequer	Nigel Lawson
Home Secretary	Douglas Hurd
Education and Science Secretary	Sir Keith Joseph
Energy Secretary	Peter Walker
Defence Secretary	Michael Heseltine
Secretary of State for Scotland	George Younger
Secretary of State for Wales	Nicholas Edwards
Lord Privy Seal	John Biffen
Social Services Secretary	Norman Fowler
Chancellor of the Duchy of Lancaster	Norman Tebbit
Secretary of State for Northern Ireland	Tom King
Minister of Agriculture, Fisheries and Food	Michael Jopling
Secretary of State for Transport	Nicholas Ridley
Employment Secretary	Lord Young
Environment Secretary	Kenneth Baker
Paymaster General	Kenneth Clarke
Chief Secretary, Treasury	John MacGregor

(Sources: **Dod's Parliamentary Companion, 1979** and **The Guardian,** September 3, 1985)

The following passage outlines some of the factors which a Prime Minister will take into account when deciding who to appoint to a Cabinet.

It is a convention that all members of the Cabinet will be members of the House of Commons or the House of Lords. If the Prime Minister wishes to appoint an outsider, then he or she will either be made a peer or will be expected to fight and win a by-election. In 1964, for example, Harold Wilson appointed Frank Cousins, a trade union leader, Minister of Technology. He became an MP by winning a by-election in Nuneaton. Being members of the Commons or the Lords means that Cabinet Ministers can explain and defend their policies in Parliament.

Most Cabinet Ministers will have had considerable Parliamentary experience. Many will previously have been Government Ministers (although not necessarily of Cabinet rank). A Prime Minister will therefore have a number of people with proven political and administrative skills from whom to make her selection.

A Cabinet resuffle?

Prime Ministers will also consider the needs of their party. Different wings or groups within the party may need to be balanced to take account of the different ideas and views on policy. Some potential Cabinet members may be future rivals for the Prime Minister's job itself. They may be included in order to deter alternative sources of power from developing within the Parliamentary party. These individuals will then be expected to agree in public with policies decided by the Cabinet (see 10.6 on 'collective responsibility'). In the case of a party coming to power after a period in Opposition, the Prime Minister will probably be guided to some extent by the composition of his or her previous 'Shadow Cabinet'. On occasions, however, Cabinet appointments have been made directly from the backbenches.

It is commonly said that some politicians are so important within a party that the Prime Minister has no choice but to include them in the Cabinet. They may even be able to demand one of the major posts such as Chancellor of the Exchequer, Home Secretary or Foreign Secretary. But this point can be over-emphasized. Ted Heath, for example, is a former Prime Minister with sizeable support among sections of the Conservative Party, yet he has not been a member of Margaret Thatcher's Cabinet. Similarly, James Callaghan did not include the popular and experienced ex-Cabinet Minister, Barbara Castle when he became Prime Minister.

(adapted from **The British Prime Minister** edited by Anthony King, Macmillan, Basingstoke and London, 1985, p. 5 and **The Cabinet and Policy Formation** by Michael Rush, Longman, Harlow, 1984, pp. 2$\uparrow$-9)

1. a What is a Cabinet 'reshuffle'?   (1)
   b Why do they take place?   (2)
2. a How many members of Margaret Thatcher's original Cabinet were still there after the September, 1985 changes?   (1)
   b How many of these were still in their original jobs?   (1)
   c How many peers were in the Cabinet in 1979 and in 1985? (1)
3. Why are all Cabinet Ministers normally members of the House of Commons or the House of Lords?   (2)
4. Identify **six** factors which may influence a Prime Minister in forming a Cabinet.   (12)

5 The Cabinet's job

As previous passages have suggested, the role of the Cabinet can vary according to the style of the Prime Minister. Margaret Thatcher, for example, is known to have by-passed her Cabinet on occasions by reaching decisions with Ministers individually or with small groups of colleagues or advisers. Those who think that 'Cabinet government' has given way to 'Prime Ministerial government' claim that such practices have become more common in recent decades. They would argue that it is now the Prime Minister, rather than the Cabinet, who makes policy. But there are limits to the activities of one person. As most Cabinet Ministers are heads of particular Government Departments, the specialized knowledge or advice to which they have access must give them a certain degree of power. The Cabinet is also able to perform a co-ordinating role. The following extract examines the main tasks of the Cabinet.

Determining policy. The traditionally accepted view is contained in the Report of the Machinery of Government

Committee (1918) which states that the Cabinet is responsible for 'the final determination of the policy to be submitted to Parliament'. J. P. Mackintosh, on the other hand, in his book **The British Cabinet**, states that the modern Cabinet has a less significant role with regard to policy-making, 'The Cabinet . . . sees the major policy decisions, but a body with an average number of twenty regularly facing a heavy agenda is not very suitable for threshing out problems and making long-term plans. . . . Parties have tended to work out quite elaborate . . . proposals when in opposition and to carry these with them into office. Once in office . . . decisions are made in the departments, in Cabinet committees, in private talks between the Prime Minister and the Ministers mainly concerned, and the differences that remain are settled in the Cabinet itself.'

Controlling administration. Obviously, a body which meets on an average for four hours every week cannot exercise close supervision of the administration. This is a matter for individual ministers. The Cabinet's control is general, and it is particularly concerned with matters which are politically important. However, certain matters are regarded as being outside the Cabinet's general control. An example is the preparation of the Budget by the Chancellor of the Exchequer; the Cabinet is merely informed of the proposals a few days before his Budget speech in the Commons.

Co-ordinating. Important decisions are reported to the Cabinet so members are able to take a broad view of developments. The Prime Minister, assisted by Ministers with no departmental duties, is particularly suited to co-ordinate the work of the various departments. When there is a dispute between Ministers, the matter can be settled finally in the Cabinet. The Cabinet can decide on priority of the legislative programme.

J. P. Mackintosh states: 'The major task of the Cabinet is not to lead the party, to manage Parliament, or to think out policies, but to co-ordinate administration, ensure that legislative proposals are acceptable to the departments concerned, to keep the senior Ministers in touch with all the various lines of activity and to give the work of the government a measure of unity.'

(from **British Government** by Glyn Parry, Edward Arnold, London, 1979, pp. 89–91)

1. Identify **three** reasons why the Cabinet may not be so important in making policy as was once thought. (6)
2. In what sense does the Cabinet have control over government activity? (2)
3. a Identify **three** ways in which the Cabinet can act as a co-ordinating body. (6)
   b Why is such co-ordination necessary? (3)
4. Giving reasons, say which you think is the most important function of the Cabinet. (3)

6 Collective responsibility

There is a convention known as **collective Cabinet responsibility**. Within Cabinet, and its committees, Ministers can express their own views, and disagreements will occur. However, once a decision has been reached, the convention requires that each member of the Cabinet must accept it and publicly agree with it. Any Minister who cannot support a decision in this way would be expected to resign. From time to time resignations do take place when a Minister feels unable to abide by a decision on a particular issue.

Very occasionally, Prime Ministers have allowed Cabinet Ministers to ignore, temporarily, the convention of collective responsibility. During the pre-referendum debate on Britain's continued EEC membership in 1975, for example, Harold Wilson suspended the convention. On other occasions, however, he had insisted on it being followed, as the next extract shows. (Wilson himself had resigned from a Labour Cabinet in 1951 in protest against charges being introduced for certain National Health services.)

Every member of the Cabinet, every junior minister, on appointment receives a document which sets out the conduct required of Ministers including broad and clearly defined rules

setting out the requirements of collective ministerial responsibility. It became my duty to draw to the attention of certain
ministers the overriding requirements of this code of
conduct, particularly in relationship to their membership of
the National Executive Committee of the Labour Party. In
1974-5 there were strains arising from certain aspects of
foreign policy, including Chile and South Africa. I wrote the
following letter to three ministers who were members of the
NEC. After some little difficulty, satisfactory assurances were
received.

> In my minute of 14 May 1974 I reminded Ministers of the
> principle of collective responsibility, as it applies to Ministers
> in their dealings with the Labour Party and in particular to
> Ministers who are members of the National Executive
> Committee ....
>
> The minute restated the rule that, where any conflict of
> loyalty arises, the principle of the collective responsibility of
> the Government is absolute and overriding in all circum-
> stances and that if any Minister feels unable to subscribe to
> this principle without reservation, it is his duty to resign his
> office forthwith .... I made it clear that it is inconsistent
> with the principle of collective responsibility for a Minister
> who is a member of the National Executive Committee to
> speak or vote in favour of a resolution ... which is critical of
> Government policies or actions, or which seeks to impose on
> the Government views or decisions which are manifestly
> inconsistent with Government policy.
>
> Your vote in support of the ... resolution at yesterday's
> meeting of the National Executive Committee was clearly
> inconsistent with the principle of collective responsibility.
> You will be aware of the embarrassment which this has
> created for your colleagues.
>
> I must ask you to send me ... an unqualified assurance that
> you accept the principle of collective responsibility and that
> you will from now on comply with its requirements I
> must warn you that I should have to regard your failure to
> give me such an assurance ... as a decision on your part that
> you did not wish to continue as a member of this administra-
> tion. I should of course much regret such a decision; but I
> should accept it.

(from **The Governance of Britain** by Harold Wilson, Weidenfeld & Nicolson
and Michael Joseph, London, 1976, pp. 44, 74-5, 192-3)

1. a Briefly explain the convention of collective responsibility.   (2)
   b What do you think is its purpose?   (3)

2. What evidence is there in the extract to suggest that the principle applies to **all** Ministers in the Government and not only to those in the Cabinet? (2)
3. a On which issue did the Prime Minister agree to suspend the convention in 1975? (1)
   b Why do you think he did this? (3)
4. a Briefly state the ultimatum presented in Harold Wilson's letter to the three Ministers. (3)
   b Was it effective? (1)
5. With particular reference to the NEC, suggest why collective responsibility may on occasions pose greater problems for a Labour rather than a Conservative Prime Minister. (5)

7 The organization of the Cabinet

The full Cabinet meets once or twice a week, plus any emergency meetings, usually at 10 Downing Street. Much of the work on the items to be discussed will have been done before the formal Cabinet meetings through: (1) meetings of the 'Inner Cabinet' – a small number of senior Cabinet Ministers, (2) informal talks between the Prime Minister and individual Ministers, (3) inter-departmental committees of civil servants (officials from various government departments), and (4) Cabinet committees.

Cabinet committees are small groups of Ministers (and sometimes senior civil servants) concerned with particular problems or topics. These can relate, for example, to defence, economic and industrial policy, intelligence and security, and so on. Their existence and composition are generally supposed to remain secret. But Peter Hennessy has estimated that in 1984 there were about 135 Cabinet committees. About 25 of these are the relatively permanent 'standing' committees, the remainder being set up to deal with specific issues or problems. The most important will be chaired by the Prime Minister. Much of the policy work is carried out in Cabinet committees. Decisions taken there may be reported only briefly, if at all, in full Cabinet. Peter Hennessy emphasizes both the secrecy and the importance of Cabinet committees in the British system of government:

The Cabinet Room at 10 Downing Street. The most senior Ministers sit opposite or close to the Prime Minister towards the centre of the table. Those seated towards the ends of the table would find it more difficult to contribute regularly to the discussion.

> The Cabinet machine [is] the engine room of British central government and the Cabinet committees its working parts... Anyone interested in understanding the real, hidden government in Whitehall – as opposed to the visible, semi-artificial version – which dominates life at Westminster, must concentrate on the Cabinet committees. Very rarely is life in the engine-room penetrated by outsiders, whether they be journalists, MPs on a select committee or scholarly researchers. Only one other nation in the western world practises private government on this scale: the Republic of Ireland.

Hennessy adds that even if the existence of all Cabinet committees were publicly known, the full process of top decision-making would still not be revealed. This is because Prime Ministers may deal with some issues by going outside the Cabinet and Cabinet committee system. Margaret Thatcher, for example, holds informal consultations with Ministers, civil servants and aides from the Downing Street Policy Unit. The Policy Unit contains the small number of outside political advisers to the PM. From 1970 to 1983 (when it was abolished) there was also a body called the Central Policy Review Staff. It was composed of equal numbers of civil servants and people from outside (mainly from universities and industry). The task of the CPRS was to investigate and report on various aspects of government policy. Unlike the Policy Unit, it was attached to the Cabinet Office, rather than the Prime Minister's Office.

The job of the Cabinet Office (or 'Secretariat') is to provide administrative and secretarial assistance for the Cabinet and its committees. The Office consists of a group of officials working at 10 Downing Street and is directly responsible to the Prime Minister. On the instructions of the PM, it prepares the agenda for meetings and distributes copies of Cabinet papers and documents to the Minister concerned. It also keeps the minutes (records of decisions, what is discussed, etc.) of Cabinet and Cabinet committee meetings, and is responsible for informing the relevant Departments of decisions made. The Office therefore has an important co-ordinating function relating to all aspects of Cabinet work. The head of the Cabinet Office is the Cabinet Secretary – a senior civil servant who works very closely with the Prime Minister.

(adapted from **How Britain is Governed** by J. Harvey, Macmillan, Basingstoke and London, 1983, pp. 140–1; **The British Constitution and Politics** by J. Harvey and L. Bather, Macmillan, Basingstoke and London, 1982, pp. 242–6; 'Whitehall's real power house' by Peter Hennessy, **The Times** April 30, 1984 and **The Cabinet and Policy Formation** by Michael Rush, Longman, 1984, pp. 40–2)

1. What is
   a the 'Inner Cabinet'?   (2)
   b a Cabinet committee?   (2)
   c the Cabinet Office?   (2)
2. How did the CPRS differ from the Downing Street Policy Unit?(4)
3. If the 'Cabinet is the engine room of the British government', why does the full Cabinet probably rarely meet for more than four or five hours in any week?   (4)
4. How might Cabinet committees
   a reduce   (3)
   b increase   (3)
   the power of the Prime Minister?

Section 11 Ministers and Civil Servants

Most Cabinet Ministers have responsibility for running the major departments of State – Government Departments. Other Government Departments are headed by Ministers who are not in the Cabinet. This section begins with an outline of the organization and work of the major Departments. The role of Ministers and their working relationships with their officials are then considered in some detail. An examination of the structure of the civil service is followed by an explanation of **delegated legislation.** This consists mainly of rules and regulations issued by Ministers under powers given to them by Parliament. With the vast amount of work undertaken by Government Departments, mistakes are bound to occur. The final passage therefore examines ways by which individuals with grievances against a Government Department can get their complaints dealt with.

1 Government Departments

When policy decisions have been made, or new laws passed, they have to be implemented. All the activities involved in running the country, and the services provided by the state, have to be administered. This is the task of the Government Departments. They will also be engaged in planning and preparing new laws and in providing advice on possible alternative policies. The following passage describes the structure and organization of Government Departments.

There are about fifty Government Departments. Between fifteen and twenty are the major Departments whose leaders will be members of the Cabinet. The Departments are named according to the work they perform, such as defence, employment, and education and science. Each Prime Minister

Major Government Departments

Department	Minister in charge	Main areas of work
Treasury	Chancellor of the Exchequer	Controlling the economy. Raising money. Control of all government expenditure.
Home Office	Home Secretary	Law and order. Supervision of police, prison and fire services. Immigration. Community relations. Drugs.
Foreign and Commonwealth Office	Foreign and Commonwealth Secretary	Representing the UK, and protecting British citizens, abroad. Diplomatic service.
Ministry of Defence	Secretary of State for Defence	Administration of armed forces. Defence policy.
Department of Trade and Industry	Secretary of State for Trade and Industry	Commercial and industrial policy. Exports. Consumer affairs. Regional policy and financial assistance. Relations with public industries.
Department of Employment	Secretary for Employment	Employment and training services. Industrial relations. Small firms policy. Factory inspection.
Department of Energy	Secretary of State for Energy	Fuel and power supplies, including nuclear energy.
Ministry of Agriculture, Fisheries and Food	Minister for Agriculture	Policies for agricultural, fishing and food industries. Food supplies
Department of Education and Science	Secretary of State for Education and Science	Overall policies for schools, colleges, polytechnics and universities Civil (i.e. non-military) scientific research. Libraries and museums.
Department of the Environment	Secretary of State for the Environment	Local government. Housing and construction. Control of pollution. Planning. Public buildings and works.
Department of Transport	Secretary of State for Transport	Public transport. Motorways and trunk roads. Road safety and licensing.
Department of Health and Social Security	Secretary of State for Social Services	National Health Service. Local authority social services. Social security benefits and pensions.
Northern Ireland Office	Secretary of State for Northern Ireland	Development of the areas concerned, including some of the services listed above
Scottish Office	Secretary of State for Scotland	
Welsh Office	Secretary of State for Wales	

can decide how many Departments there are to be and on their titles. Major re-organizations, however, are not common and some Departments – such as the Home Office and the Foreign Office – have existed for over 200 years. The major Government Departments existing in the mid-1980s are listed in the table.

Each Department has a small number of **political appointments.** These will be the Minister (often, in the major Departments, called the Secretary of State) and his junior Ministers who will assist him. The vast majority of the jobs in Government Departments, however, are filled by **permanent officials,** the civil servants. The most senior civil servant in each Department is called the Permanent Secretary. The way in which Departments are organized internally varies, but the organization of a typical Department is provided in the diagram. (The boxes with the broken lines indicate the **political appointments,** those with continuous lines the **permanent officials.**)

The organization of a Department

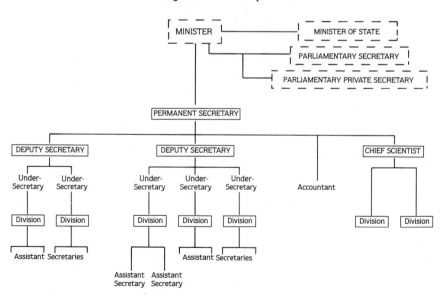

(Source: **How Britain is Governed** by J. Harvey, Macmillan, Basingstoke and London, 1983, p. 147)

Although each Department has specific responsibilities, there will often be an overlap of work between two or more Departments. Attempts to deal with youth unemployment through the provision of training schemes, for example, could involve a number of Departments, including Employment, Education and Science, Trade and Industry, Health and Social Security, and the Treasury. Effective co-ordination between the various Departments is therefore important. This is often done informally. Not all Government Departments are located in Whitehall — some are based in other parts of London. But it is relatively easy for officials from different Departments to contact each other by telephone or in person. There are also more formal methods of co-ordination. At Ministerial level there is the Cabinet, and the Cabinet Office provides a link with all Departments (see Section 10). Because most policies and government activities involve spending money, the Treasury will often set up inter-departmental committees. These committees will be composed of senior civil servants from the different Departments involved in a particular policy or activity.

(adapted from **Local and Central Government** by Kathleen Allsop (revised by Tim Brennan), Hutchinson, London, 1982, pp. 113-6; **How Britain is Governed** by J. Harvey, Macmillan, Basingstoke and London, 1983, pp. 144-50 and **Introduction to British Politics** by P.J. Madgwick, Hutchinson, London, 1984, pp. 121-2)

1. What are the functions of Government Departments?   (2)
2. Which Government Departments would be mainly responsible for each of the following?
   a Negotiating with Argentina about the future of the Falkland Islands.   (1)
   b Examining the details of a proposed cut in income tax.   (1)
   c Monitoring unemployment levels.   (1)
   d Arranging publicity about the dangers of heroin abuse.   (1)
   e Maintaining records of vehicle ownership.   (1)
3. With the help of the diagram, distinguish between a political appointment and a permanent official.   (4)
4. a Suggest how each of the five Departments referred to in the passage might by involved in, or affected by, a policy to provide youth training schemes.   (5)
   b Give **four** ways which could enable the Departments to work together on such a policy.   (4)

2 Ministers

Most Government Ministers have both **political** and **administrative** tasks to perform. Administratively, they may be responsible for a Government Department. Politically, and especially if they are in the Cabinet, they are part of a team which is collectively responsible for making overall government policy. The political and administrative functions will often overlap. As head of a Government Department a Minister has to see that the civil servants carry out their work in line with Government policy. But he also has to answer to Parliament for the work of his Department. In this way Ministers are the link between Parliament and the Government Departments. The first extract which follows looks at some of the functions of a Minister. The second shows how these functions translate into the everyday work of a Government Minister.

Many of the promises contained in the party's election manifesto are put into operation through Ministers and their Departments. This is particularly true if Acts of Parliament have to be passed. When legislation is under discussion in Parliament, it is the Minister and his junior Minister who 'steer' it through. They must have a complete mastery of the details of the legislation, which usually comes from careful briefing by civil servants. And they must be certain that the broad aims of the party are being carried out. It is easy for a party to say that it will for example 'encourage regional development', but difficult for a Minister to put such a general principle into practice.

The political view of a Minister will be reflected in the instructions and recommendations sent out by his Department. In 1965 for example the Labour Minister of Education issued a Circular to local education authorities asking them to submit plans for comprehensive education. This had been stated as Labour policy in the 1964 election. The Minister followed up the Circular with speeches, television and radio interviews, conferences, visits around the country and meetings with party workers. In this way he tried to further his political views as they applied to the Department's work.

It is especially in the House of Commons that a Minister has to prove his political ability. It is one thing to run a Department in the quiet of a Whitehall office, but quite another to face questioning and criticism in the Commons. At Question Time he will be cross-examined about the actions of his Department, and in full-scale debates he must explain and defend policy. Such political tasks demand certain qualities: the ability to speak well, to translate complicated issues into everyday language and to foresee the political effects of a Department's actions.

Because they are politicians, Ministers are answerable to the public in a more direct way than civil servants. They accept responsibility for the actions of their officials, through questioning and debate in Parliament. Even though a decision might be relatively unimportant, involving a very junior civil servant, the Minister may have to publicly justify what was done. This important convention is known as **Ministerial Responsibility.** (The principle of individual Ministerial responsibility is examined further in 11.3.)

(from **British Government** by Philip Gabriel, Longman, London, 1981, pp. 40, 42-3)

In the following extract James Prior, MP, describes his work as Secretary of State for Employment, a post he occupied from 1979 to 1981.

The roles that Ministers, especially Cabinet Ministers, may perform are multiple and demanding. Each Minister is responsible for everything that is done in his Department. This entails speaking on his Department's behalf in the House of Commons to defend the Department against criticism. He also represents his Department in inter-departmental negotiations and at Cabinet. In Cabinet he is expected to take a share of the general responsibility for decisions.

Another role of a Minister is spokesman and chief negotiator with all those groups and bodies affected by departmental measures. For example over the past few months I had consultations with the Manpower Services Commission, the Trades Union Congress, the Confederation of British Industry and other interested bodies before announcing a package of measures in the House of Commons.

A Minister is also expected to contribute to Cabinet discussions on matters not directly connected with his own Department, e.g. developments in Northern Ireland or the Fourth TV channel. In addition a Minister has another role unconnected with his Department, i.e. as a constituency MP. I am a Member of Parliament for Lowestoft and represent between 60,000 and 70,000 constituents.

A Minister's job differs in important respects from that of an MP. In addition to dealing with people, he must also deal with mountains of paperwork. Instead of dealing with close associates personally, he must delegate many tasks to civil servants without losing influence on their actions. As Ministers have collective responsibility for all Government policy they are precluded from putting Questions down in the House which is the privilege of an ordinary backbencher. He has, however, the advantage of discussing with his Cabinet colleagues responsible, any matter that is causing concern in his constituency. As you will see from my weekly programme each day I set aside a period when I can deal with my constituency post with my House of Commons secretary, Jane Knocker. Most Members of Parliament's homes are in their constituencies. Mine is at Brampton, but as a Cabinet Minister I am required to have a permanent residence in London. My wife and I live in London five days a week and return to our home in the constituency most weekends, where I usually have a constituency meeting or function to attend.

At the end of each working day at the office, I take with me a bag containing letters for signature, departmental submissions on matters of policy, Cabinet papers, etc., which I deal with in the House of Commons after my evening engagements or before breakfast the following morning. In my room at the House there is a closed-circuit TV set which records the proceedings going on in the Chamber which enables me while I am working to keep in touch with what is going on in the House.

SECRETARY OF STATE

YOUR ENGAGEMENTS FOR THE WEEK COMMENCING ON MONDAY 1 DECEMBER ARE AS FOLLOWS

MONDAY 1

9.30	Arrive Denham
10.45	Jane Knocker
11.45	MM – Conference Room A Cabinet Office
12.45 for 1.00	Lunch: Lady Plowden – IBA 70 Brompton Road, SW3 (with Richard Dykes)

3.00	RAYNER PROJECT – Mr Patrick Jenkins, Mrs L Chalker, Lord Gowrie, Mr Lester, Sir Derek Rayner, Permanent Secretary, Mr Otton (DHSS), Sir Richard O'Brien, Mr Derx, Mr Cassels, Mr Oglesby (DHSS) Mr McGuiness plus the Rayner team
6.15	John Deere Travel Award – Warwick South Earls Court (SPEECH)
7.45	Richard Cooper's Smithfield Show
for	Dinner – Claridges Dress: Dinner Jacket
8.15	
HOUSE:	TWO LINE WHIP Vote 10.00PM (pair required)
	Industry Bill: 2nd Reading

TUESDAY 2

8.15	Jane Knocker – Morpeth Mansions
9.00	DE Ministers
9.30	Backbenchers
10.00	Mr. Gordon Leak (News of the World), Interview – Caxton House
11.00	Mr Nicholas Winterton – Caxton House
12.00	Memorial Service for Lord Netherthorpe St Pauls Church Wilton Place, Knightsbridge.
1.15	British Textile Rental Association – Dining Room A House of Commons (SPEECH)
2.45	Lowestoft Delegation – Room 22 House of Commons (Jane Knocker to meet)
3.00	Mr John Cousins Mr Ipe (NEDO): Tyre Industry – Caxton House
4.00	Professor Matthews and Mr Rhode James – Caxton House
5.00	Hampshire School Trust – 23 Melton Court
6.30	Anne Lapping (The Economist): Interview Caxton House
7.00	Food Industries Consumer Council Dinner
for	Lockets (with Mr Silvester and Mr Gilbert)
7.30	(Dress: Informal)
HOUSE:	THREE LINE WHIP Vote 10.00 PM
	British Telecommunications Bill: 2nd Reading
	National Health Service (Charges for Drugs and Appliances) Regulations

WEDNESDAY 3

8.30	Mr. Saunders – Caxton House
10.00	NEDC – Millbank
1.00	LUNCH: Federation of Personnel Services – Westminster Cathedral Conference Centre (with Richard Dykes) (SPEECH)
3.00	MM – Large Ministerial Conference Room House of Commons (Mrs Prior: Waldegrave Christening – Crypt House of Commons)
4.00	Jane Knocker – Room 22
4.30	Lowestoft Delegation EETPU – Room 22 (Jane Knocker to meet)
5.00	Mr T Thompson – Caxton House
6.30	Bow Group Meeting – House of Commons (Speech) followed by Dinner – Carlton Club (with Rob Shepherd)

How does he manage to get through the day?

HOUSE:	<u>THREE LINE WHIP</u> Vote 9.30
	European Assembly Elections Bill: 2nd Reading TWO LINE WHIP (Pair required)
	Motions on European Documents on Aids to Shipbuilding; Excise Duties on Beer Wine and Alcohol

THURSDAY 4

8.30	Jane Knocker – Caxton House
9.00	DE Ministers
9.30	PM – No 10 Downing Street
10.30	CABINET
1.00	LUNCH: Mr D Perry (Sunday Express) Stafford Hotel
3.00	Briefing: First for Questions – Mr Mayhew, Mr Lester, Mr Silvester, Mr Shepherd
3.45	Lord Davis of Leek – Caxton House
6.00	Leave London by car for Southend (with Mrs Prior)
7.30	Trainee of the Year Competition – Southend College of Technology (SPEECH) followed by Mayor's Reception

HOUSE: THREE LINE WHIP Vote 10.00 PM
                Opposition Motion on Decline of the British Engineering Industry

FRIDAY 5
11.00   Miss Cresswell, Sunday Times Magazine – Brampton
3.00   Lowestoft Port Co-ordinating Committee – Council Chamber Lowestoft Town Hall
4.30   Fish Producers Organization – Lowestoft Town Hall
7.30   Dinner: Mr & Mrs Mitchell
HOUSE: TWO LINE WHIP (Pair Required)
                Second Report from Select Committee on Social Services, Session 1979/80 Perinatal and Neonatal Mortality

SATURDAY 6
9.30   Beccles   )
10.30   Halesworth)   SURGERIES
11.30   Southwold)

(from 'Note on some of the duties of a Cabinet Minister and Member of Parliament' provided by The Rt. Hon. James Prior, MP, and reproduced with permission)

1. From the list of James Prior's engagements, identify
   a a meeting with a pressure group   (1)
   b a meeting with a member of the press   (1)
   c a vote in the House of Commons for which the Minister's
      attendance was essential.   (1)
2. Describe the tasks of a Cabinet Minister in relation to
   a his or her Department   (2)
   b Parliament   (2)
   c the Cabinet   (2)
   d his or her party   (2)
   e the mass media and the public   (2)
3. From the extracts give an example of how the political and
   administrative functions of a Minister can overlap.   (3)
4. The former Cabinet Minister Richard Crossman pointed out
   that it is difficult for a Departmental Minister to avoid
   becoming too specialized in the work of his own Department.
   What are the dangers of this situation?   (4)

3 Ministers and civil servants (1)

'It's not my job to care. That's what politicians are for. It's my job to carry out government policy.'
'Even if you think it's wrong?'
'Almost all government policy is wrong,' he remarked obligingly, 'but frightfully well carried out.'

(from **Yes Minister: Volume 3** by Jonathan Lynn and Antony Jay, British Broadcasting Corporation, London, 1983, p. 116)

Government Ministers often do not remain attached to the same Government Department for very long. The average stay is a little over two years. They may be moved to another job by the Prime Minister as part of a general reshuffle. And if their party is defeated in a general election they will no longer be in the government at all. Ministers therefore rely on their civil servants, the permanent officials, for specialist knowledge and detailed advice on the work in their Department. They will work closely with the permanent secretary, the chief official of their Department, and with their principal private secretary. Over time, certain conventions developed concerning the relationship between Ministers and senior civil servants. But as the following extract suggests, some of these appear to have been changing. The traditional view that civil servants merely advise the Minister, and carry out his instructions, is also questioned.

The Minister is the politician. It is his or her job — either individually or with other Ministers — to make policy decisions. Senior civil servants are there to **advise** the Minister, to suggest alternative ways of achieving the Government's aims, and to point out potential difficulties. This is the traditional view. However, it is not always possible to make a clear distinction between **deciding** on a policy and **advising** about it. The type of advice offered may limit the scope for decision, for example. It may lead towards one decision rather than another. Offering specialist advice may therefore give the officials some influence over the policy.

Once a policy has been decided upon, it is the task of the civil servant to see that it is carried out. But, again, it may not be easy to distinguish between **making** policy and **administering** it. The way in which a policy is implemented may itself involve a series of further decisions. These decisions may have political implications, particularly when unforeseen difficulties occur.

Nevertheless, the **convention of individual Ministerial responsibility** means that it is the Minister who has to account for the activities of the civil servants in his Department. It used to be the case that a Minister was held personally and fully responsible for any mistake or incompetence that occured in his Department — even if he had not been aware of it at the time. If Parliament thought the matter sufficiently serious, the Minister would be expected to resign. However, the convention is no longer interpreted so strictly. Nowadays a Minister is regarded as **answerable** to Parliament for his Department's work. He would have to try to explain to Parliament why a particular mistake or event occurred. But he would not normally have to take the full blame for decisions taken by civil servants that he could not be expected to have known about. Besides, whether or not a Minister resigns will probably depend more on the feelings of his party, than Parliament.

Because of the traditional view that civil servants merely advised and administered, it was thought that they should remain anonymous and the details of their work kept secret. In recent times, however, the activities and identities of officials have become more widely known. Senior civil servants appear before House of Commons select committees. Their work may be subject to investigation by the Ombudsman who produces reports on alleged malpractices (see 11.7). Inside information on the operation of the civil service has also appeared in the published diaries and memoirs of former Ministers. Furthermore, the public has been made aware of certain individual officials who have been found to have leaked documents to MPs or the press.

Do these modifications to the conventions about Minister-senior offical relationships also mean that the traditional idea of a politically neutral civil service should be re-examined? It has been suggested that Margaret Thatcher has shown a greater personal interest than earlier Prime Ministers in the appointments of top civil servants. The Cabinet Secretary, however, has denied that the Prime Minister takes account of the political sympathies of those who are recommended for the top jobs. Civil servants are expected to serve governments of any party with equal loyalty. It is their job to provide impartial advice which is non-party political in form. But even here the dividing line may be unclear. Senior officials will need to be aware of their Minister's political views in order to assist him in making his party's policies, as approved by the Government, effective.

(adapted from 'Ministers and civil servants' by Martin Burch in **British Politics Today** by Bill Jones and Dennis Kavanagh, Manchester University Press, Manchester, 1983, pp. 111-8 with additional information from 'Thatcher's Mandarins', **The Times** 11 July, 1982, p.17 and 'Civil service head rules out system of political appointees' by Valerie Elliott, **Daily Telegraph** 19 June, 1985, p. 2)

1. Civil servants are expected to be 'politically neutral'. What does this involve? (2)
2. a According to the extract, what is the main task of a Government Minister? (1)
   b What are the main tasks of a senior civil servant (2)
   c How might these tasks overlap in practice? (3)
3. a Explain the difference between **individual** and **collective** Ministerial responsibility (see 10.6) (2)
   b How has the convention of individual Ministerial responsibility changed? (2)
4. In October 1984 Clive Ponting, a senior civil servant at the Ministry of Defence, was committed for trial at the Old Bailey:

> He was charged under Section 2 of the 1911 Official Secrets Act. Mr. Ponting sent copies of documents to Mr. Tam Dalyell, MP, which apparently revealed Government plans to withold from MPs details of the sinking of the Argentine battleship *General Belgrano*. He is alleged to have said: 'I did this because I believe ministers in this Department are not prepared to answer legitimate questions from an MP about a matter of considerable public concern simply in order to protect their own political position'. In a sensational verdict on 11 February 1985 the jury unanimously acquitted Clive Ponting.
>
> (from 'Court report', **Social Studies Review,** Preview Edition, March, 1985, p. 10)

Discuss the view that a civil servant should be free to disclose information to MPs if he or she believes a Minister is not acting in the public interest. (8)

4 Ministers and civil servants (2)

The conventions and images of the Minister-civil servant relationship appear to have been changing. Do these changes reveal that the

Clive Ponting, the civil servant from the Ministry of Defence, during his trial at the Old Bailey, February, 1985.

power of Ministers over their Departments is limited? Is it the civil servants who really control the work of government? Several views are expressed in the following extracts. The first presents the opinion of a senior civil servant.

> I think the job of the civil servant is to make sure that the minister is informed; that he has all the facts; that he's made aware of all the options and that he is shown all the considerations bearing on these options. It is then for the minister to take the decision. That is how the system ought to operate and that is how I think, in the vast majority of cases, it does operate.
>
> (Sir Brian Hayes in **No Minister** by Hugo Young and Anne Sloman, British Broadcasting Corporation, London, 1982, p. 21)

The following four extracts are all from former Cabinet Ministers. Their views vary — perhaps reflecting their different experiences with senior civil servants. In the first, James Prior argues that there are a number of things which civil servants can do if they are unhappy with a particular policy.

> They could slow it down by raising constant objections. They could stir up other departments to raise objections when it went to Cabinet Committee or Cabinet. They could have some discreet briefing of various organizations in the country to raise problems. And then lastly, it somehow does get into the newspapers. There would be nods and winks given that the policy was perhaps rather dangerous. If the civil service does get at odds with a minister, then it is not very easy for either to operate very effectively.
>
> (James Prior in **No Minister** by Hugo Young and Anne Sloman, p. 28)

> It's a great mistake to think there's a continous battle going on ... It is very rare that you meet real resistance or obstruction ... Generally, I found it perfectly simple to establish good relations with civil servants.
>
> (Anthony Crosland quoted in 'The Mandarins — Saints or Sinners?' by David V. Kelly, unpublished paper, p. 9)

There are two ways in which officialdom impresses its views

on Ministers. The first pressure comes from inside the Department where the officials try to make one see things in a departmental way. Ministers tend to have **only** a departmental briefing. The second pressure is inter-departmental, coming when the official committee brings its inter-departmental cohesive view to bear on the Ministers in a single official policy paper. I have yet to see a Minister prevail against an inter-departmental official paper without the backing of the Prime Minister ... or the Chancellor. And this is where one's relationship with the PM are so all-important. If one doesn't have his backing, or at least the Chancellor's ..., the chance of winning against the official view is absolutely nil.

But although Cabinet Ministers have this enormous limitation on their power of decision-taking, still their standing is infinitely superior compared with that of the non-Cabinet Minister. The unfortunate Tony Wedgwood Benn as Postmaster-General, Kenneth Robinson as Minister of Health and Peggy Herbison as Minister of Pensions have a far more difficult time than we do. And I am sure they find it much more difficult to impose their views on their civil servants. Because though the discussions of the Cabinet Committees and Cabinet very often don't have much reality and are simply rehearsing departmental points of view, nevertheless we Cabinet Ministers do have status within Whitehall, in Parliament and in the nation at large. A Cabinet Minister counts for something and a leading Cabinet Minister can certainly get his way far more easily than a non-Cabinet Minister, both in his own Department and of course in the Cabinet.

(from **The Diaries of a Cabinet Minister: Volume One** by Richard Crossman, Hamish Hamilton, London and Jonathan Cape, London, 1975, p. 200)

Departments disagree with one another very much ... Defence fights both with the Treasury and with the Foreign Office, to take a very obvious example in the field I know well. I think that a minister who complains that his civil servants are too powerful is either a weak minister or an incompetent one.

(Denis Healey in **No Minister** by Hugo Young and Anne Sloman, p. 25)

The final passage includes the views not of a Minister or of a civil servant, but of a former political adviser to the Labour Government

in the 1970s. In this position he was able to observe the relationship between Ministers and their officials.

True, civil servants do present opposing arguments, but that is their job. They are accused of ganging-up on a Minister, thwarting his attempts to change things by getting civil servants in other Departments to advise their Ministers to oppose the proposed policy. This may happen on occasions, but it is not necessarily a bad thing. Inter-departmental committees are essential because the policies of one Department will affect a number of others. Besides, civil servants owe loyalty not only to their Minister, but to the Government as a whole. It is not always easy to walk this tightrope.

Civil servants are said to manipulate their Ministers by swamping them with trivial information to keep them occupied on unimportant matters. In that way their political bosses are prevented from making any big changes. But some Ministers bring this situation upon themselves. They complain if they have not been informed of a particular decision. In fact some Ministers fail to learn that the vast majority of decisions made in a Government Department can never reach the Minister – there are simply far too many. In any case, if a Minister feels he is being manipulated, he can always manipulate back. He could exclude certain officials from a Minister's meeting, for example. Civil servants don't like that.

(Based in parts on 'Who's in charge in Whitehall?' by David Lipsey, **New Society** 24 April, 1980, pp. 155-7)

1. Which of the extracts provided above is closest to the traditional view of Minister-civil servant relations (as expressed in the passage in 11.3)? Explain your answer.   (2)
2. Which of the **politicians** represented in the extracts gives the most favourable view of civil servants from a Minister's point of view? Explain your answer.   (2)
3. Why are most decisions within a Department taken by civil servants rather than by Ministers?   (2)
4. How does Richard Crossman distinguish between Cabinet and non-Cabinet Ministers in their relations with civil servants?   (4)
5. a Why do inter-departmental committees of civil servants exist?
                                                                (3)
   b Explain how Richard Crossman and James Prior see inter-departmental pressure as a possible source of obstruction to a Minister's plans.   (4)
   c Why might Denis Healey attach less importance to such pressure.   (3)

5 The civil service

Those officials who advise Government Ministers constitute only a tiny proportion of the total number of civil servants. The following extracts examine the civil service as a whole.

The civil service consists of people employed by the central government most of whom work in the Government Departments in London and in their regional or local offices throughout the country. It also contains a number of industrial workers in government establishments such as Royal Ordnance factories (manufacturing armaments) and naval dockyards. It does not include members of the armed forces or employees of nationalized industries and local councils.

Until the nineteenth century, appointment to jobs in the civil service depended largely on influence and there was hardly any attempt to maintain general standards of efficiency. The Northcote-Trevelyan Report, 1854, recommended a system of recruitment by an open competitive examination. In the following years, the Civil Service Commission was set up to conduct such examinations, and in 1870 the system was extended to all the main categories of civil servants.

The nineteenth century reforms provided a body of civil servants selected largely for their educational qualifications and intellectual ability. But it failed to adapt sufficiently to the needs of modern society. Growing criticism in the 1960s led to the appointment of a committee of inquiry under the chairmanship of Lord Fulton. The Fulton Report, 1968, proposed a number of reforms to modernize the system. Its main recommendations can be briefly listed.

1. The creation of a civil service department.
2. A unified structure with more opportunity for promotion to the top.
3. Improved training facilities including management training for higher grades.
4. More opportunity for specialist workers such as scientists to reach top management positions.
5. More open government with less secrecy in the process of administration.

Until the Fulton Report, the civil service as a whole was under the general control of the Treasury. A major change resulting from the report was the transfer of responsibilities for all civil service matters − its organization, recruitment, training, conditions of employment, methods of work and general efficiency − to a specially created Civil Service Department. This Department, however, was disbanded in 1981. The Treasury resumed responsibility for civil service personnel and pay, but promotion and allocation became the duties of a new section within the Cabinet Office.

The service used to be divided into distinct classes with entry closely related to examination levels in the education system. Opportunities for promotion from one class to another were strictly limited. The Fulton Report recommended a unified structure with wider career opportunities. As a result, the main body of civil servants is now consolidated into a unified administration group whose work ranges from routine clerical duties in the lower grades to responsibility for management, control of staff, and advice to Ministers at the top level in each Department.

Main civil service categories

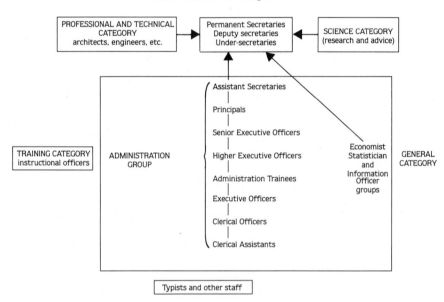

In addition to the categories shown in the diagram, every Department employs messengers, cleaners, and other support workers. There are also groups such as tax inspectors and immigration officers.

Entry into the administration group is now mainly determined by interview, together with school or college records and qualifications. The points of entry are still related to educational levels — normally at the age of sixteen (with O level or equivalent) for clerical officers, and at eighteen (with A level) for executive officers. Higher posts are filled by promotion through the various grades or by selection for the grade of administration trainee. Competition for this grade is open to honours graduates from universities and polytechnics, but trainees are also taken from the executive officer grade. Candidates are put through a series of tests and interviews.

Since the Fulton Report, greater emphasis has been put on the training of civil servants, particularly in higher grades. The earlier attitude was that specialized training was unnecessary because the intellectual and educational standards of civil servants enabled them to adapt to their jobs and learn from experience. This view dated from the nineteenth century and did not take into account the complexity of the problems of modern administration. On a recommendation of the Fulton Committee, a Civil Service College was set up and now provides training courses for higher civil servants covering subjects such as government, economics and management.

(from **Central Government and the Political System** by Keith Marder, Wheaton, Exeter, 1979, pp. 23-6, with minor additons)

The Fulton Committee's proposals were meant to deal with some of the long-standing criticisms levelled at the civil service. Most of their recommendations were accepted, but how much change has really taken place since?

A common criticism is that civil servants are too prone to 'bureaucracy' or 'red tape'. There are thought to be too many rules and regulations and too much form-filling with everything having to be recorded on paper. But one of the reasons for all this is the need to control what civil servants do. In dealing with social security claims or income tax assessments, for example, civil servants are not expected to give preferential treatment to any particular individual. By recording actions, decisions, recommendations, and so on, it should be easy to discover who is responsible if mistakes are made.

Secrecy surrounds the work of the civil service. The Fulton Committee had hoped to see more 'open government'. There have been one or two changes since then. Governments now sometimes produce Green Papers – discussion documents on controversial topics – to give interest groups the opportunity to comment on alternative proposals. But in general there is a growing concern that people do not know enough about the work of Government Departments. There are increasing

demands for more freedom of information and the abolition of parts of the Official Secrets Act (see Section 12.6).

Behind the Fulton Committee's recommendations lay the belief that the structure and training of the civil service had become outdated. Most top civil servants had been educated at public school and at the universities of Oxford and Cambridge. They had high academic qualifications, but not in subjects that prepared them for the administrative and managerial skills required for the work of modern government. Promising civil servants recruited at the lower levels were effectively denied promotion chances to the top grades. In theory, the system is now more open and more in-service training is given. According to Peter Kellner and Lord Crowther Hunt, however, the civil service has changed remarkably little. They argue that the Fulton Committee's proposals only **appear** to have been implemented. In practice they say that the non-specialist, public

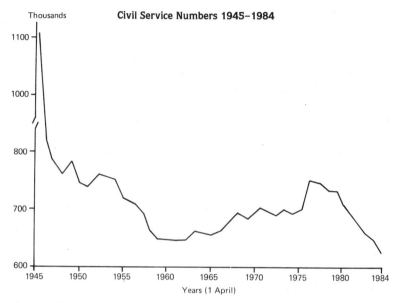

Civil Service Numbers 1945–1984

(Source: 'Economic Progress Reports' No. 168, June, 1984, p. 3 [published by the Treasury] Reproduced with the permission of the Controller of Her Majesty's Stationery Office)

Reduction in civil service numbers

	1 April 1979	1 April 1984	% change 1979–84	target 1 April 1988	% change 1984–8
Defence	247,700	200,000	– 19	170,000	– 15
Energy	1,300	1,100	– 15	1,000	– 9
Treasury, Inland Revenue, Customs & Excise, etc	126,900	113,000	– 11	104,200	– 8
Employment, Manpower Services Commission, etc	53,700	57,700	+ 7	54,000	– 6
Environment	56,000	37,000	– 34	34,600	– 6
Foreign Office	12,000	11,200	– 7	10,500	– 6
Health & Social Security	98,400	90,700	– 8	87,900	– 3
Scottish Office	10,900	9,800	– 10	9,500	– 3
Agriculture	14,000	11,500	– 18	11,300	– 2
Education	2,600	2,400	– 8	2,400	nil
Trade & Industry	19,500	14,950	– 24	14,900	nil
Transport	13,900	14,200	+ 2	14,200	nil
Welsh Office	2,600	2,200	– 15	2,200	nil
Courts, etc	16,500	17,300	+ 5	17,400	+ 1
Home Office	33,500	35,800	+ 7	41,100	+15
ALL CIVIL SERVICE	732,300	624,000	– 15	592,700	– 6

NB. Total includes small departments not listed separately

(Source: **New Society**, 17 January, 1985, p. 89)

school, Oxbridge, upper middle class civil servant still dominates the higher ranks of the civil service. Consequently, the service still suffers from incompetence and poor management. Other observers, however, claim to have noticed the beginnings of a more efficient civil service.

Margaret Thatcher's Government set out to deal with a further criticism – that the civil service was over-staffed. Its aim was to reduce the number of civil servants to 630,000 by 1984 and to under 600,000 by 1988. The extent to which this aim is being achieved can be gauged from the table and graph on page 247.

(adapted from 'Machinations of the mandarins' by Christina Larner, **New Society**, 19 June, 1980, pp. 303-4; **Central Government and the Political System** by Keith Marder, Wheaton, Exeter, 1979, pp. 26-7 and 'Honing down the civil service' by David Thomas, **New Society**, 17 January, 1985, pp. 88-90)

1. In 1984, which Department employed
   a the greatest   (1)
   b the smallest   (1)
   number of civil servants?
2. Is the planned reduction in civil service numbers on target? Explain your answer   (2)
3. a According to the graph, during which period did the sharpest decline in the numbers of civil servants take place?   (1)
   b Why do you think this reduction occurred?   (1)
4. How might
   a a civil servant   (2)
   b a social security claimant   (2)
   respond to the claim that the civil service is 'bureaucratic?'
5. Five of the recommendations of the Fulton Committee are listed in the first extract. Taking each one in turn, say how far the proposals appear to have been implemented.   (10)

6 Delegated legislation

Parliament makes law in the sense that a Bill has to pass through various stages in the House of Commons and the House of Lords. At each stage it must receive a majority vote in its favour before it can proceed further. But only about 100 new laws pass through Parliament in this way each year. These represent only a small fraction of the legislative changes that are made annually. About 2,000 rules and regulations are issued every year from Government Departments in the name of the Minister in charge. These have the force of law although they do not have to go through the various Parliamentary stages of the passage of a Bill.

This situation arises because many of the new laws which have passed through Parliament are general in scope. The appropriate Minister will be given powers in the Act to introduce more detailed provisions later. For example, the 1944 Education Act empowered the Minister responsible for education to raise the school-leaving age to 16 when this was thought appropriate. When this was done (almost thirty years later) the Minister was able to introduce the change without having to steer a new Bill through Parliment. The 1944 Act was a 'parent' Act in which Parliament had delegated to the Minister the power to make certain changes as and when he wished to do so. This type of **delegated legislation** is often made in the form of regulations called **statutory instruments.**

The amount of work that governments do makes some kind of delegated legislation inevitable. Parliament just does not have the time to debate every single change in the law. In any case, many statutory instruments are very technical and may deal with relatively minor matters which do not directly affect most people. They also provide a way in which Ministers can respond quickly to changing circumstances. Passing a Bill through Parliament can take a long time.

It does mean, however, that Ministers, rather than Parliament, are often in a position to make laws directly. In practice, it frequently means more than this. Because of the technical nature of some delegated legislation, it is the civil servants who will prepare the regulations and draw up the statutory instrument. In some cases the Minister may have done little more than put his signature to it.

Parliament does have some control over delegated legislation, although it varies in its extent. With some statutory instruments, both Houses of Parliament have to give their consent before they take effect. Others automatically come into force unless Parliament objects to them within forty days. MPs and peers have to be alert to spot those which may contain something they wish to challenge. Interested pressure groups may be able to discover, and warn MPs or the public, of an order or regulation about to be introduced. There is also a Joint (Commons and Lords) Committee on Statutory Instruments which can draw Parliament's attention to any instrument where, for example, the correct procedures may not have been followed. It cannot do this, however, merely because it questions the merits of the regulations or the policy behind it. Despite these checks there is always the temptation for the Government to use the procedures of delegated legislation to introduce an unpopular measure, as the following extract suggests.

> The Government is planning to sneak a change through Parliament in the next session which would mean sweeping powers for Ministers effectively to tax profitable nationalized industries and set their financial targets in order to raise revenue for the Treasury. To avert open warfare with the state industries, Conservative managers plan to employ the 'negative procedure' to force ministerial orders through the Commons.
>
> Under this procedure, a draft of the statutory order must be laid before the House of Commons. However, if it is not challenged within 40 days, it is passed without discussion. If it is queried by MPs then a 90-minute debate is granted, but this must take place after 10 pm. Given the Government's 143-seat majority it means these Ministerial orders could be made the law of the land with virtually no public scrutiny.
>
> (from 'Treasury to try a sneaky Commons ploy', by Mark Hollingsworth, **New Statesman**, 15 March, 1985, with minor additions)

1. What is
   a delegated legislation?   (1)
   b a statutory instrument?   (1)
   c a 'parent' Act?   (1)
2. Give **three** advantages of delegated legislation   (3)
3. What are the dangers of delegated legislation?   (6)
4. a By what means can Parliament keep a check on statutory instruments?   (3)
   b Giving reasons, say whether or not you think these are adequate.   (5)

7 Individual grievances and the Ombudsman

What protection do individuals have against the action of Government Departments? If an individual feels he or she has been treated wrongly or unfairly by a civil servant, what can be done to remedy the situation? If a Minister or official is thought to have acted illegally, it may be possible to pursue the case in a court of law. But this can be expensive. Disputes on some matters, such as rents, rates and social security benefits, might be resolved by an administrative tribunal (see Section 12.1). But many complaints are not about actions which are illegal or about matters which tribunals can decide. Many concern feelings of injustice or inconvenience thought to be caused by poor administration, such as errors, delay and rudeness. MPs provide a point of contact for constituents with grievances. By speaking to a Minister, writing to the Department, or perhaps even through Question Time, an MP may try to deal with a constituent's complaint. But he may face obstructions in getting the necessary information. And limitations of time and resources prevent lengthy investigations into the more difficult cases. It is on these sorts of occasions that an MP may refer a case to the Ombudsman.

The job of the Ombudsman – or Parliamentary Commissioner for Administration – is to investigate complaints of 'maladministration' by central government departments. The first Commissioner was

Number of completed investigations by the Ombudsman

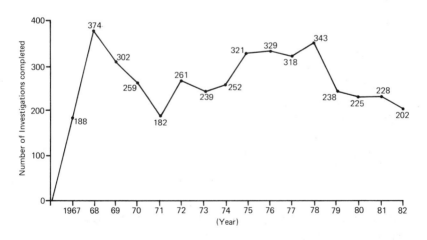

(from 'The Ombudsman: jurisdiction, power and practice' by C. M. Clothier, Manchester Statistical Society, 1980, p. 10 and updated from **Social Trends 14**, 1984, HSMO, p. 164, reproduced with the permission of the Controller of Her Majesty's Stationery Office)

appointed following the Parliamentary Commissioner Act 1967. (Since 1973 the Commissioner has also acted as the Health Service Ombudsman – investigating complaints about the National Health Service. Local Commissioners of Administration have also been appointed as local government ombudsmen.) The annual numbers of completed inquiries undertaken by the Parliamentary Commissioner are shown in the graph on page 251. The usual procedure for adopting, investigating and reporting on a complaint is indicated in the diagram opposite. The following extract describes the functions and powers of the Parliamentary Commissioner, assesses his achievements and presents some suggestions for changes to the job.

Originally the Parliamentary Commissioner for Administration could only investigate complaints passed on to him by an MP. More recently he has looked into cases sent directly to him, but only after the MP has been consulted. Over half the complaints referred to the Ombudsman cannot be investigated because they do not come within his jurisdiction. He can only inquire into those cases where a person claims to have suffered an injustice due to **maladministration** by a Government Department. 'Maladministration' can include actions which are illegal, corrupt or deliberately biased, but the most common complaints are about allegations of delay, discourtesy and incorrect calculations of tax demands or social security benefits. Some complaints, such as many of those from prisoners, allege a denial of basic rights. Other grievances are more difficult to classify – such as the complaint from a schoolboy about his pet falcon being confiscated by the Department of the Environment.

By no means all the complaints looked into are found to be justified. In 1979, the example, the Ombudsman upheld 38% of those investigated. A further 18% resulted in some criticism of the actions of Departments even though the main complaint was not accepted. This means that in 44% of cases the Ombudsman found no justification for the complaint.

In carrying out an investigation, the Ombudsman can require a Minister or civil servant to provide information and relevant

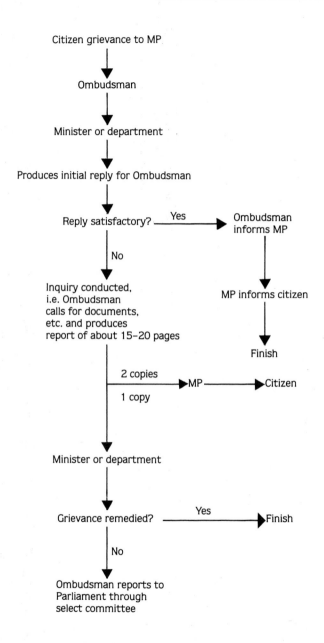

Citizen grievance to MP

Ombudsman

Minister or department

Produces initial reply for Ombudsman

Reply satisfactory? —— Yes ——▶ Ombudsman informs MP

No

Inquiry conducted, i.e. Ombudsman calls for documents, etc. and produces report of about 15–20 pages

MP informs citizen

Finish

2 copies ——▶ MP ——▶ Citizen

1 copy

Minister or department

Grievance remedied? —— Yes ——▶ Finish

No

Ombudsman reports to Parliament through select committee

(from **Examining British Politics** by A.J. Baker, Hutchinson, London, 1984, p. 140)

documents. He also has the power to call witnesses. If a complaint is found to be justified the Ombudsman will contact the Government Department concerned suggesting that an appropriate remedy is provided. The Department may be asked to re-think a decision which the Commissioner believes was unfair, or to review the procedures which led to the decision. In some cases the Ombudsman may propose that a payment be made to a complainant to compensate for expenses incurred. In many cases, however, the only remedy available is a formal apology and an agreement to try not to make the same type of mistake again. The Commissioner cannot force the Minister or Department to accept his suggestions. He can only **recommend.**

The results of investigations are also reported to the MPs concerned. In addition, the Ombudsman prepares annual reports for both Houses of Parliament. Particularly important cases may be considered by the Select Committee on the Parliamentary Commissioner for Administration, which reports to Parliament. This committee can also examine Ministers and senior civil servants if their Department does not implement a recommendation of the Ombudsman. In the end, it is to Parliament that a Minister is answerable for what goes on in his Department.

Some people believe that the Ombudsman does not have enough power to deal with grievances. The organization **Justice** would like him to be given the power to investigate 'unreasonable, unjust or oppressive action' in addition to 'maladministration'. It also suggests that he should be able to recommend appropriate changes in the law. A further proposal is that the Ombudsman should deal more directly with the public. He should be able to investigate far more on his own initiative and not have to rely so much on referrals from, or the agreement of, a Member of Parliament.

Nevertheless, a former Parliamentary Commissioner – Cecil Clothier – believes that a good deal has already been achieved. Many people have had their complaints thoroughly and independently examined. Some have obtained remedies of one sort or another. Improvements to administrative procedures have been adopted following the Ombudsman's investigations. The fact that civil servants are aware that their actions may be investigated has probably prevented the need for some complaints in the first place. But Cecil Clothier has expressed

'Is that the Ombudsman. I don't like the Government. What are you going to do about it?'

concern that not all grievances may be reaching the Ombudsman. This could be due to people not being aware of his existence or to some MPs not making the best use of his services.

(adapted from 'The Ombudsman: jurisdiction, powers and practice', address by C.M. Clothier to the **Manchester Statistical Society,** 12 March, 1980 and 'Marginal note' by Martin Kettle, **New Society,** 28 February, 1980, pp. 450-1)

1. Identify **four** ways by which individuals may be able to have their complaints about the actions of central government investigated?

(2)

2. a How many times between 1967 and 1982 did the annual number of completed investigations by the Ombudsman exceed 300? (1)

   b In 1979, in what proportion of the cases investigated did the Ombudsman find at least some justification for complaint?(1)

3. a In investigating grievances, what advantages does the Ombudsman have over an individual MP? (3)

   b At what stages in the Ombudsman's work may MPs be involved? (3)

4. a What limitations are there to the powers of the Parliamentary Commissioner? (3)

   b In what ways could his job be made more effective? (3)

5. How might

   a a civil servant (2)

   b an MP (2)

   respond to proposals to strengthen the Ombudsman's powers?

Section 12 Law, Order and Civil Rights

Previous sections have examined how laws and policies are made and how they are administered. This section looks at how laws are enforced. It examines how the legal system, the courts and the police are organized. It assesses the role played by judges and the police in the political system. The second half concentrates on the relationship between the law and individual rights and freedoms. The section is mainly concerned with the system of law in England and Wales. Scotland has a separate legal system.

1 The courts

It is the job of the courts to decide whether laws have been broken and, in criminal cases, to administer punishment if they have. The system of courts in England and Wales is shown in the diagrams and extracts which follow. It involves the possibility of **appeals** from a lower court to a higher one. For example, someone may have been found guilty of an offence by a magistrates court. If he thinks the magistrates made a legal or factual error in reaching their decision, he may be able to appeal to a higher court.

The organization of the courts system also reflects the distinction between **civil** law and **criminal** law. Criminal law is concerned with behaviour of which the State disapproves, such as murder, rape or theft. Civil law regulates relationships between individuals or individual organizations. For instance, it deals with the making of contracts and wills. A person found guilty of a criminal offence will be punished in some way on behalf of the State – perhaps by imprisonment or a fine. Punishments are not given for breaches of the civil law. Instead, the courts can award 'damages' to one party in a dispute to compensate for any losses.

Civil courts in England and Wales

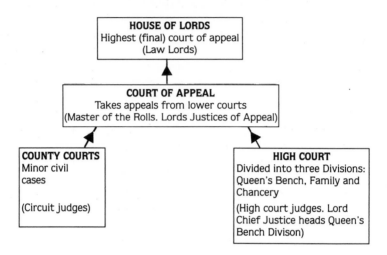

HOUSE OF LORDS
Highest (final) court of appeal
(Law Lords)

COURT OF APPEAL
Takes appeals from lower courts
(Master of the Rolls. Lords Justices of Appeal)

COUNTY COURTS
Minor civil
cases

(Circuit judges)

HIGH COURT
Divided into three Divisions:
Queen's Bench, Family and
Chancery

(High court judges. Lord
Chief Justice heads Queen's
Bench Divison)

Criminal courts in England and Wales

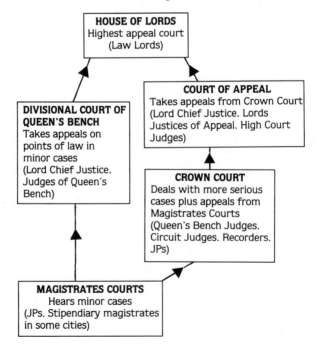

HOUSE OF LORDS
Highest appeal court
(Law Lords)

COURT OF APPEAL
Takes appeals from Crown Court
(Lord Chief Justice. Lords
Justices of Appeal. High Court
Judges)

**DIVISIONAL COURT OF
QUEEN'S BENCH**
Takes appeals on
points of law in
minor cases
(Lord Chief Justice.
Judges of Queen's
Bench)

CROWN COURT
Deals with more serious
cases plus appeals from
Magistrates Courts
(Queen's Bench Judges.
Circuit Judges. Recorders.
JPs)

MAGISTRATES COURTS
Hears minor cases
(JPs. Stipendiary magistrates
in some cities)

Civil courts

Less important cases are heard in County Courts staffed by judges who work in an area or a circuit. More important cases go to the High Court which is staffed by about 70 High Court Judges. The High Court is divided into three divisions, each of which specializes in certain types of cases. Most come before the Queen's Bench Division, headed by the Lord Chief Justice. In the County and High Courts, most cases are heard by a judge without a jury. Appeals from the County Courts and the High Court go to the Civil division of the Court of Appeal. This consists of the Master of the Rolls and 14 specialist judges called Lord-Justices-of-Appeal. Since appeals usually involve important and complex cases, three judges normally sit in this court. Where either the Court of Appeal or the House of Lords itself gives permission, there may be a final appeal to the highest court in the land which is the House of Lords. This consists of the most senior judges, the 'Law Lords'. Ordinary members of the House of Lords play no part in this work. It frequently overturns the decisions of the lower courts and its decisions are binding on those courts and thus have the status of **common law** [see Section 12.2].

Criminal courts

The great majority of criminal cases are relatively minor and carry punishments of fines, community service, probation or at most three months in jail. These come before local magistrates courts which are staffed by unpaid 'lay' Justices of the Peace (JPs). They are described as lay because JPs are not required to be legally qualified. There are about 18,000 JPs, most of whom sit for one or two half-days per week. They are not elected, but appointed by the Lord Chancellor on the advice of local Advisory Committees which work in secret and tend to receive most nominations from local political parties.

The system of appointing JPs has been criticized for being secret and for giving considerable power without public accountability. The ranks of the JPs have also been criticized for being dominated by middle-aged and middle-class males, and local Advisory Committees have been instructed to try for a more balanced social and sexual mix. In some of the larger cities full-time legally qualified magistrates called stipendiaries have been appointed. In addition to minor cases these courts, which never sit with a jury, also hold committal proceedings to establish whether a more serious case appears to exist for referral to the Crown Courts.

Crown Courts are staffed either by judges or by Recorders assisted by JPs. A Recorder is a practising barrister or solicitor who acts in this capacity part-time and deals with minor cases. The more serious cases are heard by judges who sit with a jury. A jury is a group of 12 ordinary citizens selected at random to hear cases. They are supposed to listen to the cases put by the 'prosecution' which is trying to convict the persons accused of the crimes, and the 'defence' which is trying to prove their innocence. They then have to decide whether the accused are guilty or not. When the jury has reached that decision, which must usually be unaminous (although the judge may accept a majority verdict of 10 to 2), the judge decides the punishment. The right to trial by jury is a long-established custom in English criminal law and relates to the principle of 'trial by equals'.

Appeal in less serious cases on points of law lies from the magistrates court to the divisional court. Other appeals are to Crown Courts, and from there to the Court of Appeal. The final appeal is to the House of Lords.

The courts in Scotland are basically similar in structure to those in England and Wales. There is a network of District courts which are equivalent to English magistrates courts, with JPs appointed by the Scottish Courts Administration. More serious cases are heard by Sherriffs courts. The highest civil court in Scotland is the Court of Session and the supreme criminal court is the High Court of Justiciary.

(from **Public Administration in the United Kingdom: An Introduction** by David Farnham and Malcolm McVicar, Cassell, London, 1982, pp. 161–4, with minor addition)

Other courts and tribunals
In addition to criminal and civil courts there are several other important courts, tribunals and other methods of settling disputes. With the increase in social, welfare and employment legislation it has become the practice to direct disputes arising out of such legislation away from the ordinary courts to specialized tribunals. For example, Social Security tribunals

deal with disputes arising out of an individual's entitlement to social security benefits. Rent tribunals deal with certain disputes arising out of the letting of private houses, for example deciding what amounts to a 'reasonable rent'. These tribunals have the advantage of being quick, cheap to run, accessible to ordinary citizens and having specialists in the particular area of law to settle the disputes. They are, however, sometimes criticized for being secretive and of being biased towards the interests of the State. Tribunals are not courts as such in that they are not presided over by a judge and they may only hear specific categories of disputes assigned to them by Parliament.

The European Court of Justice was established to adjudicate upon matters arising out of European Community law. It is possible for an English court to refer a matter to the European Court for interpretation. The European Court is technically the highest authority upon matters of European law and its decisions are binding upon all of our courts, even the House of Lords.

(from **The Legal Framework: Law and the Individual** by K. R. Bradley and R. A. Clark, Holt, Rinehart and Winston, Eastbourne, 1983, pp. 51–4)

1. Distinguish between
   a criminal law and civil law   (2)
   b a JP and a stipendiary   (2)
   c a court of law and a tribunal   (2)
2. a Give **two** functions of a magistrates court.   (2)
   b What criticisms can be made of magistrates courts?   (3)
3. a The House of Lords is the highest court of appeal in the country. What does this mean?   (1)
   b In what way is the authority of the House of Lords (as a court) affected by the European Court of Justice?   (2)
4. Suggest arguments for and against the use of juries in criminal cases.   (6)

2 The courts and politics

Section 7 introduced the idea that legislative, executive and judicial powers should to some extent be separate in order to prevent one person or group from gaining absolute power. Later sections have suggested a considerable overlap between the legislature and the executive. It is commonly thought, however, that in accordance with the rule of law the judiciary – the courts – remains largely independent (see 7.4). By this it is usually meant that judges are not influenced by governments in making their decisions on individual cases that come before them. The courts are also expected to be impartial in administering justice. Does this mean that judges do not or should not allow their own prejudices to interfere with their judgements? Or does it mean that judges are or should be politically neutral?

Such questions are taken up in the following extract, adapted from the work of J. A. G. Griffith. It looks at how the judiciary fits into the British political system as a whole. Professor Griffith is especially concerned with those cases where the courts are called upon to deal with matters of public controversy. These have included industrial relations, protests against authority by students or minority groups, police powers, and cases involving individual rights and freedom.

All judges are appointed to their jobs by, or on the advice of, senior politicians (the Lord Chancellor and the Prime Minister). Once appointed, however, all senior judges can remain in office until they reach the age of 75. They cannot be removed from their jobs by the government of the day. This helps to preserve the independence of judges in reaching decisions on individual cases. Nevertheless, judges are dependent on the Lord Chancellor for promotion to jobs in the higher courts. This must mean that outside pressures exist in a **general** way:

> For example, a judge who requires a reputation among his seniors for being 'soft' in certain types of cases where the Lord Chancellor . . . and other senior judges favour a hard line is as likely to damage his promotion prospects as he would if his appointment were found to be unfortunate on other more obvious grounds. (p.29)

If judges could automatically apply the law as passed by Parliament to individual cases, there would be no problem. But the job involves far more. The judges themselves 'make law'. **Statute law** (Acts of Parliament) has to be **interpreted** by the judges so it can be applied to the particular case they are dealing with. At the same time they are making **common law**. Common law is the accumulation of principles that are formed as judges make their decisions. Common law can be overturned by new statute law made by Parliament. But unless and until it is, it is supposed to be followed by the courts where relevant.

Nevertheless, judges are expected to be impartial and to be seen to be so. But it is generally believed within the legal profession that certain judges are more likely than others to be biased against certain groups or certain kinds of action. On occasions particular judges have been reprimanded by the Lord Chancellor for comments they have made in court. But judges are human and they have human prejudices. Even so, judicial opinion does not seem to spread over a wide political spectrum. It tends to be limited to a range from right-wing Labour to 'that part of the right which is associated with traditional Toryism'.

However, it is not the personal political beliefs of judges that really matter. It is the role they perform in the political system, and how they see their role, that is important. Professor Griffith is not suggesting that in political or controversial cases judges deliberately make decisions in their own interests or those of their class. He believes that they act in what they see as the interests of society as a whole. But their perceptions of this general public interest could well be influenced by the social background from which most of them come and the limited social circles in which they move. The vast majority of senior judges are from the upper or upper-middle classes, have been to Oxford or Cambridge universities, and attended public schools. They share a common background, habits and views with others of the relatively small group of people occupying positions of power in the political system. This tends to reduce the degree to which the judiciary is separate from the goverment. The courts are not opposite to the government. In practice, in most circumstances they are placed alongside it. 'Judges are part of the machinery of authority within the State and as such cannot avoid the making of political decisions.' (p.195). This is seen, for example, in the favourable attitudes of the judiciary to private property and goverment secrecy, and their dislike of trade unions and demonstrations and protests.

(adapted from **The Politics of the Judiciary** by J.A.G. Griffith, Fontana, 1985)

1. a Distinguish between statute law and common law.   (2)
   b Explain how judges can be said to **make** law.   (2)
2. a In what sense can judges be seen as independent from the government?   (2)
   b Give **one** way by which this independence is maintained.   (2)
3.   So far as this country is concerned, . . . every judge on his appointment discards all politics and all prejudices. The judges of England have always in the past – and I hope always will – be vigilant in guarding our freedoms. Someone must be trusted. Let it be the judges.
        (Lord Denning, Master of the Rolls, 1980)

        The habits you are trained in, the people with whom you mix, lead to your having a certain class of ideas of such a nature that, when you have to deal with other ideas, you do not give as sound and accurate judgements as you would wish. This is one of the great difficulties at present with Labour. Labour says 'Where are your impartial Judges? They all move in the same circle as the employers, and they are all educated and nursed in the same ideas as the employers. How can a labour man or a trade unionist get impartial justice?' It is very difficult sometimes to be sure that you have put yourself into a thoroughly impartial position between two disputants, one of your own class and one not of your own class.
        (Lord Justice Scrutton, 1920)

        (Both quotations reprinted in **Politics of the Judiciary** by J. A. G. Griffith)

   a Explaining your answer, say which of these two views is closer to those expressed by Professor Griffith.   (4)
   b Discuss Professor Griffith's claim that it is not possible for judges to be politically neutral.   (8)

3 The police

MPs are directly accountable to the electorate in the sense that their constituents can decide to vote for another candidate at the next election. The Government is indirectly accountable in that it is answerable to Parliament (which includes the elected representatives). Civil servants are under the control of Government Ministers. Judges, however, are neither directly nor indirectly accountable to the electorate. They are appointed not elected. They are not answerable to Parliament.

What about the police? The police are responsible for the day-to-day enforcement of the criminal law. They are expected to prevent crime, to apprehend those who break the law, and to maintain order in society. In 1984, 3.5 million 'serious' offences were recorded in England and Wales. The 'clear-up' rate for certain crimes, such as those involving 'violence against the person', was over 70%. For others it was considerably lower – robbery (22%) and criminal damage (35%), for instance. But to whom are the police answerable for the way in which they carry out their functions and for their effectiveness in doing so? The following passage examines this question of police accountability.

> There are 52 police forces in the UK with a total of about 142,000 police officers. The Metropolitan Police, which covers most of London, is the largest force with 27,000. Less than 1% of all police officers are from ethnic minority groups and only 9% are women. The great majority of police are uniformed officers. About 15% are employed as CID (Criminal Investigation Department) officers. In 1983 the total cost of policing in England and Wales came to £2.5 billion. It is paid for out of taxes and local rates.
>
> Outside the Metropolitan Police area, the police forces in England and Wales are by law answerable to the public through their **police authorities**. Police authorities are committees composed of two-thirds local councillors (who have been elected by the public) and one-third magistrates (who are not elected). They have a legal responsibility to maintain 'an adequate and efficient police force'. However, they have no control over 'operational matters'. Operational control lies with the Chief Constables. A Chief Constable is obliged only to 'inform' his police authority of decisions he labels as 'operational'. Sometimes he doesn't even need to do that. In any case, 'operational matters' and 'policy matters' are not always clearly distinguishable. In practice, this can give Chief Constables a great deal of scope and leave the police authorities relatively powerless. The authorities' duties do include appointing and disciplining senior police officers, setting the overall size of the force, and approving the police budget. But it is the Chief Constables who decide on the style

and strategies of policing for their areas. It would be very difficult for a police authority to dismiss a Chief Constable with whom it seriously disagreed.

However limited police accountability may be in the rest of the country, there is no local control at all over the Metropolitan Police. The police in most of London come under the direct responsibility of the Home Secretary. The Home Secretary also has some powers over the other police forces in England and Wales. He approves the appointments of top police officers and can make regulations affecting police recruitment, promotion and discipline. Guidance to local police forces is also provided through Home Office circulars.

Police activity in certain events over recent years has provoked accusations of a growing 'political' or even 'military' police in Britain. These events have included the inner-city riots such as those in Toxteth in 1981, Brixton in 1981 and 1985, and Handsworth and Tottenham in 1985. The mass policing of some industrial disputes has been accompanied by violent clashes between police and pickets. Other incidents, such as the Wiltshire police operation to prevent the hippy Peace Convoy from reaching Stonehenge in 1985, have also led to complaints about excessive use of force by the police. Questions have been raised about the increased police control of political demonstrations. There is evidence of greater police surveillance, and concern about the activities of the Special Branch (which is not under the control of local police authorities, but the responsibility of the Home Secretary). There have been worries about the increased issue of firearms to the police. In two separate incidents a five-year old boy was shot dead and a woman seriously wounded, both in their own homes. On another occasion, the police seriously injured a man they had mistaken for an escaped prisoner.

A combined effect of these developments has been to increase the demands for more democratic control over Britain's police forces. In some areas Chief Constables themselves have responded by introducing or extending their arrangements for community policing. Community policing involves a greater public presence of police officers in local areas – often on foot rather than in Panda cars. It can also involve the setting up of local police-community consultative committees. These committees give representatives of the

'Nothing for you to bother about councillor...purely an operational matter.'

public the chance to express community views and to hear police explanations of their policing strategies. They do not, however, give local communities **control** of police activities. Community policing is partly designed to reduce crime or increase the clear-up rate and partly to foster better relations with the public. Some believe that the two objectives are in any case connected. From other senior police officers the response has been to demand even greater police powers. Some of these have been granted under the Police and Criminal Evidence Act 1984. They argue that more powers are needed to combat increased crime including the growing number of incidents connected with international terrorism.

In **What is to be done about Law and Order?**, John Lea and Jock Young argue in favour of a better organized and more effective system of local democratic accountability of the

A political police force? The nationally co-ordinated police operations against striking miners during the 1984-5 coal industry dispute raised questions about the role of the police in political and industrial matters. This photograph was taken at the Orgreave Coke Works in June, 1984.

police. They believe this is essential 'for restoring mutual respect and trust between police and community'. It is also required, they claim, to create an environment in which the most deprived sections of the community can express their grievances (which are often about police matters). The authors recognize, however, that there are objections to their view. First, there is the belief that more local control could lead to the direction of policing being influenced by unrepresentative local groups. Secondly, there is the argument that policing policy is a technical matter which should be left in the hands of the professionals – the Chief Constables. Thirdly, there are those who accept the advantage of close contact between the police and local communities. But rather than risking the problems associated with local democratic control, they believe this contact can be achieved through more community policing.

(adapted in part from 'The police take a political road' by Martin Kettle, **New Society**, 28 February, 1980, pp.444–5; **What is to be done about Law and Order?** by J. Lea and J. Young, Penguin, Harmondsworth, 1984, Chapter 7 and 'Your rights and the police', **Which?**, May, 1985, pp. 226–30)

1. Explain why Londoners do not have the same say in local police matters as people in other parts of the country.   (2)
2. a Outline the difference in responsibilities between a police authority and its Chief Constable.   (2)
   b How might this division of responsibilities lead to conflict between the two?   (3)
3. a Identify two elements involved in 'community policing'.   (2)
   b How does community policing differ from local democratic control of the police?   (2)
4. a Suggest ways in which greater democratic control over the police could be achieved.   (3)
   b What problems might result?   (3)
   c In your view, would greater police accountability be justified? Explain your answer.   (3)

4 Public order and freedom of assembly

One of the areas in which police activity has increased in recent years concerns public order. On the one hand there is a need to protect members of the public from any harm caused by crowd behaviour. On the other is the question of the rights of people to meet freely with others and to engage in legitimate protest. The first extract which follows looks at legal and other restrictions to these rights.

Freedom of association and assembly refers to the right of individuals to join organizations and to participate in public meetings, demonstrations and protest marches. There are, however, many restrictions. The Public Order Act 1936 outlawed private armies and the wearing of political uniforms

Sir Oswald Mosely leader of the British Union of Fascists (London, 1936). The violent activities of the British Fascists were a major reason for the introduction of the Public Order Act in 1936.

in public. It also introduced other measures to regulate the conduct of public meetings and demonstrations. For instance it made it illegal to use threatening, abusive or insulting words or behaviour. A major reason behind this Act was to control the activities of the British Union of Fascists in the 1930s who committed violent acts against ethnic minorities to pursue political aims. A common charge arising out of political demonstrations (and brought under the Police Act 1964) is the wilful obstruction of police officers in the execution of their duty.

Under the common law, individuals can be charged with unlawful assembly and riot. During the 1984–5 coal industry dispute a number of miners were charged with riot offences but later had these charges against them dropped. The Conservative Government's employment legislation of the early 1980s can also be used to restrict freedom of assembly in industrial disputes. Under these Acts, for example, the activities of 'flying pickets' are made illegal and the number of pickets at a workplace can be reduced to six. The police and local authorities also have powers to ban certain meetings in some circumstances, and the police can decide the routes to be taken by marches.

In addition to legal controls and police powers, the effectiveness of meetings or demonstrations can be reduced in other ways. Hostile media campaigns against certain groups or proposed courses of action may produce this result. Trade union activities, for example, are often treated unfavourably in the press which has, on occasions, been forced to print corrections and apologies about inaccurate reporting.

(adapted from **The Legal Framework: Law and the Individual** by K. R. Bradley and R. A. Clark, Holt, Rinehart and Winston, Eastbourne, 1983, pp. 107–115)

There are many ways, therefore, in which the general freedoms of association and assembly can be restricted. Despite this, some senior police officers and politicians would like to see greater police powers on public order. They would like to extend the means by which not only political demonstrations, but also picketing in industrial disputes and the behaviour of football crowds, can be controlled. The following extract asks why this is so.

Official attitudes to all sorts of 'large assemblies' are hardening. The days when crowds could gather at will are over. Limits are being placed on people's freedom to gather, whether as pickets, peace protestors or pop festival goers. The balance of opinion has shifted. Pop festivals are no longer seen as sociable but as anti-social. This is true of other large assemblies. A mass demo is described, too easily, as 'mob rule'. Crowd power is clearly less acceptable than it was.

Why should this have happened? At the moment we seem to have readopted the idea of a crowd as something inherently out of control and on the rampage. This explains the bad behaviour. Or does it? A crowd of between 20,000 and 40,000 people turned up at Molesworth to protest about the siting of cruise missiles. Local farmers planned to sue CND over damage to crops caused by protesters. To the farmers' surprise, the damage amounted to no more that £300. The new fear of crowds may be rooted in quite the opposite: a crowd that is **in** control rather than out of control. The mass picket of miners which closed Saltley coke depot in 1974 was totally in control. That was the trouble. Crowd power could never be allowed to do that again, and it was not.

But what if crowds respresented not anarchy but freedom? Surely this would explain attempts to control them? Elias Canetti, the Nobel prizewinner, novelist and sociologist, took this view of crowds. Crowds, he said, free people. This is why crowds break windows and doors. They are breaking down the boundaries of people's lives. If Canetti was right, then all the current attempts to disperse crowds can be seen as attempts to limit freedom and put up boundaries. The motorway roadblocks which the police mounted to turn back miners' pickets. The razor wire at Molesworth. The stopping of public rights of way at Stonehenge. All are boundaries in the Canetti sense.

Yet, whatever the barriers the urge to gather in crowds for feast or funeral is as old as Stonehenge. In South Africa, a crowd of 50,000 blacks ignored a government ban on funerals to mourn the 29 people killed at Uitenhage. For them, the crowd is the only freedom they have.

(from 'A good crowd', **New Society**, 18 April 1985, p.71)

1. Identify **two** controls that can be used to regulate political demonstrations under
   a statute law   (2)
   b common law   (2)
2. In what ways do the provisions of the employment legislation referred to in the first extract restrict the freedom of association and assembly?   (2)
3. What are the possible dangers of a complete freedom of assembly?   (3)
4. According to the second extract, why might Governments see crowds as a threat?   (3)
5. Should public order controls be increased or reduced?
   Give reasons for your answer.   (8)

5 Civil rights

The questions about freedom of assembly raised in the previous extracts are **civil rights** issues. The following extracts will look at some other civil rights including freedom of expression, and freedom from discrimination and unlawful arrest. Earlier sections have already suggested two things about such rights and liberties. First, for a society to be properly called 'democratic' certain civil rights must be clearly upheld and practised. Secondly, unlike many other countries which have a Bill of Rights as part of a written constitution, civil rights in the UK tend to exist in a negative way. Individuals are legally allowed to do what they want provided there is no law to prevent them. Consequently, one way of discovering the extent of civil liberties in this country is to examine the restrictions on them. These restrictions may be found in statute law or common law. But there may also be limitations which arise out of other institutions in society, such as the mass media.

As the previous passages (12.4) might suggest, civil rights are subject to changes. These may occur in response to changing circumstances and attitudes. They may also come about through shifts in power and influence among different group representing different interests and views (such as political parties and pressure groups). This applies to all societies. A right won or freedom gained can be lost at a later date. In times of war or other emergency, for instance, there is often a severe curtailment of civil liberties (whether justified or not). This will be done in the interests of what is claimed to be the greater public need. But even at other times, any society will have certain limitations on individual freedoms. All laws restrict freedom in some form. A complete absence of laws would permit the 'freedom' to interfere with the freedom of others. Murder is the ultimate example.

Freedom of expression

In order to exercise the fundamental freedoms of association and assembly..., individuals must be able to express themselves freely. This means that they should be free to speak on any topic and hold opinions without official interference. It also means that individuals ought to be able to write what they want and communicate it to others, and express themselves in other ways, by dressing as they please, for example...Freedom of expression also means that individuals are free to decide for themselves whether they hold particular religious, political or philosophical beliefs and whether to pursue them actively or not.

At the same time, it is necessary to balance freedom of expression against the interests of those in society who may be put at risk by its abuse. The expression of racist views, for example, can incite racial hatred and put sections of the community in grave physical danger. Where the balance **should** lie on other issues is a continual matter of debate. Where it **does** occur at any particular time will depend not so much on what statute law defines, but how it is interpreted, for example in the courts. And this may or may not reflect the general climate of opinion in society at the time. For instance, it is a criminal offence to publish an obscene book, magazine, film, photograph or videotape. But how is 'obscenity' defined? The legal approach is to ask whether the item is likely to 'deprave and corrupt', but these terms are also rather vague. John Cleland's book **Fanny Hill** was held by the courts to be obscene whereas D. H. Lawrence's **Lady Chatterley's Lover** was not.

Other statutory limitations to freedom of expression are contained in the Official Secrets Acts, for example, and the legislation concerned with treason (which still carries the death penalty). There is also a series of common law restrictions relating to libel, slander, conspiracy and blasphemy, for instance. But there are other, less obvious, limitations, too. Section 4 showed how the range of views and opinion in the mass media tends to be restricted. As agents of political socialization the media may be discouraging the expression and spread of ideas that do not fall within an 'acceptable' range. They may do this by ridiculing or trivializing alternative views, or by ignoring them altogether. Some trade unionists, for example, believe that freedom of expression has been limited through one-sided reporting of industrial disputes.

The police and security services keep files of information about members of certain political groups. People may be wary of participating in organized politics if they suspect that their activities would be monitored and recorded. Recent data protection legislation gives individuals the right to discover **some** of the **computerized** information that is kept on them. But much information is still not stored on computers. In any case, the Act contains exceptions to rights of access which could cover most of the 'political' information on file.

Freedom from discrimination

'One justifiable curtailment on freedom of expression are the laws prohibiting discrimination on the grounds of race, colour or national or ethnic origin and on grounds of sex. Such laws have become necessary because of the unwillingness of some to accept others on equal terms.'

The Race Relations Act 1976 makes racial discrimination illegal in areas such as employment, education and housing. Similar areas relating to discrimination on the grounds of sex are covered by the Sex Discrimination Act 1975. Both Acts contain certain exceptions and the law has been only partly successful in reducing discrimination. Some of the more open abuses may have decreased, but huge gaps remain where rights are still unequal.

Freedom from unlawful arrest

One of the main elements of the rule of law (see Section 7.4) is the freedom from unlawful arrest. This means that anyone making an arrest has to show legal justification for doing so by reference to some provision in law. Although ordinary members of the public are able to make an arrest under certain circumstances, greater powers are given to the police. In some cases the police require a warrant from a local magistrate to make an arrest. But they have a lot of scope to arrest without a warrant. Not only may the police arrest anyone reasonably suspected of committing an arrestable offence. They may also arrest anyone they reasonably suspect of being about to commit an arrestable offence. The Police and Criminal Evidence Act 1984 greatly extended the powers to arrest without a warrant. For instance, the police can now make arrests for minor offences if the suspect is unable to prove his name or address. Arrests for offences against public decency, obstructing the highway, or damage to property can also be made under the Act.

There are legal remedies for unlawful arrest. For example, in civil law a person may sue for damages for false imprisonment or malicious prosecution. A prosecution for false imprisonment can also be started under criminal law by a wrongfully arrested person. Other possibilities in certain instances include attempts to gain public support for a person's release. Some cases may be referred to the European

Commission on Human Rights. This body investigates complaints not only about unlawful arrest but any grievance that comes under the 1950 European Convention for the Protection of Human Rights, which has been ratified by the UK Government. For example, the Commission investigated the British Government's ban on trade union membership for employees at the Government Communication Headquarters at Cheltenham. If necessary, cases can be referred to the European Court of Human Rights in Strasbourg, although the procedure can take many years.

(adapted from **The Legal Framework: Law and the Individual** by K.R. Bradley and R.A. Clark, Holt, Rinehart and Winston, Eastbourne, 1983, pp.117–157, and from which the direct quotes are taken, and 'Your rights and the police', **Which?** May 1985, pp.226–230)

1. What remedies are open to someone who believes he or she may have been unlawfully arrested?   (3)
2. How might the activities of the mass media
   a increase civil rights?   (2)
   b limit civil rights?   (2)
3. Why do you think the laws against racial and sexual discrimination have been limited in their effectiveness?   (3)
4.

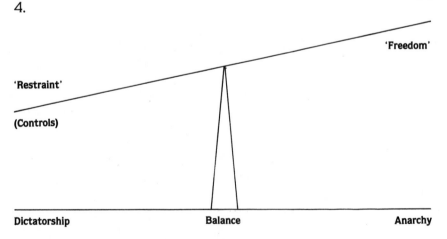

'It is sometimes said that the law ... attempts to strike a balance between total freedom on the one hand and total control or restraint of the other.'

(Diagram and quote from K. R. Bradley and R. A. Clark, pp.119, 117)
a What point about civil rights does the diagram express?   (3)
b Why would most people wish to avoid dictatorship on the one hand and anarchy on the other?   (3)

The rights and freedoms discussed in the passage above represent only a small number of the human rights that could be identified. Many countries, including Britain, have signed the United Nations Universal Declaration of Human Rights which contains 30 articles or clauses. This does not mean, however, that all societies will give equal attention to all of these rights. Those liberties thought to be the most fundamental in one society may not be considered so important in the next, but other rights may be. Consider, for example, the following extract from a letter written in response to an article in a British newspaper.

Journalists writing for leading British publications frequently use such terms as 'democracy', 'free society', and 'human rights' when referring to the British way of life. When they write about socialist countries, especially the Soviet Union, the terms they tend to use are 'totalitarianism', 'abuse of human rights' and 'bureaucracy'.

Your article 'Benefit curb turns young into "nomads"' makes no mention of human rights violations [but] it is about them. It is about the fate of more than 45,000 of the over 3m in your country. Unemployment was done away with in my country more than 50 years ago. The right to work is guaranteed by the Soviet constitution. The 45,000 Britons of whom your paper wrote are living on social security. They have been ordered to move from their homes and even from the towns in which they have been living. This constitutes a violation of another human right, the right to housing. Soviet people take this for granted. You won't find homeless people in the USSR, any more than you will find an army of unemployed.

Oleg Yarstev
Novosti Press Agency, Moscow.

(from **The Observer**, July 7, 1985, p.13)

5. a What civil rights are stressed in the second extract? (2)
   b Which civil rights do you consider are most emphasized in Britain? (2)

6 Freedom of information

In any form of democracy people must be able to participate in politics. Many will choose to participate no more than to vote at elections. But even at this level of decision-making people need access to accurate information. How can an individual use his or her vote responsibly if the information required to reach a decision is unavailable or inaccurate?

Earlier sections have shown how secretive Governments can be about their activities. Civil servants have been prosecuted under the Official Secrets Act for leaking information to the press or to MPs. There have been increased demands to replace this Act with a Freedom of Information Act. This objective is supported by a number of people inside and outside Parliament and by the pressure group 'Campaign for Freedom of Information in Britain'. This group is in favour of a legal 'right to know'. It calls for a right of access to Government documents (with certain exceptions such as information directly affecting national security). The campaign is opposed by those who believe that the work of government cannot be properly carried out without a degree of confidentiality or privacy and trust. The following passage examines the debate.

> **The Times** revealed that the Cabinet Office had refused to release the results of its unannounced study of how effective the Thatcher administration had been in making information available to Parliament and the public.

This could be seen as a symptom of the secrecy which Des Wilson, Chairman of the Campaign for Freedom of Information in Britain, has called a 'national disease'. It affects not only the central government but local government and other bodies, such as water authorities, too. Many MPs complain of the difficulties in obtaining information from Ministers. This limits their ability to carry out their jobs as the elected representatives of the people. Wilson argues that secrecy tends to hide the sources of power, encourage misinformation and make politicians and civil servants less accountable. Opponents of the Campaign, however, claim that FOI (Freedom of Information) legislation could have the opposite effect. It could reduce Ministerial accountability. Ministers are answerable to Parliament for what goes on in their Departments. A statutory public right of access to Government information, they argue, would interfere with this Ministerial responsibility. It would also lead to more by-passing of Parliament, thereby reducing the role of MPs.

The FOI campaigners say that secrecy leads to inefficiency and the greater likelihood of mistakes being made. Their opponents say more errors would occur if civil servants and Ministers knew that their files could be opened to anyone. This is because they would be less likely to record sensitive information in writing. It could also lead to the keeping of 'unofficial files' which would mean more secrecy, not less.

Without FOI legislation, however, it is argued that public participation in politics will continue to be hampered. Des Wilson states, 'Information is power'. A lack of information means a lack of power. He therefore wants to see more open government and the type of FOI laws that exist in many other democracies in the Western world. The present secretive system, argues Wilson, undermines democracy. But there is an argument which suggests that too much information could be dangerous. If the public is saturated with information it may be difficult or too time-consuming to sort out what is relevant. The idea of more open government would therefore be defeated. Opponents are also concerned about the increased risk of industrial espionage. They believe that access to official information about companies could be used by competitors to gain unfair commercial advantage. If the exceptions to a legal right of access were extended to cover these situations, then so much might be excluded that the Act would not be worth having in the first place.

However, the issues do not only involve information about matters of public policy. They also concern the rights of individuals to know what information is being kept about themselves. Individuals often have no access to files held about their children's education or to their medical records. Housing information about tenants and social services records of their clients are not usually open to inspection by the tenants and clients themselves. There is evidence of

'But why on earth would **you** want to see your file Mrs Robinson. I am the doctor.'

serious errors being recorded about individuals and remaining uncorrected because the people concerned cannot see them. But, again, there is the danger that a right of access to personal files could encourage individual officials to keep their own secret written records. This could be worse than the situation at present because if their existence was not admitted, then even other officials would be unable to check them.

(adapted from 'You the jury', **BBC Radio 4** programme, January 5, 1985 and **The Secrets File: The Case for Freedom of Information in Britain Today** edited by Des Wilson, Heinemann, London, 1984)

1. How might open access to official information affect
   a the notion of Ministerial responsibility?   (3)
   b the role of MPs?   (3)

2. What are the possible advantages and disadvantages of individuals having the right to see their personal files, such as their medical records? (4)
3. Prepare a case **either** for **or** against a Freedom of Information Act. In doing so, try to take account of the opposing arguments. (10)

Section 13 Local Government and Politics

If **central** government is responsible for running the country, why have **local** government as well? It is sometimes said that it would be impractical for Government Departments, based largely in London, to administer all the services that are required throughout Britain. This is no doubt true. But it is possible to have local offices of a Government Department where necessary. The Department of Health and Social Security and the Inland Revenue (which has local tax offices) are both organized in this way. But this is not local **government**. It is local **administration** of **national** services.

Various other justifications are made for local **government.** Local government involves the election of local people to serve on local **councils.** These **councillors** oversee the running of local services such as education, refuse collection, street lighting, leisure facilities, and many more. Whereas MPs represent their constituents nationally in Parliament, councillors represent their communities at a **local** level. It is said, therefore, that local government helps to ensure local **democracry.** Councillors are likely to have a knowledge of local conditions and needs. They are in the best position to make decisions about services affecting their communities. As elected representatives they are accountable to the local electorate. This gives people some say in the running of local services which are in part paid for by money raised locally.

Major changes have been taking place in local government, and this section provides a guide to the more important ones. The earlier passages (1-3) describe the different types of **local authority** which together make up the system of local government in Britain. They also show which of these local councils are responsible for providing which services, and how they are organized. Further extracts (3-6) examine the roles of councillors and of the officials they employ to implement their policies and administer the services. The effects on both of party politics is also considered. A changing and controversial area in recent years has been local government finance. Passages 7 and 8 therefore examine where the money for providing local services comes from and how it is spent. Central government attempts to keep a tight rein on the income and expenditure of local authorities. This raises the question of how far central control of what local authorities do clashes with the idea of **local** democracy (9). Issues relating to 'democracy' also figure prominently in the final passages (10 and 11), which focus on the role of the individual in local politics. They consider how people are represented locally, and how they can get their problems dealt with. They also suggest how the individual might exert influence over and participate in local affairs.

1 Development and change

The system of local government in Britain has been changing. In part this can be seen as a response to changes in economic and social circumstances. But it also reflects differences in political ideas about local democracy and efficiency. The following passage outlines the development of local government, concentrating on the changes to its structure over the past twenty to twenty-five years.

> Local government in England can be traced back to Saxon times. But it was not until the nineteenth century that a definite **system** of local government began to emerge. By the end of that century various types of councils had become responsible for providing services at a local level. The country was divided into a number of **counties** each of which had its own council. Within the counties, a further system of councils had developed – based on **boroughs, urban districts** and **rural districts** – which provided a range of services not carried out at county level.
>
> This system lasted until the 1960s in London, and until the 1970s elsewhere in the country. Over the years the pressure on local government had grown. It had taken on responsibility for extra services, had become more expensive to run, and central government had come to exercise more supervision. The whole structure had become outdated. One of the major problems had been the division between rural and urban areas. Growth of towns and the movements of population had made these divisions unrealistic. The system produced a lot of overlapping and duplication of functions.

The system in London was the first to be reformed – in 1963 (taking effect in 1965). The Greater London Council (GLC) was set up. And within that area, thirty-two London Borough councils were established.

The system in the rest of England and Wales was changed by the Local Government Act 1972. From April 1974 a new two-tier (or two-level) system came into being, based on **counties** and **districts**. For most of England and Wales the idea was that the top tier (the county councils) was to be responsible for general services, such as education and social services. The lower tier (district councils) would then provide the more local services such as housing and environmental health. But it was recognized that the heavily populated parts of the country – the 'conurbations' – had special problems, and so the distribution of services between the two tiers was rather different. Within these **metropolitan** areas even services such as education were to be provided by the district councils. The metropolitan counties were responsible for functions such as transport and the police.

In addition to the two-tier system, **parish** councils (in Wales, **community** councils) – a traditional unit of local government – were retained. Their functions were very limited, however.

A new system was introduced for Scotland in 1975. This, too, was based on a two-tier system – regional councils as the top tier and district councils forming the lower tier. There are also three island councils responsible for all local affairs in Orkney, Shetland and the Western Isles.

By the mid-1970s, therefore, the structure of local government in Britain looked like that shown in the diagram opposite.

Further changes to the English system were made under the Local Government Act 1985. This Act abolished the Greater London Council and the six metropolitan county councils (Greater Manchester, Merseyside, Tyne and Wear, West Midlands, South Yorkshire and West Yorkshire) with effect from April 1986. Some of the functions of the GLC and the metropolitan counties have been transferred to London boroughs and the metropolitan district councils. Other functions have been reallocated among: (1) Joint boards – composed of borough or district councillors; (2) Quangos (quasi-autonomous non-governmental organizations). These are non-

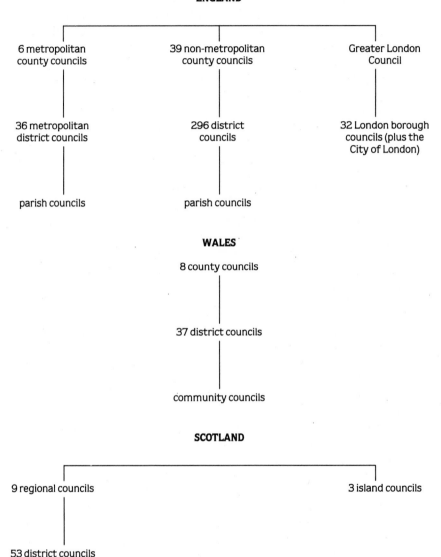

ENGLAND

6 metropolitan county councils	39 non-metropolitan county councils	Greater London Council
36 metropolitan district councils	296 district councils	32 London borough councils (plus the City of London)
parish councils	parish councils	

WALES

8 county councils

37 district councils

community councils

SCOTLAND

9 regional councils	3 island councils
53 district councils	

elected bodies which are partly independent of central government although their members are often appointed by the government. The Arts Council is an example of a quango; (3) Central government.

ANY COMPLAINTS WHEN WHITEHALL
RUNS LONDON, TALK TO HIM.

Part of the GLC campaign against its abolition.

The Government abolished the metropolitan counties and the GLC because it believed them to be too costly and too remote from the communities they served. It was also thought that a top tier had become unnecessary in the conurbations as the district and borough councils were already running most of the services in these areas. These arguments were not accepted by the GLC and the metropolitan county councils themselves. The GLC in particular conducted an intensive campaign to try to prevent abolition. It pointed out that London would become the only major city in Europe without an overall directly elected body to co-ordinate its affairs. The metropolitan counties argued that their councils actually saved money. It is cheaper and more efficient for one body to provide some services over a whole area than for each district within that area to provide its own locally. They suggested that the new system will be less democratic and accountable, and more remote and complex, as

some of the services are transferred to central government or to the quangos. They also doubted whether neighbouring district or borough councils would co-operate sufficiently, especially if they were controlled by different political parties. There was suspicion, too, about the Conservative Government's motives. At the time of the abolition proposals, the GLC and the metropolitan county councils were all Labour controlled.

(adapted from **Politics Pal** by L. Robins, Great Glen, Leicestershire, 1985, pp. 27-9 and 'Local Government in England and Wales' by Graham Thomas, unpublished paper)

Some local and national politicans believe that the new system will have to undergo further reforms in the near future. A future Labour Government might repeal the 1985 Act and, for example, bring back a city-wide council for London. The following maps, however, illustrate the present (1986) structure of local government in Britain.

Counties and metropolitan areas in England and Wales

County councils

Metropolitan areas. 1. Greater Manchester; 2. Merseyside; 3. Tyne and Wear; 4. West Midlands; 5. South Yorkshire; 6. West Yorkshire. From April 1986 there are no county councils for these areas. Most services are carried out by metropolitan district councils within these areas.

The Greater London area is divided into 32 boroughs

Scotland

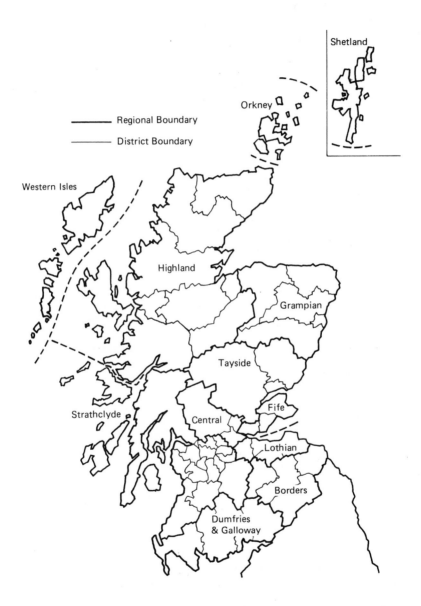

Shetland

Orkney

Regional Boundary

District Boundary

Western Isles

Highland

Grampian

Tayside

Fife

Strathclyde

Central

Lothian

Borders

Dumfries
& Galloway

(Source: 'Scottish Office brief on local government reform', reprinted in **Local Government** by Tom Brennan, Longman Resources Unit, York, 1984, p. 11)

**Example of the division of a metropolitan area (Merseyside)
into district councils**

(from **Local and Central Government** by Kathleen Allsop (revised by Tom Brennan), Hutchinson, London, 1982, p. 20)

**Example of the division of a county council (Cheshire)
into district councils**

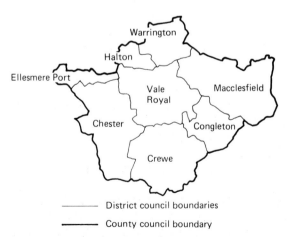

——— District council boundaries

——— County council boundary

(adapted from **English Local Government Reformed** by Lord Redcliffe-Maud and Bruce Wood, Oxford University Press, London, 1974, p. 180)

London borough councils

(from **Local Community** by Grace Jones, Nelson-Harrap, London, 1975, p. 23)

1. Which type of council provides the top tier of local government in
   a most of Scotland? (1)
   b most of England and Wales? (1)
2. Give an example of
   a a district council in a metropolitan area (1)
   b a county council (1)
3. a Why was the 1972 Local Government Act passed? (2)
   b Explain the differences in local government organization
      between metropolitan and non-metropolitan counties which
      this Act introduced. (3)
   c Why were these differences introduced? (2)

4. a What difference has the 1985 Local Government Act made to the system of local government in England?   (2)
   b Why were these changes made?   (3)
5. Outline a case for the re-introduction of a directly-elected council for the whole of the London area.   (4)

2 Functions

The services provided by each local council depend on the type of authority it is – county, metropolitan district, non-metropolitan district, etc. The following passage outlines the powers of local authorities and the kinds of services they provide. A chart shows how the main services are allocated among the different types of council.

Most local government services are **mandatory, or obligatory.** This means that local authorities must, under the law, provide them. Others are **permissive** – local councils have the powers to provide them if they decide to do so, but they are not required to. If a council wishes to perform a function which does not fall into either of these categories, it may try to get a private Bill through Parliament. If successful, the Act would apply only to that particular local authority. In addition, Parliament has delegated to local councils very limited powers to introduce **by-laws** – for example concerning the control of dogs within their areas.

The services provided by local government as a whole can be classified into three main types: environmental, personal and protective. (1) **Environmental services** are those which look after the surroundings or environment in which people live. They include street lighting and cleaning, drainage, refuse disposal and provision of parks and recreation grounds. (2) **Personal services** are provided by local authorities to improve the quality of people's lives through, for example, education, library facilties, transport services and council housing. They also include those services which aim to help those in need, such as the care of the elderly and of deprived children or the provision of 'home helps'. (3) The more obvious **protective services** are the police and fire services. But there are others, such as protection for consumers. Councils have consumer protection offices

'How many departments do I have to call to get this lot sorted?'

(sometimes known as trading standards departments), and inspectors who examine shop premises to check on standards of hygiene.

It can be seen from the chart overleaf that responsibility for providing some services is split between the upper and lower tier authorities (county and district). Where parish councils exist, some services such as the maintenance of allotments, playing fields and cemeteries may be shared with the district councils. The allocation of functions in Wales is similar to that in the non-metropolitan counties of England. In Scotland, the regional councils have responsibility for the general planning of resources, transport, roads, education and social services. The responsibilities of the district councils in Scotland include housing, health, libraries, parks and recreational facilities.

(adapted from **Local Community** by Grace Jones, Nelson-Harrap, London, 1979, pp. 22-6 and **Local Government** by Roger Opie, Wheaton, Exeter, 1979, pp. 7-11)

Allocation of main local government functions in England

Services provided	NON-METROPOLITAN AREAS		Metro-politan District Councils *	London Borough Councils *
	County Councils	District Councils		
Environmental Services Parks, gardens and open spaces	•	•	•	•
Transport planning, roads, bridges, street lighting	•			•
Town planning	•	•	•	•
Sanitation, cleansing, drainage		•	•	•
Personal Services Allotments		•	•	•
Swimming baths and playing fields	•	•	•	•
Cemeteries		•	•	•
Education	•		•	• for outer London, ILEA for inner London
Housing		•	•	•
Libraries	•		•	•
Museums and the arts	•	•	•	•
Social services	•		•	•
Public transport services	•	•	•	
Protective Services Fire service	•			
Food hygiene		•	•	•
Police	•			
Traffic regulations	•			
Road safety	•			
Consumer protection	•			•

(Source: Jones p. 26; Opie p. 9)

*Responsibility for some of the services provided by the metropolitan district councils and the London boroughs used to be shared with the metropolitan county councils or the GLC. The GLC and the metropolitan county councils ceased to exist in April, 1986. Their functions, which also included the fire service, traffic regulations, road safety, etc., are being redistributed among other bodies, including the metropolitan district or London borough councils (see pages 284–5). At the time of writing, final decisions on the reallocation of these services were still to be made.

ILEA (Inner London Education Authority) provides education for 12 of the 32 London boroughs and the City of London.

Police called to village 'summit'

POLICE were called to Great Haywood on Saturday when villagers decided to take a stand over rival claims to the positioning of a seat.

The bench was placed outside the Clifford Arms Hotel after being repaired but near-by residents were not going to accept its return lying down.

But when they tried to move it away from their homes they found themselves in the hot seat with other villagers who wanted it to stay where it was.

By 4pm tempers flared and the police arrived on the scene to cushion the effect of the verbal blows from both sides.

Last night parish councillors got round the table in emergency session to decide the fate of the seat which was provided to commemorate the Festival of Britain 34 years ago.

(from **Staffordshire Newsletter**, July 7, 1985, p. 1)

Parish councils may have have only limited powers, but their business can still occasionally arouse disagreement and conflict.

1. Distinguish between **permissive** and **mandatory** functions of local authorities. (2)
2. In relation to local authorities, distinguish between a **private Bill** and a **by-law.** (2)
3. Provide an example of each of the following types of services in a non-metropolitan area which are provided **only** by the **county** council.
   a An environmental service (1)
   b A personal service (1)
   c A protective service (1)
4. Which local authorities are responsible for education in
   a metropolitan areas (1)
   b non-metropolitan areas (1)
   c London (2)
5. a Give **two** examples of services for which responsibility is shared between the upper and lower tiers within the same area. (2)
   b Using your two examples say why you think responsibility is shared for these services. (4)
6. Why do you think parish councils are not given responsibility for providing major services such as education or the police? (3)

3 The organization of local authorities

Previous passages in this section have described how the system of local government in Britain is arranged according to different types of local councils. The following passage shows how local authorities are arranged **internally**. It will show that each local authority has a number of elected **councillors** who together consitute the **council**. The council will form a series of **committees**. Many of these committees will have corresponding **departments** which are staffed by appointed officials called **local government officers.** Each county council, for example, has an education committee and an education department. At least in theory, it is the councillors' job to decide on policy and the officials' function to implement the policy – although the officers will also **advise** the councillors.

To be eligible to stand for election as a local councillor a person must be over 21, a British subject, and will normally live or work in the area covered by the council concerned. Councillors are elected for fixed periods of four years, but can seek re-election at the end of this time. Some district councils are entitled to call themselves 'borough' or 'city' councils. These elect a **mayor** whose functions are chiefly ceremonial. Other councils elect a **chairperson.**

County councils usually hold full meetings four times a year, and other councils meet about every six weeks. The purpose of these meetings is to set out the general principles and broad lines of policy of the council. In practice this means that full meetings of the council are largely taken up with confirmations, and sometimes rejections, of decisions or recommendations already made by the council's committees.

With certain exceptions, such as those dealing with finance and education, each council can decide how many committees to set up and what they should deal with. Most councillors will be members of one or more of the committees of a council. Committees may be given some **executive** functions. This means they have power to make and implement certain decisions by themselves. Other functions will be **advisory** – the committees can recommend the full council to adopt certain

Example of the structure of a non-metropolitan district council

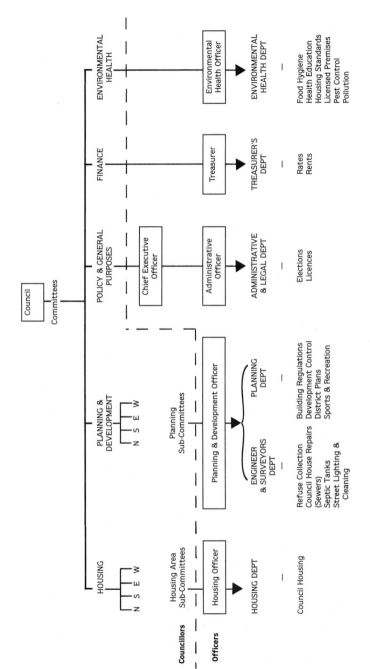

(from **How Britain is Governed** by J. Harvey, Macmillan, Basingstoke and London, 1983, p. 232, with minor additions)

policies or take particular actions. The chairperson of most committees will usually work closely with the appropriate **chief officer** (the top official in a department).

Non-metropolitan counties and metropolitan districts by law must have a chief education officer and a director of social services. Other appointments are left to each council to decide upon. But most councils – depending on their type – follow a similar pattern. It is normal practice, for example, to have a chief executive, a treasurer, chief engineer and surveyor, and a housing manager. Besides carrying out the decisions of the council and its committees, the chief officers will also offer their expert advice to the elected members. The relationship between a committee of the council (particularly its chairperson) and its chief officers is in some ways similar to that between a Government Minister and his senior civil servants in central government. In some cases, a paid official may try to dominate the elected representative. In others, an elected member may be thought to be interfering too much with the routine, day-to-day work of a particular department.

The activities of the different committees and departments of a council have to be co-ordinated. The full council can only partly fulfil this function as it meets infrequently and is too large to deal with details. There is no exact equivalent of a Prime Minister at local level, but the leader of the majority party on the council can sometimes play a very influential role. Many authorities accepted the recommendation of the Bains Report in 1972 and introduced a central co-ordinating committee composed chiefly of the chairpersons of the other committees. It may be called the Policy and Resources Committee or Policy and General Purposes Committee. Its tasks often include reviewing the work of the council as a whole, co-ordinating the budget, deciding priorities and planning future policy. Bains also suggest that co-ordination between the departments of a local authority, i.e. at officer level, should be overseen by the chief executive. As the authority's most senior official he may be in charge of a management team consisting of the chief officers of the main departments. Over the past few years, however, some local authorities have been less enthusiastic about the benefits of a Bains-type committee structure and management team of officers. Some have reverted to the more traditional model whereby major decisions are taken within the separate committees connected with individual departments.

(adapted from **How Britain is Governed** by J. Harvey, Macmillan, Basingstoke and London, 1983, pp. 228-233)

1. Briefly distinguish between
   a a councillor and a local government officer   (2)
   b a committee chairperson and a chief officer   (2)
2. Why do most councils meet so infrequently?   (2)
3. Identify **four** ways by which a local authority may attempt to co-ordinate its activities.   (4)
4. Local government and central government both involve relationships between elected members and paid officials. What **similarities** and **differences** in these relationships can be noted between the two levels of government?   (10)

4 Councillors and officers (1)

Local councillors are elected whereas local government officers are appointed. The officials are paid a salary or wage. Councillors are not, although they can reclaim travel and subsistence expenses and they can receive attendance allowances for approved duties (such as attendance at council and committee meetings). A further distinction suggested in 13.3 is that councillors make policy decisions and officers administer them. Whether such a distinction stands up to close examination will be considered in 13.5.

Councillors are expected to represent their local communities. Each successful candidate at a local election becomes a representative for a particular area (known as a 'ward' or 'division'). But he or she will also be expected to work in the interests of the district or county as a whole. Councillors provide a link between the public and the local authority officials who administer the services. In this way they are in a similar position to MPs in their relationship with the work of central government. Underlying the role of councillors, therefore, is the principle of local democracy and local accountability. A 1977 report on activities of local councillors showed that, on their own estimates, councillors spent an average of 79 hours per month on council work. More than half of this time was spent on work connected with council or committee meetings. Much of the remaining time was split between party and other meetings and dealing with their constituents' problems.

Time spent by councillors on their public duties

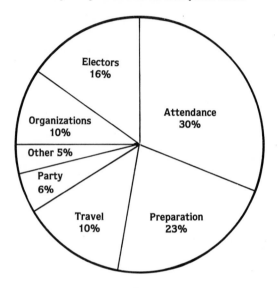

	Hours per month
Attendance at council and committee meetings	23
Preparation for meetings	18
Travelling to meetings	8
Party meetings	5
Electors' problems	13
Meeting organizations on behalf of council	8
Other	4
Total	**79**

(Source: **The Remuneration of Councillors, Vol. 2,** HMSO, 1977, reproduced with the permission of the Controller of Her Majesty's Stationery Office)

Relatively few councillors are able to devote themselves full-time to council work. It is the paid officials who administer local government services on a day-to-day basis. The officers also provide the professional and technical expertise necessary to do this.

Lawyers, accountants, engineers, town planners, educationalists and scientists, as well as people trained in management and administration, occupy the senior posts in local authority departments. At its peak in the 1970s, more than 2¼ million people were employed in local government in England – accounting for almost 10% of the working population. Although the numbers have declined since then, local authorities are still major employers. Many local government employees do not actually work in the town halls and county offices themselves, but are employed in schools and colleges, the police and fire services, engaged in mantaining roads and buildings, and so on.

In the following extract, a member of Manchester City Council presents his own view of the role of a councillor, including an account of his relationship with the officers and with his constituents.

People stand for the council for a number of different reasons; in my case the reason was to gain power in order to bring about certain changes in the way people live which I believe to be important. It certainly hasn't brought me any financial reward; my own career as a teacher has suffered. My employers give me some days off with pay but I have to take other days off without pay. I calculate that over eight years of serving on the council has probably cost me about £15,000 overall. Perhaps one and a half days a week are spent at council committee meetings plus one evening meeting. On average I spend two evenings attending public meetings and another two at Labour Party meetings. Sunday morning and afternoon are also taken up with council business, reading papers and so forth. In addition, I also have constant phone calls, and other engagements crop up. I am generally in favour of paying councillors because at present we get local government on the cheap.

What kind of people become councillors? 22 out of the 99 Manchester councillors are women. This is more than the national average. 20 councillors have one or more degrees. Most of the more highly qualified people are on the Labour side. One could not say that the council is therefore representative of society as a whole, but perhaps this is inevitable.

We have a councillor's advice bureau every Thursday. I usually meet eight people a week in this context, although I might very well be contacted a couple of times by phone on other items and personally at the various public meetings which I regularly attend. 90% of all the cases I deal with concern housing – blocked drains and so forth – but I also encounter more personal problems, occasionally those which relate to social services. I follow up these complaints by contacting the relevant officers and I usually ask for a written report on what has been done. The vast majority of cases can be sorted out satisfactorily but there are one or two which seem to drag on for years and years and one comes to accept them as a fact of life. Occasionally, one has to tell constituents that one cannot help them or occasionally I can refer their case to the local ombudsman. My view on the local ombudsman is very positive. They were set up to deal with complaints about maladministration in local government and I see their work as complementary to my own.

My dealings with council officers are generally very cordial. I frequently contact the appropriate officer myself by phone but will also frequently feed in the request via their superior officer. As a general rule I find that this is the quickest way of getting things done. I try very hard to be polite when dealing with officials and not overbearing as some councillors are alleged to be. But just occasionally one does have to remind officers of their relationship to elected members. I am not at all worried when constituents by-pass me and contact officers direct. I see my role as a 'last resort' when a constituent's attempt to gain satisfaction from dealing with officers has broken down.

I don't believe that councillors should spend the whole of their time dealing with constituency matters. They are councillors not community workers or social workers. They have to spend some of their time dealing with wider issues of policy. There are 15 committees on Manchester Council. They are concerned with formulating policy in their respective areas of responsibility. Even though central government is taking more and more power from local government there are still very important issues in terms of applying central government policy or regulations in the locality in which councillors can have a big role to play. The essence of local government is that it is **local.** Councillors represent the locality and speak for the interests of their constituents. Traditionally there has been a tension or conflict between elected members and officers. Both operate from a different set of assumptions: the officer perhaps from administrative convenience and existing priorities on occasions; the councillor on political and local community grounds. In this contest both parties have strengths and weaknesses. The councillor can say that he is the elected representative with intimate knowledge of local conditions and needs. By comparison, the officer is merely appointed and has no comparable local knowledge. On the other hand, the councillor is an amateur and part-time compared with the full-time, professionally qualified officer who has a vast inside knowledge of the local bureaucracy.

(from 'The work of a local councillor: a personal view', unpublished transcript by Bill Jones from a talk by Councillor Arnold Spencer, 21 November, 1983)

1. How can the role of the councillor be said to aid local democracy?
(4)
2. If local authorities have councillors, why are local government officers needed as well? (3)
3. From the extract and preceding comments, identify **four** differences between councillors and officials. (4)
4. Although there has been an increase in the proportion of women councillors in recent years, they are still very much in a minority. Councillors are also disproportionately drawn from the higher income, home-owning, better qualified sections of the community.
a Why do you think this is? (3)
b Approximately what percentage of Manchester City councillors are women? (1)
5. Discuss the view that councillors should be paid a wage. (5)

5 Councillors and officers (2)

The previous extract raised the issue of the working relationships between the elected members and the paid officials within a local authority. How far is it true to say that it is the councillors who make policy and the officers who implement it? The examination of the Minister-civil servant relationship in Section 11 suggested that it is often not possible to make a clear distinction between policy and administration at national level. Does the same apply to local government? The following passages explore this aspect of the roles of councillors and officers.

> Reference has been made to the widely held view that it is necessary to distinguish between policy and administration. The research report gives examples of the opinion that if only policy could be separated from administration, the former to be exercised by members and the latter by officers, this would be a solution to problems. We do not believe that it is possible to lay down what is policy and what is administrative detail. Some issues stand out patently as important and can be regarded as 'policy'. Other matters, seemingly trivial, may involve political or social reaction of such significance that deciding them becomes a matter of policy. A succession of detailed decisions may contribute, eventually to the formulation of a policy.
>
> (from **The Management of Local Government**, report of the Maud Committee, HMSO, 1967, paragraph 109, reproduced with the permission of the Controller of Her Majesty's Stationery Office)

Does this mean that officers cannot help but be involved in forming policy? Some people believe that not only is this so, but also that the officials have **increasingly** gained more power at the expense of the elected members. Kenneth Newton doubts if officers have completely taken over the councillors' policy-making role. But he does admit that the policy-administration dividing line is blurred. Many of the councillors he interviewed recognized that such a distinction is often impossible to make. The situation is further complicated in that there are quite wide differences in how councillors themselves see their roles. Some involve themselves in relatively minor matters of 'administrative detail'. Others claim to concentrate solely on broad lines of 'policy'. The willingness of councillors to accept their officers' advice will also vary. Nevertheless, the councillors generally wished to give the impression that, in the end, they are the political masters. The following views were expressed by different councillors interviewed by Newton.

> There are times when you just have to say 'That's the way it's going to be, and you know what you can do if you don't like it.' I did that a few years ago against everything the department was saying. Of course, they were absolutely right. But then so were we. We were both right in our own way, and when that happens the chairman gets his own way. (Councillor A)

I'll tell you straight I'm not interested in people's dustbins. I'm interested in power, and that's why I'm here. Officers can worry about dustbins. They run their departments in the best way they can, but they'll do it in accordance with my plans. (Councillor B)

It's their job to implement policy, not make it. (Councillor C)

I don't look at it that way. I think there's no dividing line. There's an overlap and we're all part of a team. They carry out instructions that are given to them, but it's not that easy. New policies have got to come from the council, but even then the officers have got to advise and help. (Councillor D)

A number of councillors recognized the tactics that the officials can use to try to get councillors round to their way of thinking. One councillor remarked:

It's a subtle blend of bullshit and flannel and making sure that things go their own way. Report writing, I would say, is the most important part of their job. They put out so many reports that you get swamped by it all. You've got to be on the watch for what's going on. It's all protective confetti to the officers. (Councillor E)

The official themselves may not see it in the same light. They may acknowledge the difficulties of suggesting alternatives if these do not coincide with the general policy of the controlling political party on the council.

The bloody fools. I told them clearly enough it wouldn't work. It was a textbook mistake, but they insisted on it, so we followed. Mind you I can easily see why they had to play it that way at the time. It was the only thing for them to do then. Still, I'm no party politician and I spent quite a few evenings preparing the documents. I learnt my lesson – never oppose if it's party policy. (Senior officer)

(adapted from **Second City Politics** by K. Newton, Clarendon Press, Oxford, 1976, extracts reprinted by permission of A. D. Peters & Co. Ltd)

The Bains Report agreed with the Maud Committee that it is too simple to say that councillors should **only** deal with policy, and officers **only** with administration. It stated that officers have a role to play in forming policy. It also recognized that councillors will want to involve themselves in administrative matters which affect their constituents. The ideal councillor-officer relationship was seen not in terms of a clear-cut split of responsibilities and duties, but as part of an overall management process. The difference between the roles of councillor and officer was viewed as one of emphasis or degree. This difference in emphasis can be seen, for example, in the relationship that each is expected to have with the public. Aspects of this three-part relationship is suggested in the diagram. At this stage, the influence of party politics in local government is not accounted for. This is considered in the next passage (13.6).

Relationship between councillors, officers and the public

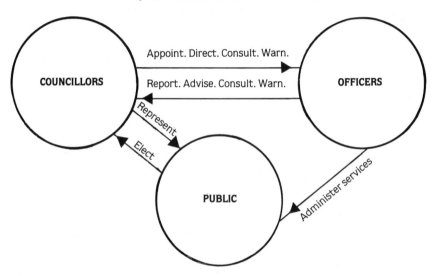

1. In your own words, explain why the Maud Committee rejected the distinction between policy and administration. (3)
2. Which of the **councillors'** views on their relationship with officials is closest to that expressed in the Bains Report? Explain your answer. (3)
3. Refer to the diagram and then identify, from the above passages, a reference to
   a councillors **directing** officers (2)
   b officers **warning** councillors (2)
4. What other information could be added to the diagram to give a fuller picture of the relationships between councillors, officers and the public? (Use the passages above plus the extract in 13.4 to help with your answer.) (3)

5. 'The issue is not whether officials have power, but to what **extent** they have power.' **(The Reorganization of Local Government** by John Dearlove, Cambridge University Press, 1979, p.54)
   a Explain this statement. (2)
   b From the information in the above passages, say whether or not you agree with the statement. Give reasons for your answers. (5)

6 Party politics in local government

Nowadays local government is dominated by party politics. The vast majority of candidates in local elections fight under a party banner and those who are elected find that much of their work within the council chamber and council committees is influenced by party considerations. Whether this is good for local government and for democracy is still a matter which is hotly debated.

There has been for a long time a school of thought which suggests that party politics have no place in local government and that services provided by local councils should be viewed 'administratively' rather than 'politically'. Those who share this view argue that councillors should be chosen from the men and women best suited for the job who will exercise their independent judgement on what is best for the local community. If party membership is a condition for becoming a candidate, they say, this will narrow the field of recruitment and exclude able people who might otherwise be willing to serve. It is also suggested that where councils operate under the party system, important decisions are taken in private party meetings and the subsequent public debate in the council chamber becomes a mere charade because all, or nearly all, of the members are previously committed to a particular point of view.

Those who favour party politics in local government argue that the provision of housing, education and other local services are highly political matters and that conflict between the parties on policies and priorities reflects views of life which are fundamentally different. Party organization, they suggest, gives a sense of direction and purpose to local authorities which

The council chamber can be a bit lonely at times.

they would otherwise lack. They contend that parties mobilize opinion and create an interest in important questions and broaden, not narrow, the basis of recruitment.

For good or ill, the effect of the party system is to introduce into local government the same principles of representative and responsible government that apply at national level. The party which holds the majority of seats governs and is collectively accountable to the electorate. If the party in power is deemed to have failed in the discharge of its responsibilities, other parties offer clear alternative policies and can be elected in their place.

(from **Local Government** by Tom Brennan, Longman Resources Unit, York, 1984, p. 12)

Not all the decisions of local councils will be made on a party political basis. But in those cases where councillors from one party occupy a majority of the council seats, that party (the **controlling group**) will usually be able to get decisions made in line with its policies. It can ensure that its own members are in a majority on every committee. This may give more power to the committee chairperson. It may also affect their relationship with the chief officers. In some councils, the situation may be complicated further by a split **within** the controlling group – for example between the 'left' and the 'right' of the party. The following extract describes such a situation.

In most councils there is a very cosy relationship. The chief officer prepares personal reports for the chairman. Decisions are taken regularly on a wide range of issues by these two people, and the chief officer does his best to 'manage' his chairman. However, in Manchester this set up did not suit the Labour Party. Party members in Manchester feel that councillors should be more accountable to them. They, after all, do all the work necessary to put the councillor into office. A tension has now risen between the chief officer and the party on occasions. The chairman is pulled in both ways: by his chief

Control of the non-metropolitan counties after May, 1985 elections

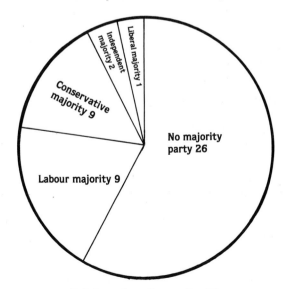

Total number of councils: 47

officer on one hand and his party allegiances on the other. The split in Manchester Labour Party has made this clash of loyalties even more difficult. Local government officers now have to read local Labour party policy carefully. It is the Manchester City Labour Party which sets down the policy and officers have found that they are expected to follow it.

(from 'The work of a local councillor: a personal view', unpublished transcript by Bill Jones from a talk by Councillor Arnold Spencer, 21 November, 1983)

But what if **no** party has an overall majority. In local government this is not now unusual. In fact after the 1985 county council elections more than half of the 47 non-metropolitan counties in England and Wales had 'hung' councils (i.e. with no single party in control). The details are given in the pie-chart on page 309.

The Alliance parties form the largest grouping on three of the 26 county councils where no party has an overall majority, and they are the second largest grouping on ten others. The following extract presents some of the effects of the absence of a single-party majority on a council.

Following the 1985 elections, a large number of the counties must adjust to the position of running local affairs with no single party in control. These hung councils — or 'balanced authorities' as the Alliance prefers them to be known — have to adopt new procedures and conventions. Cheshire, which has been hung since 1981, is seen by many as the best example of how to cope. Here the two political parties agreed new rules for relations between councillors and the officers, and for other aspects of council business. Under these, for example, each party is empowered to seek confidential briefings from the officers.

The difficulties, and some mechanisms for coping, are set out in a paper by Cheshire's chief executive, entitled **Working in a Hung Council.** This makes the point that 'it is impracticable to look ahead more than a few months, and the reality of this has to be accepted'. On the other hand, the Liberals claim that tangible benefits resulted from the 'balanced authority', although the outgoing Labour leader of the council said he wouldn't wish it on anyone, not even the Conservatives!

(from 'Election report' by John Benyon, **Social Studies Review** Vol.1 No.1, September, 1985, pp. 8-11)

1 .How many non-metropolitan county councils had a single party in control following the elections in 1985?   (1)
2. a Identify **two** arguments against party politics in local government   (2)
   b Identify **two** arguments in favour.   (2)
3. a What is a 'hung council'?   (1)
   b Why do you think the Alliance prefer the term 'balanced authority'?   (2)
   c Suggest advantages and disadvantages of a hung council.   (4)
4. From the information provided, explain
   a **how** the relationship between parties, councillors and officers in Cheshire differs from that in Manchester   (4)
   b **why** it differs.   (4)

7 Local government finance (1)

It costs a lot of money to provide local government services. For example, the total estimated expenditure for the financial year 1986-7 amounted to over £25,000 million.

Local authority spending consists of **revenue** expenditure and **capital** expenditure. Revenue (or current) spending represents the day-to-day costs of providing services. It covers wages, energy costs, and so on, and amounts to about 80% of all local authority expenditure. Capital spending goes on building new houses, schools, roads and major items of equipment that will last for many years.

Grants from central government and local rates provide most of the money for revenue expenditure. The largest single slice is paid for by central government out of national funds raised in the main from income tax, VAT (value added tax) and other taxes. The remainder is made up of money from local rates paid on business properties, domestic rates (paid by local householders), and direct charges for certain services (such as council house rents and charges for the use of swimming pools, sports facilities and car parks). Money for capital spending is mainly raised through borrowing. It is borrowed from central government or through the private financial markets. Until the loan is fully repaid, interest has to be paid each year and this comes out of the revenue spending of each local authority. Some local authorities also raise money for capital spending by selling council-owned assets such as houses and land.

The most expensive local government service to run is education. Other big spenders – including housing, social services and the police – come a long way behind. The tables show the revenue budget (planned expenditure and income) for one county council (Norfolk) and a district council within that county (Great Yarmouth).

NORFOLK 1985-6

Expenditure	£ million	Income	£ million
Education	171.7	Government grants	123.2
Social services	32.5	Rates	134.8
Police	29.7	Other (including	
Highways & transport	22.3	charges for	
Fire	7.2	services)	36.4
Administration of		TOTAL	294.4
justice	4.3		
Libraries	3.4		
Waste disposal	2.5		
Museums	1.3		
Other	19.5		
TOTAL	294.4		

GREAT YARMOUTH 1985-6

Expenditure	£ thousand	Income	£ thousand
Housing	8,128	Government grants	9,569
Housing benefits	3,399	Rates	3,016
Transport	2,422	Other (including	
Health & environment		council house rents,	
(e.g. refuse collection,		bus charges)	10,187
street cleaning)	2,358	TOTAL	22,772
Resort & related			
expenditure	1,520		
Parks & recreation	1,476		
Planning & building			
control	599		
Industrial development	152		
Other	2,718		
TOTAL	22,772		

(Local authorities must inform their ratepayers how they intend to spend their money. They usually do this by enclosing leaflets with the rate demands (bills) that are sent out each year. The details in the tables are based on information provided in this way.)

PUNCH, OR THE LONDON CHARIVARI. April 19, 1905.

THE MUNICIPAL ROAD TO RUIN.

Nervous Ratepayer. "I SAY! ISN'T THIS RATHER AN EXCESSIVE RATE? AFTER ALL, YOU KNOW, IT'S MY CAR!"

Although not forming the biggest proportion of all local authority income, the **rates,** have become a source of controversy. Owners of businesses complain about the amounts that they have to pay. The domestic rates also represent a form of taxation that householders are very aware of. They receive an annual rate demand which shows how much money they must pay to the local council. Rates are a tax on property. Each residence is given a **rateable value** by the Inland Revenue. Every year the occupier has to pay so many pence for each pound of his or her home's rateable value. For example, if the rateable value of a house is £200, and the rate in the pound is set by the council at 90p, the ratepayer must pay £180 in rates for that year (£200 × 90p = £180). Domestic ratepayers on low incomes can obtain rebates. But the Government is thinking of compelling all householders, however low their incomes, to pay at least 20% of their local tax bills.

Rates are collected only by the district councils and London borough councils. But outside the metropolitan areas most of the money is passed to the county councils to help pay for the services they provide. The county council tells the district councils in its area how much money it will need each year. This is called a **precept.**

Demands for reform or replacement of the rating system are frequently made as many people see it as an unfair system of local taxation. The poor often pay a larger proportion of their income in rates than do others. Many entitled to rebates do not claim them. Furthermore, a person's rates bill may bear little relation to his or her income. It also takes no account of the number of separate incomes in any particular household. For example, a family of four each with a job, and all living in the same house, may be paying only the same amount as a person living alone next door. Nevertheless, the rating system is generally well understood. Rates are cheap to collect and it is very difficult for people to avoid paying them. And, at least until recently, it did help local authorities to maintain some independence from central government. This is because it is the local councils themselves which are responsible for deciding the level of rates for their areas.

However, the Conservatives have been promising to reform or abolish the present rating system since 1974. This commitment was strengthened in 1985 after widespread dissatisfaction from Tory supporters in Scotland following large rate increases for some people living there. A major problem, though, is what to replace it with. All the alternatives which have been suggested have their own difficulties. A **local sales tax** would involve an increase in the price of goods sold in the shops. This would have the effect of taxing the poor at the same rate as the rich. It could also mean people choosing to shop in a neighbouring district where the rate of sales tax might be lower. The Layfield Committee in 1976 recommended that local authorities should obtain some of their money through a **local income tax.** Margaret Thatcher is unlikely to support this idea as she is against more taxes on people's incomes. One system being considered by the Government is a **poll tax.** This would involve levying a tax on everyone on the electoral register. However, it could discourage people from registering. It would also require a big increase in the rebate system as many people would be unable to pay the full rate. There has been a suggestion that a poll tax could be combined with a revised form of property tax. But it is unlikely that any major change to the present system of rates will be made before the next general election. Some Ministers are thought to have doubts about the wisdom of a poll tax.

1. Identify **four** sources of local authority income.   (2)
2. If the local rate set by a council is 80p in the £, how much would a householder pay in rates if the rateable value on her home is £300?   (2)
3. a How much money were Norfolk and Great Yarmouth councils each due to receive from ratepayers in 1985-6?   (2)
   b Why the difference?   (2)
4. a Outline a case for abolishing the rates.   (4)
   b Outline a case for keeping the rates.   (4)
5. The introduction of a poll tax would mean that every person qualified to vote would have to pay the tax. What are the possible benefits and problems with this?   (4)

8 Local government finance (2)

In the late 1970s the Government became concerned about the amounts of money local authorities were spending. It considered that some councils were not responding to its requests for economies. Since then central government has been tightening its control of local government finance. One way it can do this is by controlling the amount of money it grants to local authorities. About half the money for local authority **revenue** spending is provided in this way. Government grants come in two types – **specific grants** and a general or **block grant.** Specific grants are made for particular services, such as the police, transport and to help pay the cost of rate and rent rebates, or housing benefits. The block grant – or 'Rate Support Grant' – is the main government grant to local authorities, and is not restricted to any particular service.

Under legislation introduced in 1980 the government calculates its grant on the basis of how much it thinks local authorities in each area ought to be spending. Between 1981 and 1985 the Government also gave local authorities individual 'spending targets'. Any local authorities overspending on these targets would have their grants reduced in the following year. In 1985 the Government decided to abandon its practice of setting individual targets. But it still maintains control through its power to reduce and to redistribute the amounts of grant. For example, the Government's grant proposals for 1986-7 shifted the balance slightly in favour of the metropolitan areas at the expense of authorities in the rest of the country.

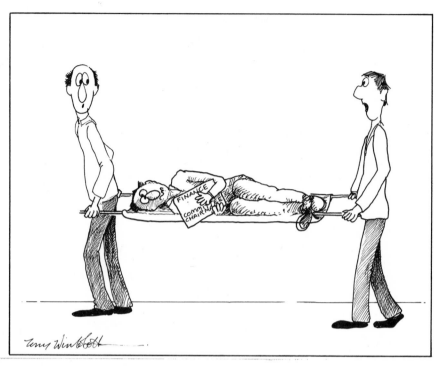

'It's the worst case of rate-capping I've ever seen.'

A further control on local authorities' ability to raise money operated for the first time in 1985-6. Councils which had been penalized for exceeding government spending limits were effectively prevented from raising extra money through their rates to compensate for reductions in central government grants. This measure of imposing a ceiling on the amount which a local authority can raise through its rates it known as **rate-capping.** In 1985-6 eighteen authorities were rate-capped. For 1986-7 twelve were penalized in the same way (see table). Rate-capping has been criticized for reducing local authority independence. It takes away a council's opportunity to make its own expenditure decisions. According to the three main organizations which represent the interests of local authorities (the Association of Metropolitan Authorities, the County Councils Association and the District Councils Association) it presents a serious threat to the principle of local democracy.

Rate-capped local authorities 1985-86

ILEA	Greenwich	Leicester	Southwark
GLC	Hackney	Lewisham	South Yorkshire
Basildon	Haringey	Merseyside	Thamesdown
Brent	Islington	Portsmouth	
Camden	Lambeth	Sheffield	

1986-7

Basildon	Hackney	Lambeth	Newcastle
Camden	Haringey	Lewisham	Southwark
Greenwich	Islington	Liverpool	Thamesdown

One local authority which wasn't rate-capped in 1985-6, nonetheless found itself in dispute with central government, as the following passage shows.

Local authorities are expected to balance their budgets when planning their expenditure and income. But in 1985 Liverpool City Council, after delaying to set a rate for that year, eventually budgeted to 'overspend'. Their planned expenditure was more than their expected income. Grants to the council from the government had been reduced, and the council refused to make large rate increases to make up the difference. It also decided against cutting back on certain services, particularly its massive housing renewal programme.

> The main reason for Liverpool's present 'overspending' stems from its housing programme, launched with ruthless speed since May 1983. So far 3,800 new council houses have been built or started, a further 3,000 improved and around 27,000 private houses improved. All the authority's resources are focused on one style of development — traditional houses and bungalows with spaces for cars, parks with railings, and corner shops. Families are rehoused in the same neighbourhood.
>
> Last week the Birchalls — Mary, Christopher and five children — moved into a new house. 'We've got the same neighbours, but it's a totally different feeling,' said daughter Teresa. 'We've got a garden for the first time in our lives.'

At one stage it had seemed that not only Liverpool's housing programme but its entire range of services was under threat. The council was rapidly running out of money to pay the wages of its employees. However, the council arranged to borrow money from a Swiss bank in order to help balance its budget. The 49 Labour councillors who had voted for the 'illegal' budget were told they would have to pay £106,000 out of their own pockets for losses incurred in delaying to set the rate. (Similar **surcharges** were also placed on some Labour councillors in the

Part of Liverpool City Council's housing renewal programme, September 1985. In the background high-rise slums from the 1960s.

London Borough of Lambeth for the same reason.) The councillors said they would not pay the surcharges and they lodged an appeal in the law courts. If the appeal fails, they will be disqualified from serving as councillors for five years.

(adapted from 'Rate rebel councillors face surcharges of £230,000' by Richard Evans, **Financial Times,** 10 September, 1985, p. 1; 'Liverpool party faces probe' by Robert Taylor and Jonathan Foster, **The Observer,** 24 November, 1985, p. 2 and 'Struggle on the scrapheap' by Robert Taylor and Jonathan Foster, **The Observer,** 22 September, 1985 p. 7 [and from which the direct quote is taken])

1. What is the difference between the two types of government grant to local authorities? (2)
2. a What is meant by a **surcharge** on local councillors? (2)
   b Why were some Liverpool and Lambeth councillors informed that they were to be surcharged? (2)
3. Why do you think Liverpool City Council deliberately budgeted to overspend in 1985? (4)

4. a What is 'rate-capping'?   (2)
   b How many of the rate-capped local authorities in 1986-7 had been rate-capped in the previous year?   (1)
   c How might rate-capping be seen as 'a threat to local democracy'?   (3)
   d In what **other** ways has central government attempted to control local government finance?   (4)

9 Central control or local democracy?

Although local authorities are responsible to their electorates, they derive their powers from Parliament.
(Government White Paper on Rates)

People do not like town hall 'bureaucrats', or paying their rates. But they do like, and value, the schools their children attend; the home help their elderly parents receive; the security of decent police and fire services; street lighting, a reliable bus service; their public libraries. If the government gets its way, some part of each of these services will go.

(Jack Straw, Labour MP, in **Sunday Times** 18 December, 1984)

The previous passage (13.8) reported a concern that the increased central government control over local authority finance is reducing the scope for local democracy. Some local authorities have even complained that if they keep within spending or rate-rise levels they may have to break laws which require them to maintain minimum standards in their services. But a decline in local authority independence is not confined to financial matters. Some people saw the abolition of the GLC and the metropolitan county councils, and the transfer of some of their functions to unelected bodies, as further evidence of this process. Local authorities have been forced to sell council houses. The Government has encouraged them to privatize services such as refuse collection. And legislation is planned to prevent 'political' advertising by local authorities.

However, there has always been some central control of local government. And any government will want to control public spending as part of its overall economic policy. The problem is how to do this whilst preserving local democracy. Providing services effectively and economically may not always fit well with the need to ensure that councils are accountable to the local electorate. The following extracts explore these issues of central government control and local democracy. The first looks at some of the **reasons** for central control and the **methods** used to achieve it.

Local authorities are not free agents. All of them have been created by the central government and they are only free to act within the powers given to them by the central government. Those powers, and their responsibilities, are laid down by numerous Acts of Parliament. Central government also makes sure that local authorities exercise their powers in a way the central government can accept.

Why is it necessary to have central control? Many local services are really part of a national pattern. Thus it is vital for central government to ensure that all local authorities keep in step. For example, in the provision of education – although there are variations among local authorities – a similar pattern must be maintained throughout the country. Otherwise, children in one authority would have less opportunity than children in another. Some policies, too, must be co-ordinated if they are to be rational and efficient; and central government acts as a co-ordinator in these cases. The planning work done by local authorities is an example of a service in which such co-ordination is vital. A lot of money for local government comes from grants made by central government which will want to make sure that it approves the ways in which that money is spent.

How is central government control exercised? **(1) Financial control.** The government can control local authorities through its power to withold or reduce grants and to audit (check) local accounts. The fact, too, that central government cannot or will not grant unlimited amounts of money – coupled with the use, if required, of rate-capping powers – places a ceiling on local authority spending. **(2) Ministerial approval.** Ministers and government departments have the right to approve or reject some local schemes. For example, comprehensive school reorganization plans had to be approved by the Department of Education and Science before they could go ahead. In particular, the Department of the Environment links local authorities in England with the centre and keeps a general oversight of local issues. The Welsh Office and the Scottish Office have similar functions. **(3) Inspection.** Some local government services are open to inspection. Education, police and fire services are the ones most regularly inspected. **(4) Appeals.** People who feel they have been unjustly treated by their local authority can often appeal to the government Minister for his ruling on the matter. Appeals are most often made to the Secretary of State for the Environment against planning decisions and the compulsory purchase of private property. **(5) Legal controls.** The central government must see that laws passed by Parliament are obeyed. Local authorities, like people, are not exceptions to this rule. If a local authority breaks the law by exceeding its powers (in which case it is said to be acting **ultra vires**) it can be prosecuted in the law courts for doing so.

(from **Local Community** by Grace Jones, Nelson-Harrap, London, 1979, pp. 33–4, with minor additions)

1. Identify **three** reasons for central government control of local authorities   (3)
2. From the information provided, say which method of central control you think is generally the most effective. Give reasons for your answer.   (2)

The following two extracts present rather different views on the questions of control and local democracy. The first was written when some of the recent increases in central control were only being considered.

Is local government to go on being local **government** or is it to become a set of mere local offices of a great central bureaucracy? Hitherto, in this country, we have had local government, for the very good reason that the services local councils provide are on the whole personal. They need to be adapted to local people. They must be accessible: if someone has a problem he needs to know that somebody locally has the power to decide. What is more, people need to be able to influence the kind of services that are provided. They need ways of calling those who run the service to account.

Traditionally, local government has met all these needs because it is locally elected and because it has independent tax-raising powers: the rates. Unfortunately, it is under threat from the centralizing fantasies of Ministers and civil servants.

They itch to take on tasks that are not required of them and are better performed by others. They dragoon Parliament into giving local authorities increased responsibilities without increasing the tax base on which they rely. They then use the subsequent need for increased support as an argument for increased central control.

Increasing the financial independence of local authorities and reducing their reliance on central grants would support the principle that different functions should be performed by different levels of administration. The duty to provide and maintain a service should be performed by local authorities. Central government should deal only with those overall policy, resource and regulatory functions that Ministers and their departments can sensibly perform. When central government tries to do more it becomes a tyranny.

(from 'Rates – safeguard of democracy' by Tyrrell Burgess, **The Observer** 12 August, 1979)

3. Why does Tyrrell Burgess support the principle of local democracy?   (3)
4. According to Burgess, how should responsibilities for local services be split between local government and central government? (2)

Local authorities are neither particularly democratic – voting turnout is low – nor accountable. They are shunned by the many, manipulated by the few, run by small groups of politicians and officers. Electors are allowed to express their views only every four years. Local government is not local. The results of local elections generally reflect national political moods.

Councils could cut costs without cutting services, but have hardly tried. Billions have been poured into housing, and wasted. Some £300 million in today's prices was wasted in clearing slum houses in London that could have been renovated. Yet local authorities are now demolishing estates built within the past 15 years. Waste and poor service are widespread. Planning costs the nation some £700 million annually. Apart from the green belts and conservation, we get little from it. There are expensive and inept computer systems; home helps cost up to twice as much as private domestic help; and there is little relationship between spending on education and the results achieved. Few councillors could run a corner shop, let alone large councils. Few officers have ever worked in a cost-demanding environment, and management is generally weak.

Frustrated ratepayers have turned to the government, which has adopted the conventional approach of extending its control. But this is wrong: the government has too much power already. Local government should be handed over to consumers, the electorate and ratepayers. We should turn housing over to the tenants, give education to school governors and parents, and streamline the planning system. There should be elections of a third of councillors every year, referenda on major spending proposals, and there should be a statutory duty requiring councillors and officers to ensure that services are economical.

Finally, we need more open and accountable local government, so that **we** can see what **they** are doing for our children, our elderly folk, and our dustbins, with **our** money.

(from 'Whitehall v Town Hall' by Alex Henney, **Sunday Times**, 18 December, 1984)

5. How does Alex Henney attempt to support his view that local government is
   a not 'particularly democratic'   (1)
   b not accountable   (1)
   c not local   (1)
   d wasteful   (1)
6. Discuss Henney's proposed solution to what he sees as the deficiencies of local government.   (6)

10 The individual and the local community (1) Representation and influence

As earlier passages in this section have shown, the formal way in which individuals are represented at local level is through their councillors. There are over 70,000 parish or community councillors. But the major council work in England and Wales is carried out by the 25,000 or so elected members at the county, district and borough levels.

Provided they have reached the age of 21, most people are entitled to stand for election for the council in which they live or work. All councillors are elected for a four-year term of office. In the metropolitan districts one-third of the seats on the council come up for election each year except during the year when county council elections are held. In the counties, the London boroughs and the parishes, all seats are contested together once every four years. Under the 1972 Local Government Act, non-metropolitan district councils were allowed to choose which of these two arrangements to adopt.

On many councils, it is difficult to get elected unless the candidate has been selected to stand by a political party. Most people aged eighteen or over are eligible to vote in local elections. But the turnout (usually around 40%) is significantly lower than at a general election. Local issues may sometimes be important in determining voting behaviour. But voting generally seems to reflect the levels of support for the different **national** parties at the time.

Sections of the local community may have their interests represented or looked after informally by groups such as tenants' or residents' associations and other local pressure groups. These may provide ways in which individuals can participate in the affairs of their local community. They are considered in more detail in 13.11. The following passage suggests ways in which individuals can try to get their problems or grievances dealt with by their local authority. It also suggests how they can try to influence local policies.

> The most common problems taken to councillors concern the failure of a department of the local authority to provide some service which the elector feels he or she is entitled to. Very often, these things are quite local and routine – council house maintenance, street lamps not working, roads in need of repair, rubbish not collected, housing applications, and so on. In such cases, a councillor may have a look personally to check the facts of the case, and sometimes, pass the query on to another councillor if his own council isn't responsible. But most commonly, he will contact the head of the department concerned to press for action or to ask for further information. The Commissioner for Local Administration – the local ombudsman – is a sort of backstop who investigates cases

where people believe they have suffered as a result of local authorities failing to carry out their duties properly.

If a problem involves a **policy decision** – about parking meters, secondary school reorganization, a planning decision or swimming pool charges, say – the sort of help a councillor can give you is unpredictable. The councillor will have to decide whether anything can be done, and whether (in his view) it would be in the interests of the area generally. He will then have to seek the views of the senior staff of the relevant department, and lobby his fellow councillors on the appropriate committee. He would then have to arrange to guide the proposal through his party group, the committee and perhaps the full council. The chances of getting what you want are quite small with this kind of issue. Many issues involve **planning** decisions – a controversial area often involving long and complicated procedures. Your only real recourse against an unhelpful councillor is to vote him out at the next election.

ACTION CHECKLIST

1. Find out which local authority and which department is responsible for the service you have trouble with.

2. Telephone or write to the department concerned. Keep a record of what happens and who you speak to.

3. If you're dissatisfied, contact the councillor who represents you on the council. If you don't know who this is, ask at your local public library.

4. Still unhappy? Try the chairman of the committee, or party leaders, and get help from a relevant local pressure group. And it could be worth contacting your MP. Another ploy: write a letter to your local newspaper.

5. In the last resort, consider legal action, an appeal to a tribunal or Minister (where appropriate), or to the local ombudsman.

If you want to to have a say in local **policies,** your voice on its own may not have much effect. Getting more influence will mean devoting time and effort to:

- keeping up with local events. Local newspapers and radio report some council affairs, but not usually routine matters. You can find out more by attending meetings of the council, or, more interesting, its committees.

- joining a local organization with a stronger voice than yours on its own. Ratepayers', residents' and amenity associations (some of which put up candidates in elections) are quite common, and there are voluntary organizations dealing with many services which a local authority provides. Temporary organizations are quite common too, to fight particular compaigns – often about development plans, roads or the closure of some local public service. Some councillors, though, are wary of pressure groups because they may exercise too much influence on small parts of the local authority's work, at the expense of others.

- joining a political party. This is almost certainly the most effective way of keeping up with and influencing local affairs. Councillors report regularly to ward and branch meetings, so you can get an inside view of what is happening. Policies and reactions to local events are also discussed, so you can have a hand in making the decisions. And councillors can least afford to disregard the views of their own parties.

(from 'Local government', **Which?** January, 1979, pp. 11-12)

1. Identify **three** reasons why joining a political party is probably the most effective way of influencing local affairs.   (3)
2. Why do you think the turnout at local elections is lower than at general elections?   (3)
3. Why do you think a council's committee meetings would usually be 'more interesting' than a meeting of the full council?   (2)
4. How might writing to an MP help in getting a local authority to deal with a problem?   (2)
5. A local resident contacts her local councillor because her dustbin has not been emptied for a month. Another contacts her councillor because she wants to prevent the construction of a lay-

by and bus-stop near to her house. Which of these two individuals is more likely to get a satisfactory solution to her problem, and why?   (4)
6. Discuss the view that local pressure groups benefit local democracy.   (6)

11 The individual and the local community (2) Participation and influence

Section 1 pointed out that not many people are politically active. Even at the local level, very few people stand for council elections. Rather more may be involved occasionally or regularly in local pressure group activity, but they will still form a minority.

> How local government works is a mystery to most people, according to the results of a survey of 112 local authorities. Many councils are trying to increase the amount of participation in their decision-making processes, says the report. Schemes include regularly consulting residents' associations, involving community groups in deciding on local amentities, giving special treatment to particular estates, consulting ethnic minority groups and establishing local information centres. But in spite of such efforts – and many councils are making no effort at all – local government is still remote for most electors.

> (**New Society**, 17 January, 1985, p. 110)

Nevertheless, local political activity does seem to have increased over the past twenty years. There have been growing demands to decentralize decision-making – to bring it closer to people at local levels. The idea is that individuals would have more control over their own communities and their own lives. In some areas political parties – notably, but not exclusively, the Liberals – have been active in promoting community politics. The following passage looks at some of the ways people may participate in the affairs of their local community other than those provided by the formal structure of local government.

Community groups can provide a two-way link between the local authority and the public. They are close to public opinion.

Members of the Peckham Action Group protesting against Council plans to demolish local housing.

At the same time they can discover the views and plans of local councillors and officials and the difficulties they face. Such groups, however, are not always easy to set up and keep going. They demand a lot of time and energy and they need to be well organized. They must also be prepared to meet a lack of interest or enthusiasm from some people in the community, at least initially. But many have got off the ground and have become a focal point for a variety of community activities and initiatives.

Tenants' associations have developed in many areas. They put pressure on local authorities to deal with housing problems such as general repairs, inefficient and costly heating systems, damp, lack of play facilities, and fairer rents. Tenants' associations representing people living on different estates in the same district sometimes combine to form a federation of tenants' associations. **Planning action groups** form to secure participation for local people in decisions affecting their environment. Some have forced the authorities to re-think their plans for new roads, car-parks and office blocks, or to improve areas of bad housing. Similar issues may be adopted by

community associations, particularly those formed in some run-down inner-city areas. In other areas community associations have often been formed over single issues – a pedestrian crossing, an adventure playground, and so on – or to organize a particular event such as a local festival. If successful, they may then develop into more permanent pressure groups in their locality. Other community groups include squatters' groups, women's aid organizations, claimants' unions, pensioners' groups and community health groups. Some may be local branches of national pressure groups. The National Women's Aid Federation, for example, is a country-wide organization that wants better legal rights for all married women. Locally, it campaigns for facilities for women who are victims of violence.

Most community groups are voluntary organizations run by unpaid local activists. They often lack the resources and the power to get themselves taken seriously by the local authorities. At planning inquiries, for instance, they are unlikely to be able to afford the expert professional support available to local councils or commerical interests. The individuals most active in community groups often believe strongly in what they are trying to do for their area. But there is always the possibility that some may have more selfish motives. In any case, most community groups cannot claim to represent the entire community. Neither do they have to consider the whole range of needs and problems facing a town or locality. Local councils, on the other hand, have to try to establish priorities from many competing needs and interests. Some councillors therefore see community groups as a nuisance, or even as a threat to their jobs as local representatives. Others may be glad of their assistance in bringing to light local problems and needs. Some councillors actively encourage them as a means of helping to change things through grassroots action.

Yet the limitations of such groups perhaps still leaves a need for local communities – particularly in urban areas – to be able to get their problems dealt with or their views heard. Closer links with the local authority may be required. In some districts **elected neighbourhood councils** have been formed. Neigbourhood councils are composed of individuals elected to represent a particular street or block of flats. They do not have formal legal powers. But they can present the views and concerns of their neighbourhood to the local council. They may

BRADFORD: A LOCAL ISSUE

In June 1982 18 flats in Newby Square were damaged by floods and the tenants demanded compensation. Further surveys revealed serious structural faults. Now the tenants are fighting to be rehoused and to have the flats demolished – but for the local council the decisions are not that easy.

Sandra Graham and the Newby Square Action Group.

The size of the problem

Due to shortage of money Bradford has built no new council houses for two years. If Newby Square is demolished they will lose 670 flats, and homes will have to be found for tenants on existing estates. A housing survey revealed condensation, poor heating, noise, leaking and rotten window frames in the square.

What can the council do?

In 1968 Newby Square cost £2½m to build and the council is still paying off this loan at £151,097 per annum. Cost of demolishing the square would be about £4 million – more than it cost to build! Other options include conversion to offices, lowering the maisonettes to single storey, selling to a private developer. The total housing budget is £48,908,700.
Leeds recently had to demolish a tower block of similar flats. *Liverpool* sold a high rise block to a private company for £1!

Who takes the decision?

Twenty-one elected councillors on the Housing Committee decide all major housing issues, aided by full-time council officers under a director of housing.

Where will the money come from?

To raise money to demolish and rebuild, the council would have to raise *rents* or *rates* or both. The government is penalising councils that they consider are spending too much money and this year Bradford must pay a penalty of *£5.7 million* because they are already over their spending target. On top of this the government has *reduced* the money (*block grant*) it gives to Bradford by *£24 million*.

16 years of misery on condemned estate

1968: Newby Square is built to replace the clearance area known as Little India off Manchester Road.

1982: June 30 – Tenants begin rent strike over demands for compensation for damage to carpets and decorations after flooding hits 18 ground floor maisonettes. They complain that officials failed, despite repeated requests, to carry out an inspection.

August 7 – Housing Services Special Sub-Committee agrees that council should help pay for redecoration and replacement of carpets. Tenants are urged to take out insurance on the property.

August 21 – Tenants occupy Newby Square council office, angry over slow replacement of carpets. Council said it was under no legal obligation to compensate flood victims but would do so 'as a goodwill gesture'.

August 24 – Sit-in continues. Protesters accuse Housing Chairman Coun. Ken Hirst of 'lying', and challenge him to meet them.

August 25 – Coun. Hirst says protesters 'can sit there all winter if they want . . . We will not be blackmailed'.

September 14 – National Anti-Dampness Campaign – Shelter-backed – says flats should be repaired or bulldozed. Coun. Hirst says inspection of flats within previous three years had produced 'clean bill of health'. Protesters open their own complaints office.

September 20 – Housing Committee meeting disrupted by hecklers asking why Newby Square question was to be discussed in private. Coun. Hirst asked to resign, and Labour councillors criticised for not supporting tenants earlier.

September 21 – Coun. Abdul Hameed visits the square and reports his 'alarm' at claims that asbestos had been used in construction.

September 25 – Sit-in ends after council agreed to make goodwill payments of £4000.

1983: June 20 – World in Action features 70,000 properties built throughout Britain by Bison Concrete. Interview with former Bison executive who admitted destroying documents dealing with construction faults.

July 13 – Six councillors call for release of month-old report on Newby Square.

July 21 – Report shows that defects would take 'millions' to remedy.

August 2 – Council decides to demolish flats.

October 27 – Tenants assured rehousing office would be set up on the estate.

1984: April 17 – Tenants stage sit-in at housing department and refuse to leave before seeing Director of Housing.

May 30 – Rehousing office opens on the estate. By now 350 families have already moved.

(from **Politics and You**, BBC Publications, London, 1985, p. 8)

also support local initiatives such as play schemes and help to organize social events.

(adapted from 'Community groups information', **Local Government School and Community Kit,** published by Community Service Volunteers, London, 1978 and **Tackling the Town Hall** by Roger Jefferies, Routledge & Kegan Paul, London, 1982, pp. 33-4)

1. a Identify **three** types of community group examined in the passage (1)
   b How do they differ from neighbourhood councils? (2)
   c If local government electors can vote for candidates to serve on local councils, what is the point of neighbourhood councils? (3)
2. a What do you understand by the term **community politics?** (1)
   b What are the advantages and disadvantages of community politics? (6)

Read the extract **Bradford: a local issue** and answer the following questions.

3. What are the different problems facing
   a the Newby Square Action Group? (2)
   b Bradford Council? (2)
4. Identify **three** different methods used by the action group during their campaign. (3)

Concluding Note: Power and Democracy

1 Two theories

The very first extract in the book suggested that when studying the British political system it was necessary to bear in mind the question 'Where does power lie?' Relationships of power have been examined, directly and indirectly, throughout the book. For example, where does power – or the balance of power – lie in the relationship between Parliament and Government? Or between Parliament and the judiciary? Or between Ministers and civil servants, pressure groups and Parliament, the police and the public, central government and local government, councillors and local officials, an MP and his or her party? The list could be extended a lot further. It is not always easy to locate power, however. And its distribution may change over time and in response to changes in other aspects of the political system and of society as a whole.

Section 1 – whilst showing that the term 'democracy' has different meanings to different people – also outlined what might be expected in a **representative** democracy. Subsequent sections may be used as a guide in helping to assess how far such features are found in the British political system. But an assessment of democracy might also consider the opportunities people have to **participate,** at different levels, in the political process. Again, various passages have looked at this aspect of politics.

However, are governments always as concerned with democracy as with what they may see as the need to preserve order and stability? In the words of 'Sir Humphrey Appleby', the 'senior civil servant' in the BBC television series **Yes Minister,**

> Government ... is about stability. Keeping things going, preventing anarchy, stopping society falling to bits. Still being here tomorrow ... Government isn't about good and evil, it's only about order and chaos.
>
> (**Yes Minister Volume 3** by Jonathan Lynn and Antony Jay, 1983, p. 116)

And if there is any truth in this statement, do governments have the **power** to see that order **is** maintained?

These twin themes of power and democracy, then, underlie much of the examination of British politics in this book. They are very much connected. In fact some people gauge the extent to which a political system is democratic by seeing how far power is dispersed throughout society. They ask, 'To what extent is power shared amongst different groups and individuals?' There are different ways of attempting to answer this question. The following extract explains two.

One view is that power is widely distributed and rests ultimately with the electorate. An alternative view of power in Britain presents a very different perspective arguing that power is concentrated in the hands of a small minority, the ruling class.

Both theories might agree that a democracy is a political system which is based on government by the people. But the first view would emphasize that it is not possible for people in a large complex society to be directly involved in every decision which affects their lives. It would say that in practice the only way government by the people can work is in the form of representative democracy whereby a few represent the wishes and interests of the many. The two main institutions of a representative democracy are political parties and pressure groups. Political parties represent the nation as a whole. To be elected they must reflect public opinion in their election promises. To gain re-election they must reflect the wishes of the people during their term of office. Pressure groups represent the wishes and concerns of sections of society. They put pressure on governments to further their members' interests. In a democracy governments do not consistently favour any one pressure group but take account of the wishes and demands of all pressure groups when passing legislation. By means of political parties and pressure groups both the public in general and particular sectional interests in society are represented. This is the way, acccording to the first view, that a representative democracy works.

The second view is closer to the ideas put forward by Karl Marx in the nineteenth century. He believed that the state represented the interests of a ruling class made up of those who own and control industry. This view therefore rejects the idea that governments like Britain's are democratic. Governments attempt to provide a framework in which private industry and particularly big business can grow and prosper. This is the main stated objective of the Thatcher government. Its economic policy aims to produce a fitter and leaner British industry and an end to what it sees as overmanning, restrictive practices and the abuse of union power. Governments protect and secure markets abroad for British goods. They provide assistance to firms wishing to export their products, and they make financial contributions to private industry.

If these efforts to help private industry succeed, the owners rather than the workforce stand to gain most. Marx believed that workers were exploited and oppressed because a part of the wealth they produced was taken from them in the form of profit. If this is the case then there is always the possibility of conflict and rebellion. One way of keeping people in their place is to give them the impression that those in power represent their interests and act on their demands. According to supporters of this view, this is what the state in Britain has done. It has provided a range of benefits for workers – such as old age pensions, unemployment benefit, a national health service and free education – which is largely paid for from taxes on the wages of the workers themselves. It gives them the impression that their interests are being represented. These measures can be seen as 'sops' to keep the masses quiet and to damp down their frustration and resentment. This – together with agencies of socialization such as education and the mass media – produces a fairly passive workforce to earn profits for the owners of private industry. Thus governments help the poor a little and in doing so help the rich a lot.

(from **Sociology: A New Approach** edited by Michael Haralambos, Causeway Press, Ormskirk, 1983, pp. 100-1, 106-9, with minor additions)

1. From your study of the British political system, say which, if either, of the two theories of power presented in the extract you prefer. Give reasons.   (10)
2. Draw up a list of some of the features you consider essential in a

democracy. Then briefly examine whether, and to what extent, each of these features exists in the British political system. (10)

2 The wider study of power

Different theories exist about the distribution of power in society. A comprehensive study of power would involve crossing the traditional boundaries between academic 'subjects'. This book, for example, has been designed to meet the requirements of students taking courses, and preparing for examinations, in the field of 'Politics and Government'. It has therefore concentrated on those areas specified by the examination boards. These areas mainly relate to the political system in Britain, including the structure and processes of government, and the role of individuals and groups within it. But questions about power are also of interest, for example, to historians, economists and sociologists. Their concerns may overlap with those of the political scientist. But each of these is likely to approach the issues from a different perspective and be involved in analysing different aspects of power. Something of the flavour of a wider approach may be gained from the following passage, which also identifies some of the problems involved.

> Studying power in British society is not a simple matter. It goes further than analysing decision-making by governments or the social class background of the top decision-makers. It involves being drawn into philosophical and theoretical debates about the relationship between society and the individual within it. And social thinkers have argued about this for centuries. Analysing power inevitably involves making controversial and personal judgements about what it really is and how it should be studied.
>
> British society is very unequal. Private property, such as the ownership of land or shares in companies, is largely concentrated in a very few hands. There are vast inequalities in incomes. Standards of housing, education, working conditions, employment prospects, and the quality of life in general, vary tremendously. These inequalities relate to class, gender and ethnic differences within society. But sociologists recognize that such inequalities produce and reflect unequal power

relationships. The wealthy and privileged groups in society are in a better position than others to control their own lives and those of the rest of the people in society.

A problem, though, is how to discover the extent to which these privileged classes actually **use** their potential power, and **how** they use it. It is not difficult to show that a small number of people occupy the controlling positions in industrial companies, the large banks and the other financial institutions. It is relatively easy to demonstrate that these people have similar class and educational backgrounds, share interests, hold similar attitudes, and often know each other well. It may also be the case that they have much in common with those who hold the top posts in government, the civil service and the armed forces. What is far more difficult, however, is to study in detail 'what these people do and how they do it' (Dearlove and Saunders, p.218).

There is another problem. Some sociologists believe that the analysis of power is not just about the study of top people in business and government, or whether power is widely distributed or concentrated in the hands of a few. They suggest that power stems from the overall structure of society itself, rather than from the activities of particular individuals. To see what this means, the structure of society can be likened to the organization of a school. In most schools the relationships between the teachers, other staff and the students form a structure in which some have more power than others. Like the rungs on a ladder, they are positioned one above another. The power that a headteacher can exercise over the teaching staff, or the teachers over the pupils, does not depend so much on the personal qualities of any of the individuals involved. Rather, it stems from their position in the school system, from its structure. As long as they remain within the school, the extent of their power is largely decided for them by the way the school is organized. In a similar way, power within British society may be seen as arising out of the way the society is organized. And the structure of British society is complex. It is therefore perhaps useful to view power 'in the context of a system of domination which no one group totally controls or consciously manipulates'. (Dearlove and Saunders, p.218).

Finally, it should be remembered that Britain exists – and increasingly so – within wider international economic and political structures. Wherever power may lie **within** Britain, it must also be seen to be exercised, for example, by the transnational business corporations, by the institutions of the EEC and by the international financial institutions. Economically and militarily there are also close links with other countries, notably the United States.

(adapted from **Introduction to British Politics** by John Dearlove and Peter Saunders, Polity Press, Cambridge and Basil Blackwell, Oxford, 1984, pp. 217-8; 'Society Today' in **New Society,** 21 February, 1985 and **Ownership, Control and Management in the Class Structure** by D.R. Roberts, unpublished M.Phil. thesis, University of Bradford, 1982)

Index